Too Marvelous for Words

JAMES LESTER

Too Marvelous for Words

THE LIFE AND

GENIUS OF

ART TATUM

OXFORD UNIVERSITY PRESS
New York ❧ Oxford

Oxford University Press

Oxford   New York
Athens   Auckland   Bangkok   Bombay
Calcutta   Cape Town   Dar es Salaam   Delhi
Florence   Hong Kong   Istanbul   Karachi
Kuala Lumpur   Madras   Madrid   Melbourne
Mexico City   Nairobi   Paris   Singapore
Taipei   Tokyo   Toronto

and associated companies in
Berlin   Ibadan

Published in 1994 by Oxford University Press, Inc.,
200 Madison Avenue, New York, New York 10016

First issued as an Oxford University Press paperback, 1995

Oxford is a registered trademark of Oxford University Press

Library of Congress Cataloging-in-Publication Data
Lester, James.
Too marvelous for words : the life and genius of Art Tatum / James Lester.
p. cm.   Includes bibliographical references and index.
ISBN 0-19-508365-2
ISBN 0-19-509640-1 (pbk.)
1. Tatum, Art, 1909–1956. 2. Jazz musicians—United States—Biography. I. Title.
ML417.T2L47   1994
786.2′165′092—dc20
[B]   93–4284

10 9 8 7 6 5 4 3 2 1

Printed in the United States of America

This book is dedicated to the hundreds of jazz musicians whose lives and contributions also deserve books but will probably never get them.

Acknowledgments

THIS BOOK COULD not have been written if a large number of people had not been willing to rummage around in their memories and to take the time to share their memories with me. Many of the people I talked with went even beyond that and gave me critically important encouragement, of which I needed large dollops. Some spent hours talking to me, others briefly gave me leads to others I needed to contact. But all were important and significantly helped to make this book.

I want to list here the people who agreed to talk with me, partly for the record but mainly to let them know how grateful I am to them. And I would be just as grateful even had the book not been published, because I found talking with most of them a warm and fascinating experience, a window on a world I'm sorry I never knew intimately and a world which is for all practical purposes gone (an alarming number of this group died after I interviewed them, though not necessarily immediately). I have the strong feeling that I've received a rare gift from a select group of humans.

The order of the list is merely alphabetical:

Mrs. Ernestine Allen, Scott Alsop, Don Asher, Eddy Barefield, Harper Barnes, Louis Bellson, Keter Betts, Mrs. Dotty Bigard, Eddie Bonnemere, Harold Brown, Ray Brown, Tom Brownell, Weldon

Burnett, Joe Bushkin, Jacki Byard, Red Callender, Mrs. Olivia Calloway, Benny Carter, Al Casey, Fred Cate, Page Cavanaugh, Doc Cheatham, Mel Clement, John Cleveland, John Collins, Willis Conover, Stanley Cowell, Bill Cummerow, Alan Dale, Stanley Dance, Russ David, Bob Davis, Mrs. Olivia Davis, Barrett Deems, Buddy DeFranco, Dave Dexter, Jr., Kurt Dieterlie, Robert Doerschuk, Dorothy Donegon, Jim Doran, Bill Douglass, Frank Driggs, John Eaton, Art Edgerton, "Sweets" Edison, Herb Ellis, Leonard Feather, Bob Fitzpatrick, Diana Flanagan, Charlie Fox, Bud Freeman, Dave Frischberg, Billy Fuster, Milt Gabler, Leonard Gaskin, Jim Gavin, Mrs. Lois Gayle, Mrs. Virginia Gear, the Reverend John Gensel, Martha Glaser, Claire Gordon, Elwood Gray, Harry Gregory, Adelaide Hall-Hicks, Lionel Hampton, Jake and Denisa Hanna, Jon Hendricks, Al Hibbler, Milt and Mona Hinton, Mrs. Elizabeth Hochman, Malvin Hoffman, Major Holley, Joseph Howard, Felicity Howlett, Dick Hyman, Merle Jacobs, Deannette James, Jimmy Jones, Steve Jordan, Dick Katz, Harold Kaye, Orrin Keepnews, Brooks Kerr, Ellis Larkins, Steve Lasker, Bernice Lawson, Delbert Lee, Floyd Levin, Ernie Lewis, Nellie Lutcher, James Maher, Adam Makovich, David Mann, Ellis Marsalis, Tim Masters, Steven Mayer, Russell McCown, Marian McPartland, Charlie Meenes, Rusty Monroe, Max Morath, Dan Morgenstern, Mrs. Henry Morrison, Eli Newberger, Big Nick Nicholas, Gene Norman, Red Norvo, Les Paul, Mozart and Rudolph Perry, Mel Powell, William Randle, Dave Reed, Ben Rifkin, Norman Ross, Seymour Rothman, Jimmy Rowles, Marshall Royal, William Savory, Phil Schaap, Duncan Schiedt, Loren Schoenberg, Barbara Seiger, William Seraile, George Shearing, Dale Sheets, George Simon, Ilomay Sims, Johnny Smith, A. B. Spellman, Joe Springer, Royal Stokes, Sylvia Syms, Karl Tatum, Arline (Tatum) Taylor, Steve Taylor, Jack Towers, Jeannie Trevors, Bobby Tucker, Barry Ulanov, Earle Warren, George Wein, LeRoy "Snake" White, Kevin Whitehead, Gerry Wiggins, Martin Williams and Theo Wilson.

Pat and Paul Kaplan took care of me on trips to New York, and Ruth Sward offered me West Coast lodgings when I needed them. I want to give special thanks to Jim Doran who encouraged me in the strongest way when I was thinking of giving it up; to Jim Maher who introduced me to Sheldon Meyer at Oxford University Press; and to my wife Valerie who, as her reward for suggesting the idea to me, has had to live with this book for five years.

Annapolis, MD   J. L.
14 May 1993

Contents

"The true genius is not helpfully communicative. . . . In reality, he lacks the key to verbal communication of his inner motivations, except within his art. . . . He does not seek self-knowledge, gives no account of himself, neglects and consumes himself. . . . He burns up, but does not defy the burning: rather, he ignores it. He does not see himself in relation to the world. He doesn't see himself at all."

HILDESHEIMER, *MOZART* (on the difference between the true genius and the would-be genius)

Too Marvelous for Words

Introduction

". . . a creature who, for all his fame, still
stands in need of a little understanding."
LYTTON STRACHEY (referring to Shelley)

ART TATUM'S NAME is now a secure part of American popular culture, and almost everyone understands that to put someone on Tatum's level is to bestow the highest praise. A play reviewer can write: "Stoppard handles words the way that Art Tatum used to handle a keyboard," and the compliment is widely understood, even by people who never heard Art play the piano. More than thirty-five years after his death, his name is still a metaphor for excellence, and not just in America but the world over. I recently met a young jazz pianist and her mother, both from Azerbaijan in the former Soviet Union, and they were offended that I thought they might not know who Art Tatum was.

But who was Art Tatum?

In 1988 I set out to find a good biography of Tatum. I wanted to learn something about where such a giant had come from, who his own idols had been, what experiences had made him the figure I knew, what sort of a person he was, what sort of life he had when he wasn't playing. It astonished me to discover that no biography of Tatum has yet been published. No fellow pianist, no jazz writer, no family member, in the thirty-seven years since his death, has yet undertaken a written record of his life. No wonder that if he exists at all for lovers of jazz he exists as a distant, an almost abstract figure, a black eminence waving his hands over the keyboard and thundering through the jazz world.

Art Tatum has not been forgotten, certainly not by the experts. Billy Taylor's 1983 book, *Jazz Piano,* has more entries in the index for Art Tatum than for any other name, and Gunther Schuller, in his 1989 book, *The Swing Era,* Volume 2, gives more pages to Tatum than to any other soloist. The Smithsonian collection of recordings *Jazz Piano,* released in 1989, has more tracks of Tatum's playing than of any other pianist. There are currently several concert pianists (for example, Steven Mayer) who pay their respects to Tatum by frequently playing transcriptions of his recordings in their programs, along with the standard classical piano repertoire. I recently attended a performance by Stanley Cowell, a significant post-Tatum jazz pianist, who devoted his whole concert to playing Art Tatum arrangements. Unfortunately there were far more of us in the audience over fifty than under forty; Cowell was preaching to the converted. (Cowell has gone on, incidentally, to compose a piano concerto dedicated to the memory of Art.)

But nothing has come along to tell us who he was. My aim has been to write the book I was unable to find in 1988, to do my best to answer the question of where he came from, and to put into a coherent narrative all the fragments of information about his life that now exist only in isolated sources and in personal memories. My intent has not been to provide a reference work, documenting his career, the chronology of his public appearances, the dates and places of his recordings. I wanted to get the musician into focus as a person.

I regret that I didn't start sooner. There is some excellent material about Tatum, the musician, already in print. There is an admirable discography (Laubich and Spencer) and three technical analyses of his performance style (Howard, Howlett, and Schuller). Even the dedicated searcher, however, will turn up little about the people and events in Tatum's life. Several brief biographical sketches, most of which cover the same ground, can be found in chapter or magazine article form, and there are short paragraphs buried in other narratives. But each of these comprises only a few fragments of his story, and when I had read through them all I longed to find out how they really fit together.

Tatum, I soon realized, was more a worthy than a promising subject for a biography. I was particularly interested in personal interviews with people who had known him or worked with him, of course, but 1988 was a very late date on which to start collecting living memories about Art Tatum. His contemporaries, those who were still with us, were in the general vicinity of eighty years old and were showing a marked tendency to shuffle off this mortal coil, all too often before I could reach them. One of his two living relatives and his widow, for reasons which I could never persuade them to reveal to me, were uncooperative.

Getting acquainted with people who knew Art personally, from early schoolmates to those who spent his last days with him, has been far and away the most enjoyable part of writing this book. Of course, there is often no hard evidence against which to evaluate personal accounts of incidents, and one either finds the account plausible or one does not. As an audience for many stories, I've found myself involved in a lot of what may be sifting fiction from fiction. If they were good stories, and not outrageously improbable, I have included them.

It is especially frustrating that there is no almost no record of the man's own report of himself, in his own words. No one I've talked to ever received a letter from Tatum, and his very limited vision makes it plausible that there may be no letters (although I can't be sure that his relatives don't possess some). Many potential interviewers saw him as a bit aloof and unapproachable—and never approached him. Barry Ulanov knew and interviewed a large proportion of top jazz figures in Tatum's era, but told me that he "gave up as fruitless any attempt to get a long narrative from him," as he would have liked to. The 1930s and '40s abounded with jazz greats who were more than willing to talk, and the reluctant or retiring ones got passed over. The few published interviews with Tatum have a curious quality; in them, he sounds genial and cooperative but gives almost no information in reply to the interviewer's questions. Without some expression of his own attitudes it is almost impossible to imagine his inner world, the place from which he emerged from time to time to astound us. Musically, we don't need to know about that, but having it would let us feel much closer to the man.

WHEN I SPOKE about Art with Ellis Marsalis, a jazz pianist and teacher, and father of (among others) Wynton and Branford Marsalis, he remarked that no one could write about Tatum properly who hadn't "gigged," or worked as a jazz musician himself. I want to say here, at the beginning, something about my credentials for writing a biography of a jazz pianist.

The last time I wrote about jazz was in 1941. I was in the eighth grade and wrote a prize-winning essay on the "comeback" of Louis Armstrong. (Little did I realize that the comeback of which I wrote was to be only the first of several—it was in fact impossible to keep Louis down.) For my prize I chose a biography of W. C. Handy, composer of, among other things, the "St. Louis Blues" (St. Louis is my home town). I tell you this to make it clear that I am not a jazz academic, not a jazz critic, not even an occasional contributor of articles on jazz in any form. My connection with jazz has been as an avid listener and as a moonlighting performer, on both piano and trombone.

Music in our household was determined by my mother's taste which ran to Wayne King and Guy Lombardo, the simplest and most pre-digested music of its time. I was a child during the Depression, and the radio in our house was generally tuned to those "sweet bands" that seemed to console America in that often sad era. Somehow I found my way to the right stuff by the time I was on the brink of being a teenager. I was buying (and I now confess to the world occasionally stealing) 78 rpm recordings of the jazz bands of Will Hudson, Jimmie Lunceford, Count Basie, and other hot bands of the late 1930s, and listening secretly after bedtime to radio station WIL for the best jazz program on the air in St. Louis. Having started piano lessons at around age eight or nine, at my own instigation, I had found the world of "Pine Top" Smith, Meade Lux Lewis, Fats Waller, Teddy Wilson, and of course Tatum, by the time I was thirteen (not, I admit, without pausing briefly to pay attention to such society pianists as Eddy Duchin and Carmen Cavallero—blame it on my youth).

I have been playing semi-professionally since 1941. I think my first paid appearance as a performer was at a block party in the Italian section of St. Louis. I was on piano and the band was on a six-foot high platform in the middle of the street. We played with such vigor that my fingers bled under the nails (not for the last time). I learned boogie-woogie and it made me very popular at parties, but as time went on it was Teddy Wilson whom I tried more and more to sound like. I loved Wilson's crisp and polished style, the clarity and sparkle of his melodic lines, the variety and interest of his left hand, the tenths constantly in motion, and those crystalline runs that sounded so spontaneous and yet inevitable at the same time. His sophistication and rich musicality, and maybe also his introverted character, appealed to my own personality much more than did "getting into the gorilla bag" (the phrase is Oscar Peterson's) with boogie-woogie. Finally, there was the fact that Wilson sounded accessible to me. I could hear what he was doing, and with enough work it seemed it might just be within reach. Tatum, of course, never was within reach, and I turned to him purely for musical experiences and not for a model. Tatum was there to define the limits of the possible, as he still is.

Since then I have held union cards in six major cities, as a pianist and a trombonist. In an Army Special Services unit in 1946 I played lead trombone in the big band, piano in a small group featuring the tenor player Warne Marsh, and wrote the book of arrangements for the band. I did several arrangements for the George Hudson band in St. Louis, the pride of the black community there, and was introduced by Hudson as a potential arranger to Lionel Hampton. In more recent years I've played hundreds of dances and private parties, in big bands and in smaller groups. My unknowing mentor Teddy Wilson once heard me play and commented (so I'm told), "He really seems to know what he's doing"—faint praise, perhaps, but from such a source it meant worlds to me. (There is a line in a novel that describes how I sometimes feel about my own playing, in which one of the characters says about another: "He seems to know what he's doing even if he can't do it.")

My vocation has been elsewhere, as a psychologist, but I have gigged. Those are my "credentials" and combined with my interest in Tatum they have given me the brashness to pursue the writing of this book. At least it seems brash to me; as an editor of *Down Beat* once remarked to a feature writer, "Tatum is a really big subject."

ART TATUM, COMING from out of nowhere (this is not a slight on Toledo, Ohio, but a comment on the disparity between his background and his accomplishment), set a precedent and a standard by which generations of jazz pianists could not escape judging themselves—even though by such a standard failure was almost guaranteed. Jimmy Knepper, the New York-based jazz trombonist, put this idea simply: "Tatum, Parker, and a few others got jazz out of the simple stage and now it's imperative to be a virtuoso."

Tatum was indeed a virtuoso, on several levels, and there is absolutely no dispute about his technical brilliance. It is the element of his playing that is easiest to assess, since his playing practically demands to be measured against the standards of the whole Western tradition of the concert piano, and to my mind at least Tatum is best understood in the light of that tradition. Consider some educated descriptions of his playing:

> . . . almost every one of Tatum's performances is from a pianistic-technical point of view a marvel of perfection . . . his playing must be heard to be believed, and in its technical perfection it is something beyond verbal description, at least this author's verbal capacities. The note-perfect clarity of Tatum's runs, the hardly believable leaps to the outer registers of the piano (he is not known ever to have missed one), his deep-in-the-keys full piano sonority, the tone and touch control in pyrotechnical passages clearly beyond the abilities of the vast majority of pianists

to merely render the notes in some nominal way—these are miracles of performance which must be appreciated aurally." [Schuller, *Swing Era,* 482]

Tatum's style was notable for its touch, its speed and accuracy, and its harmonic and rhythmic imagination. No pianist has ever hit notes more beautifully. Each one—no matter how fast the tempo—was light and complete and resonant, like the letters on a finely printed page. Vast lower-register chords were unblurred, and his highest notes were polished silver. . . . His speed and precision were almost shocking. Flawless sixteenth-note runs poured up and down the keyboard, each note perfectly accented, and the chords and figures in the left hand sometimes sounded two-handed. Such virtuosity can be an end in itself, and Tatum was delighted to let it be in his up-tempo flag-wavers, when he spectacularly became a high-wire artist, a scaler of Everests. Tatum's bedrock sense of rhythm enabled him to play out-of-tempo interludes or whole choruses that doubled the impact of the implied beat, and his harmonic sense—his strange, multiplied chords, still largely unmatched by his followers, his laying on of two and three and four melodic levels at once—was orchestral and even symphonic. [Balliett, *Ecstasy,* 113]

Listening to a really good pianist one might say, "I could never do that." But confronted with Tatum most musicians have said to themselves, "*Nobody* can do that!" "To have heard him play," one pianist wrote, "was as awe-inspiring as to have seen the Grand Canyon or Halley's comet. . . ." It seems to me, however, that Teddy Wilson, a contemporary, close friend, and first-class player himself, put the paean to Tatum in its clearest form:

Maybe this will explain Art Tatum. If you put a piano in a room, just a bare piano. Then you get all the finest jazz pianists in the world and let them play in the presence of Art Tatum. Then let Art Tatum play . . . everyone there will sound like an amateur. Pianists with regular styles will sound like beginners. Art Tatum played with such superiority that he was above style. It is almost like a golfer who can hit a hole in one every time he picks up the iron. It was a special kind of ability he had. If I had to choose an all-'round instrumentalist, in a classical vein, or in a more modern vein, I'd choose Art Tatum.

The famous Tatum runs are certainly what first jump out at you; they are, someone said, like the arc left against the night sky by a Fourth of July sparkler. They can dominate your attention, and they have given generations of pianists a sense of inferiority. But it has to be said, and then underlined, that to stop there is to miss most of what is significant about Tatum. As one record reviewer put it: "Art Tatum's performances demand much of the listener. He is not easy and cannot be fully discovered with one or two surface listenings. Of course, you get the gloss, the flash, his elegant sound. But there is so much more." What can be missed by a casual listener is the tremendous structural complexity in what he did, and the very advanced (for jazz) harmonies that he used. (Chapter 7 includes a discussion of Tatum's performance style.)

Tatum's virtuosity is not for everybody, however. His dazzling command of the keyboard has been a wedge that has divided opinion about him. There has been a minority of critics who find in him an unnecessary ornateness or even floridity, a shallowness, "an excess of hyperbole." One of the most polite expressions of this point of view was that "his tendency to display his accomplishments sometimes gets in the way of a performance." The cultivation of virtuoso skill has always exposed players to the same criticism: NO SOUL. Performers back to Franz Liszt and beyond have suffered this criticism: decoration, not substance; effect, not content. In the case of jazz musicians the complaint is that showy displays of musical athleticism take the place of musical thought and usurp the place of more significant improvisation. Jazz criticism is a murky, subjective thing, but one important criterion has always been originality; whenever skill seems to have replaced imagination, or prepared devices take the place of creativity, a reputation suffers. Because of his virtuosity, it has never been easy to judge Tatum by this particular criterion.

It is clear, though, that what Tatum did, as Knepper suggested, was considerably more than add one more to the variety of jazz piano styles. His harmonic and rhythmic innovations affected the whole context for jazz playing, and not just for pianists. In the scope of his influence he is comparable to Louis Armstrong before him, and to Charlie Parker who came after. He is, however, impossible to categorize as to style—he seemed to develop along a track of his own even though he was thoroughly aware of the action on all the adjacent tracks. And he is difficult to assess clearly because it's hard to know what standards to apply. Whitney Balliett with his reliable deftness of language summed him up in 1968, and captured a central truth about Tatum's career : "No one ever knew exactly what he was or what to do with him. He was said to be the greatest jazz pianist who ever lived and he was said to be not a jazz pianist at all. He was admired by classical pianists . . . by jazz musicians, and by dazzled, tin-eared laymen. People poked fun at his ornate style . . . and then wept at his next brilliance . . . nobody has decided yet what kind of a pianist he was" (Balliett, *Ecstasy,* 111). The clearest light can be thrown on Tatum, I think, if we see him as a displaced person, a kind of outsider, keeping alive an old tradition (piano virtuosity) in an alien country (jazz).

In the descriptions of many listeners, hearing Art Tatum for the first time was somewhat like living through an earthquake—it astonished, it alarmed, it could shake one's foundations. Inflated as that may sound in the 1990s, when performance expectations are vastly different from what they were in Tatum's era, it was overwhelmingly true in the 1930s and 40s. Musicians traveling from city to city were already telling each other in the late 1920s about the unbelievable piano playing they had heard in Toledo, and he was well on his way to becoming a living legend before he made his first solo recordings in 1933. The impact on his listeners was made all the greater by the knowledge that Art Tatum was nearly blind.

I liken Tatum to an earthquake advisedly. Earthquakes are not only impressive but they can be destructive. I never heard anyone say that Tatum inspired him or her to play the piano. A really accomplished musician *might* find encouragement. Mel Powell, who had intensive classical training as a child and later won rave reviews as a teen-age pianist and arranger with Benny Goodman, told me his first experience with Tatum's playing was positive: "What it probably did was to encourage me to see that that kind of sheer instrumental virtuosity that I'd been cultivating in the other world of music not only had a place [in jazz] but was the summit." More than a few musicians, however, were anything but encouraged by him; Rex Stewart, who is best known for having become a star in Duke Ellington's trumpet section, reports that after his first encounter with Art Tatum he somehow felt he was inadequate at filling Louis Armstrong's shoes (with the Fletcher-Henderson band of 1928), and he "toyed with the idea of giving up the horn and going back to school" (Stewart). Bobby Short, who is best known as an entertainer rather than a jazz pianist but who is none the less talented for that, was once "stopped in his tracks" by Tatum:

> . . . one day Len [Short's manager] took me into Lyon and Healey's music store to listen to a Tatum record. His technique was like Horowitz's. He was a wizard, I listened to the recording and I was shocked to hell! When it was finished, the salesman said, "Do you play the piano, son?" Yes, I did. "Would you play for us?" I crossed over to the piano and sat down, and because I was so impressionable and depended on my ear for so much, found that I couldn't play the piano at all. Not a note. Tatum had undone me to that extent. I could not get my fingers to react to my mind, because my mind was suddenly overflowing. I'd been stopped in my tracks.   [*Black and White Baby*, 157–58]

The pianist Lennie Tristano noticed this phenomenon in some of his listeners and called it "kinesthetic paralysis." Even Oscar Peterson had to go through this experience. In an interview (with André Previn) Peterson described his very first encounter with the Tatum technique. In his teens his father—perhaps thinking that Oscar was getting too big a head about his playing ("I thought I was pretty heavy at school, you know—I'd play in all the lunch hours with all the chicks around the auditorium.")—sat him down to listen to the Tatum recording of "Tiger Rag," one of Art's early recordings which simply blew everyone away, including the ascendant Oscar: "And, truthfully, I gave up the piano for two solid months; and I had crying fits at night." Oscar Peterson!? (In a different interview, with a *Time* researcher, Peterson said he gave up playing for three weeks. Whichever it was, Oscar was clearly shaken up.)

Some people who thought they were becoming piano players gave up the instrument for another; for example, Les Paul, the renowned guitarist, told me: "When I saw Tatum, and heard Art Tatum, I quit playing the piano. . . . I just sez, that's not for me. 'Cause this guy, I'll never be able to beat a blind black man playing piano like that. . . . This guy is just way, way too good, and he's got so much going." Everett Barksdale, who later had the little-envied job of playing guitar in Tatum's Trio in the '50s, heard him in Detroit in 1926 when he still considered himself a piano player: "This is unbelievable, I don't believe anybody can do that thing on the instrument," he remembered thinking, and "so that was the end of my piano career." And many of the pianists who kept going carried the scars for years; I have heard Johnny Guarnieri, who had an entirely respectable career as a jazz pianist, first in a small Artie Shaw group and later as a solo performer, say that he was fifty-five years old before he realized he didn't have to play like Tatum. Many pianists spent years of their careers "chasing after him," trying to reach his level of accomplishment, even trying to play exactly like him, to the detriment of tapping their own creativity or finding their own style.

Tatum's astonishing technique not only stunned jazz musicians (and paralyzed a few) but also won the admiration of some of the prominent concert artists, conductors, and composers of the day— such artists as Gershwin, Leopold Godowsky, Paderewski, and Rachmaninoff. Most important to Tatum, Vladimir Horowitz admired and praised him, often extravagantly. Itzhak Perlman, the violinist, said in a television interview that from the moment he first heard Tatum on record he "absolutely fell in love with him." When the great Soviet violinist David Oistrakh arrived in America, one of the first things he wanted to do was shop the record stores for Tatum recordings.

Gershwin "listened with rapture" to Tatum, especially when the songs were Gershwin's own, such as "Liza" and "I Got Rhythm." He once gave a party especially for Tatum at his 72nd Street apartment in New York. One of the guests was the famous concert pianist Leopold Godowsky (from whom Fats Waller is alleged to have taken some lessons), and one who was there reported that "Godowsky listened with amazement for twenty minutes to Tatum's remarkable runs, embroideries, counter-figures and passage playing" (Levant, *A Smattering of Ignorance*, 195).

With the technical ability to make concert musicians pay attention, and with the improvisational creativity to make jazz musicians go anywhere to hear him (John Lewis of the Modern Jazz Quartet once spent $1000 in a week listening to Tatum on 52nd Street), he had the potential for being a giant in either world. What did he really want? How did he really see himself? There was no question in which world he would have to make his career. Partly because of his blindness (although we don't really know how much that handicapped him in learning composed pieces), but mainly because of the barriers a black musician faced in his time, jazz offered Tatum the only viable way forward in music. He took it and ran.

Early Development

*"And so will someone when I am dead and gone
write my life? (As if any man really knew
aught of my life, Why even I myself I often
think know little or nothing of my real
life . . .)"*   **WALT WHITMAN**

ART TATUM, JR., was born on October 13, 1909, in Toledo, Ohio. Teddy Roosevelt had just been succeeded by William H. Taft as President and times were not bad. World War I was still five years away, the Great Depression, twenty years. That remarkable and complex instrument, the piano, had escaped the confines of royal or upper-class music rooms and every household that could afford one had a piano in the parlor, like a household pet. In 1909 an American production record of 364,545 pianos was set, and American manufacturers (294 of them) for the first time turned out more pianos—considerably more—than the European builders. Large numbers of elephants were dying to provide ivories for them.

Jazz as a field of music had itself just been born and ragtime music, essentially a piano form, was a national rage. The men who would turn ragtime into the style known as "stride piano," the style that would be dominant when Art would begin playing professionally, had already begun their own development: James P. Johnson (born 1891) was eighteen, and Willie (The Lion) Smith (born 1897) was twelve. Several other pianists who would later have a powerful influence on Art's development as a jazz pianist were toddling toward kindergarten in 1909: Earl Hines (1903) was six, and Fats Waller (1904) although only five was already playing hymns on a harmonium to accompany his father's street-corner preaching.

A number of people destined to shape American jazz were born at about this time. The year 1909 saw the birth not only of Art Tatum but of Benny Goodman, Lionel Hampton, Gene Krupa, Ben Webster, Lester Young, Dickie Wells, and Jay McShann. Only slighter older than Art were Bunny Berigan, Red Norvo, Benny Carter, Rex Stewart, and Albert Ammons, and babies born only a year or two later than Art included Mary Lou Williams, Artie Shaw, Roy Eldridge, Stan Kenton, and Teddy Wilson. All these talented people would help to create the vehicle of jazz, and would ride it together well into the twentieth century. Many of them will show up in Tatum's story. All of them would outlive Tatum by a wide margin.

ART WAS THE second of four children, the oldest of the three who lived; sister Arline came nine years later and brother Karl eleven years later. Both parents were born in the South and were part of the first generation of southern blacks to be born into freedom rather than slavery. They probably moved to Toledo, separately, around the turn of the century. The great emigration from the South in search of jobs and a more liberated life style for blacks had not yet started. In 1902 there were only some 750 blacks in Toledo (according to Russell McCown, who was born in that year and claims to be the oldest living native of Toledo; he can still remember seeing in person the Indian Iron Tail, whose head is enshrined on the nickel). By 1909 there were still fewer than 2000 blacks out of a total population of about 168,500, a proportion of not much more than 1 percent. The black community in Toledo in 1909 must have been compact and well known to one another.

Art, Sr., was born in Statesville, South Carolina, and was twenty-eight when Art, Jr., was born.[1] He was a mechanic of some sort, and he had regular and steady employment during most of Art's life, first with the gas company and later at the National Supply Company, a steel-pipe factory, where Karl said he was a "shipper." Money was managed conservatively, but was apparently never a problem, at least not until Art, Sr. died in 1951 (of complications from an industrial accident). Karl has said his father "was tall and brown-skinned, and there wasn't any foolishness about him," and Arline has described her father as ". . . tall and imposing. Everybody used to think he was a doctor, because of his personal blessings" (Balliett, *American Musicians*). According to Arline he was a solid and devoted father, if rather strict about discipline and morality: "Even though the youngsters communicated mostly with their mother, Mr. Tatum's presence was always felt. He was the disciplinarian. He believed in the good and the dignified life. . . . He believed in responsibility" (Rothman, "The Art of Tatum"). All of that is reflected in his membership in the Grace Presbyterian Church, the Frederick Douglass Community Association, the Indiana Avenue Branch YMCA, the NAACP, and the Knights of Pythias.

There is almost nothing to give us a clue as to Art's relationship with his father, except for a few of Arline's remarks—for example: "Don't let a football game get on the radio or the TV Art bought us when they first came out, and they'd sit in the front room yellin' and carryin' on . . ." (Balliett, *American Musicians*). Mr. Tatum, Sr., loved sports, as Art, Jr. did for his whole life, and Art loved to share sports events with his father. Arline told me, "My Dad used to go to ball games, he'd meet Art in Cleveland or New York or wherever there's a big game, you know, Art call him, say, 'Hey, Pop, you wanna come to Cleveland, you wanna come to NY, So-and-so's playing,' you know."

In spite of Arline's remarks about the "presence" of her father, in the view of a neighbor, Ernestine Allen, "You didn't see too much of his father. That's the reason I didn't know what kind of work his father did. You didn't see too much of him. But he was there, because he took care of 'em." Another neighbor, a contemporary of Arline's, couldn't remember Mr. Tatum at all, and thought he might have died quite young. Perhaps his presence was more felt than heard. It seems clear that in the daily life of the Tatum family the mother was the figure who made things run.

Mildred Hoskins ("a little bitty thing" but "very strong" according to Mrs. Allen) was born in Martinsville, West Virginia, probably in 1890. Her obituary in the *Toledo Blade*, July 14, 1958 says she was sixty-eight when she died; that would make her nineteen when Art, Jr., was born. Mildred worked, as a domestic in white Toledo homes. In spite of working, it seems likely that she, as would be the case in most traditional families, had the major responsibility for Art, Jr.'s upbringing. Mrs. Allen described her as "a very staid, strong woman, and she had a lot of high principles."

Karl probably came closest to living up to her ideals, to being the way she wanted a son of hers to be; Karl was stable and studious and eventually took a college degree and had a career as a social worker. But Art (she always pronounced it "A-u-t," just like "ought") in fact was probably her favorite child. Again according to Mrs. Allen, "She loved Art the most, 'cause she always talked about Art." She was a warm and outgoing woman; Arline told a reporter: "She had a way of opening her home and her arms to all." When Arline talked about her with me it was mostly in the present tense and I could almost feel her presence in the house, turning out solid meals for the family, keeping the cookie jar filled for neighborhood children, and humoring everybody's individual quirks. From the tone of published accounts even in his young adulthood Art, Jr., relied heavily on her judgment and opinions. It was she who made sure that money was saved out of anything Art, Jr., earned, first from his paper route and later from his piano playing around town, and she who when he was old enough bought him his first car. (Art seems to have had a love affair with cars, and once told friends that his greatest regret in life was not being able to drive.)

When Art was born the family was living at 820 Mill Street,[2] but they moved while he was still a child to 1123 City Park Avenue, just off Dorr Street, a main thoroughfare into downtown Toledo and only a few miles from Toledo's riverfront. Art grew up largely in the house on City Park. Mrs. Allen, who lived next door to the Tatums as a child, has said this was a respectable, middle-class neighborhood at the time, one of the best neighborhoods in which a black family could live, and that "Considering the times, they lived well—they had a very neat, clean house, and the kids were always well-dressed and they were very neat, the yard was always impeccably groomed and everything." Toledo neighborhoods were far less segregated by color than they appear to be now, and on both Mitchell Street and City Park Avenue the Tatums had white neighbors, and white friends, as well as black.

By almost all available reports the Tatums were a solid and church-going family, with strong conventional values. Religion was important, and in 1919 Art, Sr., and Mildred were charter members of the Grace Presbyterian Church, across the street from the house where the children were raised. In fact, Mr. Tatum's obituary says that Grace Presbyterian "was founded . . . in his former home on Mitchell Street." In any case it prospered and grew and soon had to move from City Park to a larger location, but the Tatums remained active in the church. On the other hand, Art, Jr.'s parents seem never to have opposed his interest or his involvement in the late-night and alcohol-drenched world of jazz, and that seems unusual in a traditional, church-going black family in the early part of this century. Mrs. Allen recalls that it was common knowledge in the neighborhood that in Art's adolescence and early adulthood he was devoted to drinking bootleg beer, and the fact that this doesn't seem to have caused any family problems seems mysterious to me. However, what I might think as a white person, about how a black family might have operated early in this century, is surely based mainly on stereotypes. Talking to Arline I realized that while the Tatums had high moral standards they were also flexible and realistic. Arline told me:

> I couldn't stand nobody did a lot of drinking. I used to go
> out sometimes with a lot of my girl friends and they used
> to like to drink. But my stomach would never hold a lot of

this junk, so therefore my Dad, I'd come in here and my Dad would go downstairs, he'd keep tomatoes and Vienna sausage and all that kind of stuff down there, you know, for me, 'cause he knew if I'd be out there with them girls I was gonna be sick. He'd go down there, he'd get up out of his bed, go down there and get some ice and put tomato juice on it and all like that, bring it upstairs to me. But Momma say, "No way." Momma say, "I told her not to do it. No way." But she knew he was gonna do it, what'd she care anyway, she knew Poppa was gonna do it. Poppa'd get up outta bed and take care of his girl.

Some of their realism about alcohol probably came from living in a partly glass house—one childhood acquaintance told me, "Their Daddy drank pretty good, their Momma, too." But everyone agreed they were respectable and hard-working—"nice people."

It has been said (for example, in the entry for Art Tatum in the *Biographical Dictionary of Afro-American and African Musicians,* Eileen Southern, ed.) that both parents played musical instruments, in at least a basic fashion: Art, Sr., the guitar and Mildred the piano. Arline also reported this when the *New Yorker*'s Whitney Balliett interviewed her: "[My father] played the piano and he loved the harp—the Jew's harp. My mother played piano, too, and a little violin, and sometimes they'd have a session together. Church music" (*American Musicians*). However, Arline said nothing of this in her Rothman interviews, and several people I talked with who had known Art as a child had no recollection of either of his parents' ever playing. There is a claim that Mildred gave Art his first piano lessons, but his brother Karl doesn't believe she played enough to give Art lessons; and in any case there is no evidence to show that she was capable of taking him very far. Whether or not Art's parents played, it seems pretty certain that Art's first exposure to music was to church music, as it was for so many other black jazz musicians. The earliest input to the dawning musical consciousness of the future jazz giant was probably the sweet and simple harmony of hymns.

Art's partial blindness must have been like a boulder in the stream of his development, forcing the flow into channels different from those of the other children he knew and grew up with. His visual impairment began early, but it's not clear whether or not he was born with some kind of handicap. Rex Stewart wrote that Art was born with milk cataracts on both eyes, and Karl, too, says cataracts from birth were the cause of his handicap. However, Arline's account is that Art was born with sight but developed diptheria, measles, and scarlet fever when he was three, and one of the residuals of these bouts was a severe visual handicap.

One person I talked to surprised me with yet a third explanation for Art's limited vision. Ernie Lewis[3] described a visit to the Tatum house in the 1940s and a conversation with Art's mother, in which she took full responsibility for Art's disability. She reported she often let him sleep, as an infant, on the front porch of the house, which faces toward the east and the rising sun. Mrs. Tatum seems to have felt that the infant Tatum's eyes were burned as he slept in the early morning there on the porch. She forgot about him while doing the housework:

> She was a talkative lady, she'd talk, talk, talk, she'd tell you everything. She told me how Art became blind. As a baby, she left him outside and the sun, or the reflection from the glass, hurt the nerve in his eye. It didn't seem to bother her, the way she talked to me. She's a very talkative woman, she'd talk, talk, talk the whole time I was there. She talked herself into it, and then right out of it, and just kept right on talking. She didn't tell me anything about cataracts or diseases. She just told me that he had gone to sleep, and she had him out there on the front porch, she went to do her housework, and she forgot about him being out there in that sun. I can understand her doing something like that, the way she was talking.

But in point of fact Mildred's explanation seems unlikely to be true. Early morning sunlight would be at too low an angle to be injurious, and if painfully intense light were reflected, say from a window, a normal child would almost surely throw an arm over his eyes or turn over. However, children with measles are indeed dangerously vulnerable to damage from light, and if this was not understood by Mrs. Tatum it could be that measles combined with mornings on the porch *did* play a part in producing Art's visual impairment.

It is truly puzzling that Mrs. Tatum made no mention of either the cataracts or the childhood disease stories. Art himself almost never mentioned them, either, although one writer once reported of an interview with him, "He said he wouldn't mind if I told that he had had a cataract operation when he was a young boy." He didn't like to have attention focused on his handicap, and if questioned about it he often invented a story. Several people heard him tell others, later in life, that his blindness was the result of a football accident. One of them was Rex Stewart:

> I've heard him go into the routine: he was playing halfback for his high school team on this rainy day; they were in the huddle; they lined up; the ball was snapped . . . wait a minute—there's a fumble! Tatum recovers . . . he's at the forty-five-yard line, the thirty-five, the twenty-five! Sprinting like mad, he is heading for a touchdown! Then, out of nowhere, a mountain falls on him, and just before oblivion descends, Tatum realizes he had been tackled by Two-Ton Tony, the biggest fellow on either team. He is carried off the field, a hero, but has had trouble with his eyes ever since. [184]

Somehow the money was found for a series of eye operations (Stewart says there were thirteen of them), and such a series fits much better with the cataract theory than with the childhood diseases one. As a result of these operations, when he was eleven he was at least able to see things held close in front of him, and possibly to distinguish colors. That, however, was not the end of the story. At some point, probably in his early twenties, Art was mugged.[4]

> It was one night in his early Toledo period when Tatum lost what little eyesight he had gained through the painful series of childhood operations. After a session at the Cha-

teau [the Chateau de France, a popular Toledo restaurant and nightclub], friends would drop Tatum off at City Park and Dorr Street. He enjoyed walking the short, familiar block to his house in the cool of the morning. Art whistled with the same trueness of note that he played piano, and people along the way grew to recognize this early morning song as coming from their brilliant young neighbor-pianist. One morning they heard the song suddenly interrupted. This brought the B. F. Adamses to the door in a rush, in time to see the blind pianist struggling with an assailant who had blackjacked him. As Mr. Adams raced down the stairs of his home, the assailant broke away and fled. Art was helped into the house. The blackjack had caught him in the eye. Dr. B. E. Leatherman came immediately and administered emergency treatment. The next morning Art was taken to the hospital. The eye had been damaged beyond repair. From then on the other eye got worse.

[Rothman, "The Art of Tatum"]

More recently Arline has told me that Art knew who his attacker was, and that it was the nephew of the man who owned the place where Art had been playing.

I think the guy must have known where he lived anyway. And he must have followed them in the car, maybe intending to get Art when he got out. And the white people next door that we called Grandma and Grandpa, Grandpa Adams jumped up out of his bed, he had his pajamas on, he was comin' out to git the guy, and he jumped out. Art sort of sit down on the walk, it sort of made Art sick, I think. Then he [Grandpa Adams] hollered up here and kept callin' Momma and Poppa, and he walked Art on up here, and by that time my mother and dad was downstairs. He said, "Somebody hit Art, right out there in front." And they set Art in a chair, not this chair but a chair right here by the door, and my mother called the doctor. And he got up outta his bed and come here—I think if I'm not mistaken he taken his eye out and did something to it. He got operated on the next day at Flower Hospital. He went to

Flower to have his operation, long, long years ago. I think he was one of the first colored that had been in that hospital.

Later on he said who it was. And my Dad went over there—my Dad's quiet, but don't hurt us kids! My Dad went over there looking for that dude. He didn't find him but he told the guy that owned the place, which was his uncle, he told him, "You better tell him to leave town, because he will do no good staying in this town." Of course, my mother called the police right away. But he didn't come back there, so his uncle said—just disappeared.

While the attacker got very little money from Art, since Art had a habit in those days of keeping any significant cash from a job in his shoe, he did succeed in undoing, in a few seconds, much if not most of the gain of those expensive and unpleasant eye operations. No further efforts were ever made to improve Tatum's vision. Much later Art's wife allegedly offered to donate one of her corneas as a transplant for him, but Art was too afraid of the operation to go through with it.

In spite of this gloomy story, by all accounts Art refused to take his limited sight very seriously and instead took it, so to speak, in his stride. Arline, nine years his junior, was almost possessively protective of him, even though it was totally unnecessary.

And I was absolutely crazy about Art 'cause he couldn't see good. And sometimes like if Art would go near Indiana or Division or somewhere down thataway I'd get my girl friend who used to live down the street, just go down the street and see if Art made it down there. I would go and stand in the door—Dorothy Royal, that used to have music down on Belmont, used to have a tavern, she didn't allow any kids in there. But she'd know when I walked in, I wouldn't go no further than the door, see if he's in there. He'd tell Momma, "Well, I'm goin' down to Dorothy's," you know. He used to have a chauffeur, and the boy'd come and pick him up, and they'd go on down. And he'd tell Momma usually where he was; I'm goin to Johnny Crocket's or I'm goin' to Dorothy's or I'm goin' to the pool room—he loved to shoot pool.

Lynn Mathews, he used to be a policeman there, and he had a son called Lynn. They lived the next street over, on the same street that Art was born on. Lynn had a goat, and Art and Lynn, boy, they used to get out there in that field and they had that goat every day, playing with it. They didn't let nobody play with the goat but Art and Lynn and this one other boy. They'd get out there and they'd have a time with this goat. See, I had an aunt that lived right at this field, aunt and uncle, on my Dad's side. And I used to would go there and sometime I'd sit in the window and watch 'em. I watched Art everything he did, you'd better believe it.

But for his own part Art minimized his handicap and managed to have a nearly normal childhood. His teacher Mrs. Morrison summed it up: "He was as near normal as a kid could be and yet be blind. Bless his heart." According to Arline and others, it kept people near him most of the time, and Art seems to have liked that. Rothman wrote, "He was completely social; he wanted to be with people, and he wanted them to enjoy him." Young boys as a group are not conspicuous for their compassion, or for making allowances for handicaps—they are more likely to make fun of them. Yet he was successfully social, and not just when he was playing the piano. Family and friends have reported that he played a lot of marbles, and Eddie Barefield, a musician who lived near Tatum in the early 1930s, told me that Art was able to play pool amazingly well. Eddie, in fact, believed Art could see better than he let others believe. He tells a story about sitting at a bar with Art and having Art interrupt the conversation to move closer to an attractive woman who had sat down some distance away. Russell McCown, who was older than Art but who lived in his neighborhood, claimed that Art was able to play basketball largely by sound; he knew where the others were from the sound of their voices, and could even take respectable shots at the basket. There was just one thing, Rothman reported: "In the middle of the game he might suddenly quit, race into the house, sit down at the piano and play continuously for an hour."[5]

Art must have won his age-mates over in some way, as he was clearly able to do with people all the rest of his life. Whatever the facts may have been about his participation, sports were clearly one of Art's strongest and most long-lived interests. Brother Karl was athletically gifted and was able to do what Art could not—throw himself fully into sport—and Art was always proud of Karl's prowess in school.[6] Art had a phenomenal memory and on the street corner he was often the court of last appeal for some dispute about a sports event or an athlete's record. For the rest of his life Art's passion for sports was second only to that for music, and both were far ahead of anything else. There's reason to think, as we will see, that his interest in sports had a lot to do with a strong competitive streak.

There are many stories about how later in life Art would turn his impairment into a joke. Interestingly, these usually involved an automobile. In one of these stories, Art was being driven home (in the 1931 Model A Ford bought with money his mother saved out of his earnings) from an engagement in Toledo, when the car was flagged down by a policeman for speeding. Art managed to change places with the driver before the cop appeared at the window, and when the officer asked him whether he knew how fast he had been going, Art replied that he didn't know, because he was blind and couldn't see the speedometer. Eventually the officer recognized Tatum and the two young men got off with a warning. In another story from a later time, Art staged a great argument with the blind singer, Al Hibbler, in front of others who didn't know him well enough to know this twist to his humor; the "argument" was about who should do the driving if they went on tour together.

Art's first schooling was at the Jefferson School in Toledo, but it seems impossible to be precise about dates. He completed the eighth grade at Jefferson in 1924, aged fourteen, but no records for him have been located later than 1919, when he was ten. In 1917, Ruth Brockway's class had nine members, ranging in age from seven (that would be Art, whose eighth birthday came after the start of the school year) to sixteen. While this was apparently a class for the blind, other handicaps may have been represented. For what it's worth, Art, Jr.'s average achievement, taking reading, English, spelling, and arithmetic together, was a 77 out of 100, which put him somewhat below the average for his class (still, he was the youngest, and also these years, 1917 to 1920, were probably the years when he was having his series of eye operations). He was judged better at arithmetic than at the other subjects, and that continued to be his best subject over the three years. Bill Cummerow, another visually impaired Toledan who was some years behind Art in school, has told me that all blind children in Toledo had to take piano lessons, but Ms. Brockway's gradebook has, sadly, no entries in the column for music. There is good reason to think that Art's very special abilities were already manifest by age seven, but perhaps Ms. Brockway had no ear for music.

A lucky accident[7] recently turned up the teacher who had Art for English and American history in the seventh and eighth grades (1922–24), still alive (in 1992) and able to share vivid memories of those two years. Art learned Braille at Jefferson, and it seems typical of his enthusiastic, optimistic nature that he taught Braille to Arline and Karl, because he enjoyed reading that way and thought they would, too. But it was the school's policy to keep handicapped children in regular classes as much as possible, so Art spent much or even most of his time with sighted students. Mrs. Morrison's classes ran to forty-eight or fifty students, so there would have been little time to give Art special attention. And yet he had no trouble keeping up.

> He was a mischievous little chap. He took Braille with another teacher at the same time, so he came to my classes only when Braille was not necessary. He was not a genius type, you know, as for grades, but he was interested in school and I would say that he was a good solid C student. I was always told that he was not born blind, that his father was—this may be not so, I was told that his father was one of these cult people that didn't believe in dealing much with doctors. But anyway when we had him he could see—he could see to get around. And I remember him as

well as—he didn't go home for his lunch and neither did I. Most of the children did go home for lunch, so oftentimes he and I, or very few, were the only ones in the building, and I'd hear him sometimes on the drums, and I heard him on piano. Every chance that kids got they took to the piano, and he took to the piano more than anybody. And another thing—in those days we diagrammed sentences. At noontime what he loved to do, I would fill a blackboard—the pupils liked to take as long a sentence as possible, with dangling participles and phrases and so on— well, he and I there with our lunch had a chance to do that and fill a whole side-board. I did not do the work for him, I would just say, "Now where should this go"—we always called him Arthur, we never called him Art—"where should this go, down which word should this go?" And he was excellent at it, and just loved to have the kids come back from their lunch and find the whole side-board covered with his work. But he was a good boy, a mischievous boy—he had a sweetness about him that I enjoyed, otherwise I wouldn't have worked with him every noon-time. It was really fun to work with him, because he had a keen mind and he was so pleased when he could find just exactly where the lines went. I remember lots of pupils I taught . . . I loved teaching. Of course, children in those days didn't pack a knife for you, either. He was a "nice," as teachers call them, a nice boy that you would enjoy having around . . . There were others we had a little trouble with, but never with him. He wasn't a sissy by any means. He was well-liked by other pupils, too.

In November of 1924, aged fifteen, instead of entering Woodward High School he was moved to Columbus, Ohio and enrolled at the School for the Blind. By a coincidence no odder than most, the trumpet player Harry "Sweets" Edison, with whom Art eventually recorded, grew up across the street from this school. (Several brief acounts of Art's childhood refer to it as the Cousino School, but the Ohio Historical Society has no record of a school with that name,

Karl doesn't remember that name, and Sweets didn't recognize it either.) Clearly, the Tatums wanted to do everything they could for their son, and the move to Columbus was made easier by the fact that there was a cousin there who could keep tabs on him. The existing file on Art at the school tells us nothing about his performance there, or how he was seen by teachers, but Arline has reported that once again he showed a great capacity for making friends. Years later he still had contact with schoolmates from the School for the Blind in different cities, and whenever he was in one of those cities he would look up his classmate "for a big laughing, hand-clapping, finger-snapping session."

Several authorities assert that Art studied violin as well as piano in Columbus, and the singer Jon Hendricks, who grew up several houses away from the Tatums, told me that he saw Art's violin in the house. Arline, too, has put a violin under Art's chin, without mentioning the Columbus School for the Blind:

> You know, I was up there looking to see when I came home one day if his violin was still around. Now, where it is I don't know. Yeah, he could play the violin pretty good. He liked violin. Oh, I can't think of this boy's name, he's a white boy. He went to school with Art, over at the blind school, over at Jefferson. He played the violin, and him and Art were great friends. And Art came in here one day, and he said, "Momma, I want you to hear something." So Momma said, "What is it?" So him and the boy came in here one day, Art got with this violin, Momma, she smiled and everything, everything we do that's great she'll let us know she likes it. And she said, "Well, where'd you learn that?" What is that boy's name? He's blind too. I been trying to think of his name, 'cause I was gonna look and see if I could find him somewhere in the telephone book, you know, 'cause he was such a good friend of Art's.

In September of 1925, less than a year after starting in Columbus, the school records show that Art was no longer enrolled in the

School for the Blind. He almost certainly returned to Toledo, and at some point (perhaps immediately) entered the Toledo School (or Conservatory) of Music, which no longer exists. I have found no records that would document how long he studied at the Conservatory (some say two years). It seems safe to guess that Art had stopped school by 1927 at the latest, whether he had finished high school or not. By this time he was already extraordinarily accomplished on the piano, and there seems to have been no question about the idea that he would at that point begin a career as a professional pianist.

Russell McCown, who knew him as a boy, has said that he never knew Art to have a date or in any other way actively to seek contact with girls. Russell is convinced it was entirely because of his absolutely over-riding interest in the piano, and never mentioned his visual impairment as a handicap where girls were concerned. Women were not absent from Art's later life (his illegitimate son was born when he was twenty-four, and later he was twice married), but for the biographical record he must have entered his twenties with lots of experience at the piano and very little experience with women.

Whenever Art finished school, the next natural and in fact unavoidable stage would have been the finding of a suitable job. For Art, most of the options available to others were closed by his visual impairment. However severe that was, somewhere between 70 percent and 90 percent, it meant that what were opportunities for others—jobs such as waiter, bellman, Pullman porter, mechanic like his father—were passageways locked against him. Without his musical talent (such a tame word for Art Tatum!) he would have faced a deadeningly limited range of possibilities. Even with his talent he could probably never have found a way to realize more than a small share of it without a vehicle like jazz. Within jazz he could improvise a career, make a career out of improvising, invent a path for himself, take advantage of fast-changing musical developments, and even influence the course of those developments. The coincidence between his birth and the birth of jazz was surely more important for his life than for many of the others who were to become jazz musicians.

CLEARLY, WE WOULD like to know more than we do about Art's growing up. Unfortunately, the adults who knew Art as a small child are gone, his peers who knew him as an adolescent are nearly gone, and many of those who knew him as an adult report that he almost never discussed his past, or his private thoughts and feelings. Even Billy Taylor, who was a kind of protégé of his, has said that he never felt the freedom to ask Art much of anything about himself or his past. Mel Clement, a Washington-based pianist who knew Tatum well over a long period, also reports that although they spent many nights together, talking and playing, Art never talked about his personal life or his past. It was always music or sports. One gets the impression that somehow Art actively discouraged any discussion of his past or his personal life.

Nevertheless it seems clear that Tatum grew up among stable people and was part of a family and community with a settled life style. What we can see from this distance is a person who from the beginning stood out as cheerful, fun-loving, energetic and out-going, very fond of people but at the same time fiercely independent and competitive. The newly invented automobile was a powerful symbol of independence for him, and the futile impulse to drive one popped up repeatedly in his life. But it was the existence of the piano that gave him his actual independence. One can see even in his early life how his musical skill became, on the one hand, his ticket to a self-sustaining life and his escape from confinement within the prison of blindness, and on the other hand an asset to his sociable personality and a way to keep others around him. Music gave Art more than musical pleasure; it literally held his life together.

Anecdotes of Art's later life almost all show the same characteristics as do his childhood. He always joked about his impairment, but he was also intensely independent about it, did not like to have it mentioned as a handicap and, for example, would prefer to pre-plan his entrance to the piano in a club rather than have someone lead him there. He was simply inexhaustible and had a life-long habit of staying up all night after a gig, usually seeking an after-hours club in which to listen and play until daybreak or later. He loved sports all his life and always insisted on a radio in his hotel room so he could listen to football and baseball games. And he seems almost never to have been by himself, at least not by choice. There was no trace in his early youth (or later) of that dramatic and demonic self-destructiveness that seemed to haunt some other jazz musicians, for example, Charlie Parker, Billie Holiday, Chet Baker, or Miles Davis. In his adult years he lived as simple and safe a life as a jazz musician might, filled with much the same pleasures as were his growing years. His friends, as ever, were devoted to him (one said he was "simply a lovely man to know." As Orrin Keepnews wrote not long after Tatum died, ". . . few if any lives [in jazz] were on a more even keel than Tatum's."

"The only harm he ever did," Earl Hines said, "was to himself." But that seems to have been the result, not of a demon he couldn't control but of a zest for life and a carelessness about taking care of himself. Lots of jazz musicians took little care of themselves, and in fact several of the elderly black musicians I talked to said, in effect, I never expected to make it to forty. I'm reminded of the jazz musician who had reached the age of seventy and was being toasted at a banquet, who reflected in his speech, "If I'd known I was gonna live this long I'd have taken better care of myself." If Art's life-style was hardly healthy, it also wasn't extreme for his line of work; it just caught up with him earlier than with some others.

The parallel with his close friend and mentor, Fats Waller (who died at 39), is remarkable. What Andy Razaf said of Fats would seem to apply just as well to Art Tatum: "Life to him was just one long crescendo, and he had to live it fast; but he never consciously hurt anybody but himself . . . I shall always remember him as a great, happy guy who lived a happy, carefree life that ended much too soon" (quoted in Ulanov, *A History of Jazz*).

Early Musical Development

"Talent learns from others, a genius from himself." **ARNOLD SCHOENBERG**

"He mastered the piano as if by magic, the secret of which will never be discovered . . ." **FETIS**, describing the pianist Thalberg

TATUM WAS CLEARLY a musical prodigy, responsive and reactive to sound and to music from a tender age. Early on he began wanting to play the piano more than anything, he set himself the highest standards and he was willing to work at achieving them, and his visual handicap was no handicap at all when it came to music. He had an extraordinary memory (for music, of course, but also for voices, for sports information, and even for remembering hands of cards in bridge and pinochle), and he must have begun storing up musical ideas from an early age.

No one is still alive who can say for sure exactly when his musical talent first started to manifest itself.[1] One reference work (Miller) asserts that Tatum "began his musical activities on the violin at age thirteen, but a year later switched to piano . . . ,"[2] and that relatively late age seemed to be confirmed even by Tatum himself, in one of his rare public statements; late in his career Art appeared on the Steve Allen television show, and the following exchange took place:

> ALLEN: Art, when did you begin playing? When you were a kid?
>
> TATUM: (*pause*) I started when I was about 12 or 13, I guess. I started on the violin first. I was very poor [on the violin], incidentally. . . . I studied violin for about two years, and I studied piano for about four days, and I was a much better pianist in four days . . . (*trails off*).
>
> [The Tonight Show, June 2, 1955]

Clearly, Art didn't mean to say that he studied piano only for four days, but rather that he was immediately better on piano than on violin. In any case maybe Art was answering a different question from the one Allen asked, and was describing his first actual lessons, although neither Arline nor Karl has ever suggested to an interviewer that Art's first musical experiences were on the violin. Furthermore, not only is it unthinkable that an innate talent like Art's could lie dormant for thirteen years, but a number of eye-witnesses have put his first musical steps at a much earlier age. For example, by what appears to be Arline's account (quoted in Rothman, "The Art of Tatum"), he was showing interest in the piano in his family's living room by the time he was three, and showing unusual talent by six. According to another story , his mother noticed his first efforts at the piano at age three: "When Art was three, his mother took him along to choir practice. After they returned home, she went into the kitchen to prepare dinner and heard someone fumbling with a hymn on the piano. Assuming that a member of the church had dropped by and was waiting for her to come out of the kitchen, she called out, 'Who's there?' No one answered, so she entered the parlor, and there sat three-year-old Art, absorbed in playing the hymn"[3] (Stewart, "Genius in Retrospect," 185). He had picked out the melody of one of the hymns he had heard at church choir-practice earlier in the day, and after that he frequently amused himself at the piano. Remembering that his blindness had set in at least by the time he was three, and that his life must have been severely limited by that fact, it is easy to imagine that discovering what he and the piano could do for each other must have been enormously significant to him, no matter at what precise age it happened.

Mrs. Bennett was an aunt who lived close by and who has given another eye-witness account of Art as a small child at the piano: "In the beginning Art's mother used to set him on the piano stool to let him amuse himself while she did the housework. He was about four years of age at the time, but he learned to play. He used to hit the bass notes with his elbow then the bass chord with his left and the melody with his right hand. It was amazing the music he could play in this manner, all by ear, of course" (Spencer, *An Appreciation*).

Amazing, indeed! If this story can be believed, Art was apparently struggling to play "stride" piano before he could reach even an octave—or for that matter before stride piano had been invented. There is another story that echoes this one. A woman who had been at the Jefferson School at the same time as Art recalled that often at recess Art would go to the piano in the kindergarten room and play, and that she and others would stand and listen to him rather than go out doors and play. "Art was so little that he couldn't yet span an octave," she said. "He would use his left elbow for the low note and arch his arm over the keys to reach the top notes of the octave with his fingers."

Assuming even a kernel of truth in such stories I have to see in them at the very least a really fierce and early desire to master the keyboard. He showed a sense of rhythm, too, and wanted to keep time with his foot. But since his foot didn't reach to the ground, "it was kick, kick, kick, until he had kicked a large spot of varnish from the piano." Mrs. Bennett capped her description with the comment that, "He was playing pretty well for a small boy!" Mrs. Bennett must have had too little experience with piano players, small or large, to let her grasp what a phenomenon was unfolding in her neighborhood.

There is more evidence about the age at which Art started playing in the remark of Russell McCown, a childhood friend who was seven years older than Art: "My earliest recollection of Art Tatum, my folks returned from a concert at the church one night, they were talking about this little five-year-old blind boy playing the piano. I found out his name was Art Tatum. He could play anything he heard—and then he'd play it his way."

Limitations on his vision must have led to his paying increased attention to what his ears were telling him, and there are some signs in the stories that are told that he was innately superior at interpreting sounds. Early on he could tell what coin had been dropped on a table by the ring of it, or what note two spoons produced when hit together. His childhood acquaintance Rudolph Perry told me, "He had an ear—if he heard something outdoors, he could hit it on the piano. Airplane, anything, he could hit it on the piano." And another childhood friend, Steve Taylor, reported:

> His ear was so acute, until if he would hear a bumblebee he could reproduce that sound on the piano. Even an airplane flying in the air—I heard him do that! If there was thunder and lightning outside, he could reproduce the thunder on the piano. He came to our church sometimes, played there, some hymns, then we'd have a little demonstration, how he could reproduce these sounds and all that sort of thing.

Later in his life observers claimed that he could identify the dominant note in even a flushing toilet, or could tell what brewery a dropped beer can came from. In this respect he was showing what is almost certainly an inherited gift, and there are many similar accounts about the lives of other musical prodigies; Renée Fisher's book, *Musical Prodigies,* is full of interesting stories of this kind. (I like the story Gene Lees tells of Oscar Peterson, on tour and traveling in a bus, asking the driver, "Could you drive a little faster or a little slower? I can't sleep in B-natural.") As his interest focused on the piano, Art became enormously sensitive to its sounds. He complained about any out-of-tune notes on the family instrument, to the extent that his father indulged in the relative extravagance of having the piano tuned every other week or so. Arline reports that he also hated to hear even a well-tuned note in the wrong place, whether he or anyone else had played it. "Art could be sound asleep in his room, but if I hit a wrong note he was up and bellowing at me."

Art's highly unusual sensitivity to pitch worked hand-in-glove with his phenomenal memory. We've already heard about his ability to reproduce hymn melodies at a very early age. His friend Russell McCown has another testimonial: "One time the Jenkins Orphan Band came up here from the South, you know, Art stood on the corner, listened to them, then he'd go home and play anything he'd heard." Art's ability to remember people, over periods of many years, purely by the sound of their voices amazed many in later years. Mrs. Morrison visited him backstage in the 1940s, when he was working on 52nd Street, the first time she'd seen him since he left the eighth grade some twenty years earlier. Without any introduction she said, "Arthur, do you remember me?" With almost no pause he replied with the name of the American history textbook she had used in his class. And it wasn't only memory for sounds—later on this same skill helped make him an acknowledged champion at the card games he loved to play.

Art did, at some point, have a real piano teacher, by the name of Overton G. Rainey. Rothman (1985) places O. G. Rainey at the Jefferson School, which would mean that he got hold of Art quite early. And John Cleveland, of the Toledo Public Library, told me he believed that Art studied with Rainey in the Toledo public schools and in private lessons. However, Mrs. Morrison doesn't remember him, and A. B. Spellman says that Rainey was a teacher not at Jefferson but at the Toledo School of Music and that Art started with him only after his return to Toledo from the School for the Blind in Columbus, in his mid-teens.[4] Doerschuk and John Chilton, like Spellman, assign Rainey to the Toledo School of Music. In other words, we don't know how early in Art's training Overton Rainey got hold of him.

We do know that Rainey, like Art, was both black and visually impaired. He sometimes added to his income from teaching by working in bars near his home, playing sheet music he had learned in Braille. Bill Cummerow, another partially blind black pianist, who took lessons from Rainey five or six years after Tatum had moved on, says that Rainey did not improvise at all, and didn't encourage an interest in jazz in his students. Cummerow remembers that Rainey was both impressed with Art's gift and critical of him for not doing more with it—by which he probably meant aiming at a concert career rather than jazz. He criticized Bill for tapping his foot when he played and saw it as an unfortunate habit that went along with an interest in jazz, telling Bill: "Art used to do that, too" (shades of the spot Art wore in the varnish on the family piano). Rainey was also outspokenly critical of Art, as he watched him move out into the world, for drinking too much. All the same, Bernice Lawson, a teacher of piano who knew Art much later in Los Angeles, often heard him speak of Rainey, giving him credit for having been a major influence on him. To judge by the results, he certainly did something right.

The period between Art's first picking out hymn melodies and his completion of work at the Toledo Conservatory, say between the ages of six and sixteen (1915 to 1925), comprised the years when the lights came on in his head, when he developed a conception of what a piano was for and what he might do with it, and when he established his fundamental approach to it. All during this period one could say, as Charles Dickens said about an early transatlantic steamer, that he was "giving rich promise of serious intentions." By the end of the period he had a command of the keyboard that he could hardly have improved upon, a command that one concert performer (Steven Mayer) has said was the equal of the greatest pianists of the nineteenth century. Mayer particularly compares Tatum to the concert artist Josef Hofmann. And yet this period of Tatum's life is one of the most frustrating to try to understand, or even to throw any light on. The idea that Rainey was able to ground him in the classical tradition, and establish the keyboard habits that were the basis of the most outstanding technique in jazz piano playing, seemed farfetched to me—until I learned that the concert pianist Anton Rubinstein had only two teachers: his mother and "one other unknown person."

The case of Rubinstein, and that of Blind Tom, convinced me that with enough raw talent it can be done.

Rubinstein's achievements are well known. Blind Tom is a less visible figure, who may provide an even better illustration of raw talent.[5] He was born in America, blind, the twenty-first child of a slave, in 1849, at the height of the European "virtuoso frenzy," and he was "thrown into the bargain" when his mother was sold to a certain Colonel Bethune. Very early he showed an extreme sensitivity to sounds: "he would caper joyfully when sounds pleased him, or bang his head against the object, roll his sightless eyes, make time bodily with a heard rhythm." He imitated vocally the cries of animals, the sounds of clocks or even storms, almost anything he heard. As a small child he could join in when the Colonel's daughters sang and he even progressed quickly to harmonizing with them. When he was five the master acquired a piano and Tom listened to the girls practicing; then late at night he would sneak into the big house to pick out sounds on the piano. He learned, according to reports, every piece in the girls' repertoire, and then began devising his own pieces, based on natural sounds: "This is what the wind [or the birds, or the trees] said to me," he would explain. Colonel Bethune began exhibiting Tom when he was eight, as a prodigy who could play an amazing repertoire of his own songs "but could also reproduce immediately, upon a single hearing, anything played on the piano, no matter how complex. He could also name any notes that someone else played, and could improvise on a theme suggested by a member of the audience." An Albany, New York, newspaper reported on his concert there: "With his right hand he plays 'Yankee Doodle' in B♭. With his left hand he performs 'Fisher's Hornpipe' in C. At the same time he sings 'Tramp, Tramp' in another key—maintaining three distinct processes in that discord, and apparently without any effort whatever." Most of the rest of Blind Tom's life was occupied with appearances demonstrating his unique and totally untutored talents, in concerts and on the vaudeville stage. He was widely presented in Europe as well, where some of the best known professional musicians of the day heard him, tested him, and (so it is reported) validated his authenticity. If we take all this as even an approximation of the facts, then Blind Tom stands as evidence of the raw, un-polished, largely genetically given abilities that must form the base, in greater or lesser degree, of every famous musician's talent. He also illustrates the fact, as do many others (for example, Alec Templeton, Lennie Tristano, George Shearing, Ray Charles, Marcus Roberts), that blindness need be no handicap to a keyboard artist. Tom died in 1908, the year before Tatum was born, and it's likely that Art never heard of him.

It's clear that Art went from groping for melodies to being some-one in demand for all kinds of public performances in a short span of time. In fact so did most musicians who made a name for themselves: Mary Lou Williams was playing the piano at afternoon teas when she was still so small she had to sit in someone's lap, Ahmad Jamal gave a concert at age eleven, Benny Goodman had his first paying job at age twelve, Fats Waller was a theater organist at fifteen—examples like these could be extended at will. Tatum's pattern was not at all rare, but how terribly unsatisfying it is not to be able to look in on it! By what stages, by how much work, with what help if any, did he climb the ladder from keyboard guesswork to professional competence? How did he acquire a technique which looked like waving his hands over the keys but which brought concert musicians to hear him? How did he learn to bring such chordal and harmonic innovations into his playing? To whom was he listening, and what ambition was driving him? Most people I asked about this could only say that it looked like his achievements were entirely his own, and that in fact may be the nub of the truth. To a large degree he simply flowered, and in his flowering he became *focused* in a way that most people can hardly understand. Almost all of his life experiences had music at their center.

The best we can do is assume that Tatum's move, from piano student to professional jazz musician, took place by the same stages and small increments familiar to most musicians who have traveled this path. We can assume, too, that his movement along that path was phenomenally fast. His ability and his love of the piano were obvious to many people early in his life, although few other than Rainey could really assess that ability, or realize that this was a world-class musician. Francis Williams, a childhood friend of Art's, was another aspiring piano player. He listened to Art and, figuring that there must be something lacking in him since he couldn't do what Art did, gave up the piano for the trumpet. It was only years later when he was on the road playing trumpet that he got some perspective. He would always ask the local musicians to take him to hear their best piano players. Inevitably the best seemed pale to Williams, since he was comparing them with Tatum. Eventually it dawned on him that there simply was no one around who could play even remotely like his friend. Even Tatum's family, who sacrificed to support his interest in the piano, seems to have been surprised at how the world esteemed him. Once when he was playing in Detroit, as a mature artist, his sister and her husband went to the club where he was appearing to hear him. As they approached the club they found a crowd outside waiting to get in to hear Art. "What's happened? Has Art been hurt?," they wanted to know (Rothman, "Toledo Years"). It was only by way of traveling professional musicians who came to town and heard him that the full extent of what was growing in Toledo began to be recognized. (For that matter, it's only recently that the city of Toledo has given him any public recognition. In 1988 they put on an Art Tatum Day and practically no one came. More recently the city has named one wing of a new branch library after him. Most recently, in 1991, Toledo found funds for a month-long festival in his honor, featuring lectures, seminars, and the first performance of a piano concerto by Stanley Cowell dedicated to the memory of Art.)

Soon, probably before he had reached his teenage years and therefore possibly before he had ever had a formal lesson, he was asked to play at parties both at school and in people's homes. Most jazz musicians can tell similar stories about this time in their lives. Russell McCown related a very early memory, in which he describes Tatum as younger than twelve:

> My first encounter with him as a musician, I was working
> for a man who was having a gathering down at his place, at
> Howard Farms, that's a place southeast, down toward the

lake. This man, his name was R.H. Winters, I worked for him about 7–8 years, I was working in the stock room, he was an electrical contractor, we were good friends also—so, he wanted me to get him Art. I knew Art, he'd hang around the corner with the boys. Wherever we went he played. I was able to get him, no problem. So I got him Art, he went down there, he sat down at the piano—Art started saying, this piano's out of tune. He'd hit where the note should be, you know—but he said, I can't play this piano. So I brought him back to Toledo, and Mr. Winters paid him anyway. Mr. Winters gave him a lot of money for that day, $25, but he couldn't play the piano. Later on, Art would be playing around—he formed a little combo of his own when he was about 12 years old, 3–4 pieces, played at dances and stuff like that.

Certainly as a teen-ager he was providing the music for social occasions—probably the one-steps, two-steps, cake-walks, and rags that were still so popular then. A cousin recalled it for an interviewer: ". . . everyone wanted Art to play the piano so they could sing and dance. No amount of coaxing could get Art to perform so someone else would take over the piano. After the player tired or got up for some refreshments Art needed no more persuading. He would then sit down and play to his heart's content. He was, naturally, very popular with the young crowd" (quoted in Spencer, "An Appreciation"). This looks like another characteristic of Art's that lasted the rest of his life. In more than twenty-five years of nightly after-hours sessions with other jazz pianists, in Toledo, Columbus, Detroit, Chicago, New York, and Los Angeles, among other cities, Tatum was almost always the last to play (and the last to go home).

We have an eye-witness report that by 1925 he was in command of all the elements of his hair-raising style. The bassist June Cole, who was then playing with the popular McKinney's Cotton Pickers orchestra, claims to have heard him playing in a gambling house in Toledo in 1925 "at his full technical prowess." (Art, aged sixteen, spent most of 1925 at the Columbus School for the Blind, so this incident probably took place in the fall after his return.) Cole was doubling, after his night's work with McKinney, as a singer in a late-running gambling joint called Big Noble's. He remembers quite clearly the night when, just after he had finished "Dear Old Southland," with Todd Rhodes of the McKinney band accompanying him, "this young blind fellow came up to me" and, very quietly and shyly, asked, "'Mr. Cole, could I play that number for you again later?' I said he could, and I can still remember just how good he was." According to Cole, the big, crashing chords, the sweeping runs, the richly elaborate fill-ins were part of the Tatum style even then. "He used to play behind me all the time after that, and he didn't have to ask permission again" (Keepnews, "Art Tatum," 154).

Even if we know next to nothing about how Tatum practiced, or how much, we can make some good guesses about the music he was exposed to. And we can assume that he tried to master much of what he heard. If his listening habits in his early life were anything like his later habits, Tatum listened to everything that was available to him, not only to pianists and not only to jazz. He would have been exposed to the gamut of American musical bric-a-brac, by way of piano rolls, recordings, and radio: hymns, the parlor pieces which were so popular in his time (by composers such as Victor Herbert, Ethelbert Nevin and Edward MacDowell, for example), ragtime and novelty piano ("Kitten on the Keys" was published in 1921), and on to the early Paul Whiteman recordings (the first ones were in 1922) with their quasi-symphonic treatment of popular songs. He could have heard the young Vladimir Horowitz (only five years older than he) on record while he was still in his teens, and he was a very strong fan of Horowitz's from early on (it eventually became a mutual admiration). Certainly while he was working with Rainey and again at the Toledo Conservatory he would have listened to performances of classical works, possibly as an aid to learning some of them himself. In his mature musical performances Tatum often tossed in quotations from outside of jazz, a Sousa march or "My Old Kentucky Home," and much of it was material that he must have stored away in these early listening years. These flourishes amused some and irritated others, but they certainly revealed the range of stuff that had gone into the memory banks.

Recordings of jazz, too, were available early in his life. He was eight when the Original Dixieland Jazz Band made its first recordings in 1917 (one of which was "Tiger Rag," which was also one of Tatum's first recordings, sixteen years later), nine when Jelly Roll Morton first recorded, and thirteen when the New Orleans Rhythm Kings made their first record. The style of jazz piano that Art took most to heart, New York stride, was available on piano rolls from at least 1917, when James P. Johnson made his first roll; and Fats Waller recordings began to be available in 1922. The first commercial radio broadcast took place in 1920, when Art was eleven, and air time quickly became given over predominantly to music, especially the varieties of "jazz" which were springing up around the country. He certainly would have heard the early big-band jazz of Fletcher Henderson and Duke Ellington, both of whom were recording in the middle 1920s, and Earl Hines and his band were recording and broadcasting from Chicago soon after that.

He not only listened, but like most of the other jazz musicians of his era he often taught himself to duplicate recorded performances. Where Art was different was in how quickly he could learn, and totally master, something he had heard only a few times. Francis Williams said he simply could not tell, from the next room, whether it was Art or a piano roll he was listening to. Some of the piano rolls Art listened to may have been produced, without his knowing it, by two pianists (Williams liked to say that since Art played with seven hands that still gave him a three-hand advantage). That would have set him a severe performance challenge and it may have helped to set his aim and expectations for himself exceedingly high. (When Willis Conover, the Voice of America's jazz expert, asked Tatum about the rumor that this was so, "Tatum laughed and said no." "It still sounds possible," Conover said.) If indeed it happened, then it's amusing to think that it may have found its reflection years later, in another story that may or may not have happened: "Oscar Peterson . . . tells the story of the days when he was considered a young genius, and his father brought home an Art Tatum recording. The two listened, and then the elder Peterson asked, "What do you think?" "They're great," the young Peterson responded in awe. "Who are those two guys?" (Rothman, "Toledo Years").

IN ANY CASE, from perhaps the age of ten on, Art Tatum was a familiar figure in Toledo's black community. His childhood friend Rudolph Perry, who was about three years younger than Art, told me, "Everywhere he went if there was a piano, he'd sit down to it . . . He'd be in a house playing, you could tell it was him 'cause nobody else ever sounded like him, people would stop out in the front of the house," and Russell McCown said, "Art was playing around here, no matter where you'd go, no matter what else was going on, Art was up there playing the piano." Perry recalled Art playing at the YMCA near his house: "Art used to play at the Y, they had a little baby grand there, we all used to sit around and watch him. We'd go around there to swim and all like that, and he'd wind up playing the piano." Another friend, Steve Taylor, was there:

> When we were kids the Indiana Y was built on the corner of Elizabeth and Indiana—brick building right in the center of the 8th Ward, where all the black people lived, and in the lobby of the Y there was a beautiful grand piano. Now, Art used to come there—wasn't too far, he only lived about two blocks from the Y. So he used to come up there and play this piano, and people would just gather around, and listen, to this terrific execution—he was a virtuoso, that's all there is to it.

So Art played wherever there was a piano and people to enjoy it—like Mallory on Everest, he went to the piano because it was there. And as he grew up that piano-playing instinct and his love of socializing led inexorably from the Y to the speak-easy. There was little enough entertainment for blacks (even less than for whites, no doubt) in Toledo in the 1920s, and local speakeasyies became havens for young people fenced in by the surrounding white community and preached to by fundmentalist ministers. Jon Hendricks's sister, a schoolmate of Arline's, remembers a local joint where Art held forth:

On Friday and Saturday this man, his name was Mr. Clark, he'd rent this place, and all of us would go, there was just a piano in there, and Art would play the piano. And later on they got slick, they were selling the corn whisky, by the pitcher! And he would play. You didn't pay to go in, it was just you'd be in there because you'd buy this pitcher of corn liquor. And he would just play until about 12:30—it started sometimes about 7:30, everybody'd be there drinking, it was the only thing to do. And of course I shouldn't have been there, I was too young! All of us, we were all in school. We'd go there, just lucky we never did get caught. And we'd stay there, and Art would play. Art was the only one would play there.

FELICITY HOWLETT, in her doctoral dissertation on Art Tatum, sums up what information she was able to find about his early musical development : "The basic training for the musical legend that Tatum became had its roots in a little formal instruction, a prodigious amount of listening and learning from piano rolls, radio and records, and a lot of time at the keyboard, whether at home or in the street."

A Professional in Toledo

"You play what you hear, and he heard more than any of us . . ." **DON ASHER**

"I cannot say to any person what I hear—I cannot say it to myself—it is very wonderful."
WALT WHITMAN

TOLEDO IN the 1920s had no shortage of local talent, and it was also on the circuit for touring musicians. Art almost certainly took in all the touring musical acts, since age was no barrier to going into a theater. He was apparently looking for chances to play in clubs at as early an age as they would let him in. At first he simply asked for permission to sit in during intermissions, and one can easily imagine him wanting to measure himself against the professionals. Exactly when and where he played his earliest paid appearances has not been documented. He was probably being booked by club owners as early as fifteen or sixteen (1924–25), but he was certainly being paid for playing at social functions even before that, including appearances at prominent local sites such as the Toledo Club and the Rotary Club.

Harold Payne, another acquaintance of Art's in the 1920s and a banjo player at that time (the guitar had not yet become popular with jazz musicians), remembers playing a variety of jobs around Toledo with him, including a dance at the University of Toledo. He and Tatum played, he recalled, "anywhere there was a piano, bootleg liquor, and a chance for tips, places like La Tabernella, Chateau La France, Chicken Charlie's, Darfey's . . . Dorothy Royal's Blue Lantern, and spots long forgotten" (Rothman, "Toledo Years"). Payne also recalls one time when Art had agreed to provide music for a dance but completely forgot to hire the musicians. At the last minute he had to hire two "terrible" horn players ("the worst in Toledo," Harold told me). At the dance Art was asked to "give the horns a rest," so Harold and Art played for a while together (Tatum and banjo—it boggles the mind!) and then the crowd demanded Art Tatum solos for the rest of the evening.

As he began to realize the possibilities, at some point Art got together a six-piece band to work professionally. The group included several musicians who went on to play with nationally known groups: Milton Senior (alto and clarinet) joined McKinney's Cotton Pickers, one of the finest of the midwestern bands, in 1928; and Harold Fox (violin) eventually worked with Wilbur de Paris. The rest of the members of the group were Bill Moore (bass), Lester Smith (guitar), and Fats Mason (drums) (Spencer, "Appreciation"[1]). Two of the then well-known Toledo night-spots where the group played were the Chateau La France (a converted mansion) and the Tabernella. Both were popular, whites-only restaurants, and they were also famous during those years, which were Prohibition years, as rum-runner hangouts.

Rex Stewart, the trumpet player who eventually became so well known playing with Duke Ellington's orchestra, has described vividly hearing Tatum in 1926 or '27, when Tatum would have been seventeen or eighteen. Stewart was in Toledo with the Fletcher Henderson band, where he had recently replaced Louis Armstrong, when Milt Senior, already known and respected by the Henderson musicians, persuaded Henderson and some of his players to go to hear the teenage Tatum, playing in a club in an alley in the middle of Toledo's

Bohemian district. They were somewhat reluctant, since almost everywhere the Henderson band went there was someone trying to bring a local musician to their attention, and few of these tips produced a real musical experience. However, this one did: "To a man, we were astonished, gassed, and just couldn't believe our eyes and ears. How could this nearly blind young fellow extract so much beauty out of an old beat-up upright piano that looked like a relic from the Civil War?" (Stewart, "Genius in Retrospect").

Coleman Hawkins was an unknown sideman of Henderson's on that night in Toledo. Stewart maintains that Hawkins was so taken by Tatum's playing that he immediately dropped his slap-tongue style and began creating a different style based on what he'd heard Tatum doing. What Hawkins did with that new style eventually led to his being judged one of the giants of the tenor saxophone, as well as to a line of disciples who made the saxophone the dominant instrument in jazz. This is just one example of the kind of indirect influence Art Tatum has had on the development of jazz. Stewart himself said that Tatum's playing led him to consider seriously giving up the trumpet and returning to school. And Henderson, like so many after him, refused to play after Tatum. Stewart quotes Henderson as saying, "I am pretty sure that we are in the presence of one of the greatest talents that you or I will ever hear."

This account by Rex Stewart of the devastating impact of hearing Tatum at the piano has elements in it that have been repeated in many later accounts of first impressions of Tatum. Above all, there is the sense of hearing piano playing that is totally off the scale normally used to rate pianists. Very early on, Tatum had bounded out of the normal frame of reference, not only for pianists but for jazz musicians on any instrument. I want to repeat, for readers who have grown up in a post-Tatum world, that his accomplishment, even at an early age, was of a different order from what most people, from what even musicians, had ever heard. It made musicians re-consider their definitions of excellence, of what was possible. Besides inducing awe and wonder, it shook people's foundations, made them question themselves, confused them about their own worth. Even Oscar Peterson, probably the most highly honored and rewarded jazz pianist in the world, has said that for years he was unable to play properly if Tatum was in the room.

With Tatum's really exceptional impact on listeners in mind one might be a little skeptical of another bit of Stewart's account—except that it's entirely consistent with the many reports from later in Tatum's life which describe him as totally lacking in arrogance or ostentation: "To our surprise," Stewart wrote, "this talented youngster was quite insecure and asked us humbly, 'Do you think I can make it in the big city [New York]?' We assured him that he would make it, that the entire world would be at his feet once he put Toledo behind him. Turning away, he sadly shook his head, saying, kind of to himself, 'I ain't ready yet.'"

By 1928 New York had become mecca for jazz musicians, and midwestern musicians from then into the 1940s felt the intimidation of heading east to face the jazz establishment. For Tatum it would mean confronting the masters of the style on which he had cut his teeth—James P. Johnson, Willie (The Lion), Smith, Fats Waller—and others whose names he probably didn't even know, for example, Luckey Roberts, Clarence Profit, Marlowe Morris, Donald (The Lamb) Lambert, Jack (The Bear) Wilson, Willie (The Leopard) Gant, and Stephen (The Beetle) Henderson. I don't think it's too fanciful to imagine, however, that Tatum's remark, about not being ready, was not a sign of being "insecure" but rather expressed his feeling that he wasn't yet fully confident of his ability to destroy, to "wipe out," to "cut to pieces," as musicians like to say, any and all comers. Nearly, maybe—he was certainly getting tremendous feedback from the touring musicians who came through town. Among others, Duke Ellington, who was well on his way to his own eventual fame, heard him and encouraged him:

> Friends had been talking about him, telling me how terrific he was, yet I was unprepared for what I heard. I immediately began telling him that he should be in New York. Quite a lot of what he was doing was taken right off the player piano rolls, and I felt that the action and competition would do much good in helping to project that part of

himself which was covered up by the carbon-copy things he did so perfectly. Also, I knew that once in New York he would be drawn into the Gladiator Scene with some real bad cats. I could just see The Lion, cigar in the corner of his mouth, standing over him while he played, and on the verge of saying, "Get up! I'll show you how it is supposed to go!" [Ellington, *Mistress*]

Ellington himself had been daunted by his encounters with the New York pianists (there is a story that he recognized early that he would never play stride piano like The Lion and told someone he was going to "go back home and write some music I can play").

Harold Payne says that Tatum's reply to Ellington was, "I don't think I'm really ready for New York." At some point around 1930 or 1931 the arranger and bandleader Don Redman came through Toledo, and by this time Tatum was whistling a different tune; he told Redman, "Tell them New York cats to look out. Here comes Tatum! And I mean every living tub with the exception of Fats Waller and Willie the Lion" (Spellman, 15).

It was apparently another year before Art got his chance at New York. Several authors have claimed that his first trip east was in 1928 but I can find no basis for that claim. The redoubtable (but not undoubtable) Rex Stewart even brings Paul Whiteman into the picture: "It was probably at Val's that Paul Whiteman 'discovered' him a year or so later, when Art was nineteen [i.e., in 1928] and took him to New York to be featured with the Whiteman band. But insecurity and homesickness combined to make him miserable, and after a short time, he fled back to Toledo." In fact, researchers for the Time-Life record issue searched the Whiteman archives and found no references to Tatum. If Whiteman had ever presented Tatum, a black, on the same stage in the 1920s or '30s it would have been historic and widely reported. I personally interviewed Kurt Dieterlie, who had been concert master of the Whiteman organization and is one of its few surviving members, and he had no recall of any connection between Whiteman and Tatum. Art's pilgrimage to New York was not made until 1932.

During his years of apprenticeship in Toledo, probably in 1927 at age seventeen or eighteen, Art won a local amateur contest and as a result began appearing on Toledo's radio station, WSPD. Amateur contests were a popular form of entertainment in those days; Jon Hendricks told me that he and Art often competed against one another around Toledo, "in theaters and churches and bazaars and banquets—all kinds of places. He was in the same position as me—he had a talent that was in demand. As I say we were on a lot of amateur shows. Sometimes I'd come in first, sometimes he'd come in first, then the next time I'd come in first." These contests were also a very important funnel for bringing real talent out of obscurity and to the attention of the professional world; other artists whose first big breaks came as a result of such contests include Fats Waller, Ella Fitzgerald, Sarah Vaughan, Oscar Peterson, and more recently Bobby Enriquez.

At WSPD, Art's first spot was from 9 to 9:15 in the morning, providing background and intermittent music for an announcer (Ellen Kay) who presented shopping information. But Harry Gregory, who lived near Art in the 1920s and who often walked him to the radio station, says Art didn't like having to be at the studio before noon, since he seldom got home from his round of after-hours clubs before five or six in the morning. Fairly soon—and inevitably—his talent impressed the station with the need to give him more room. During most of 1928 and 1929 he had his own fifteen-minute program at noon daily on WSPD. Commercial radio was a new and extremely important entertainment medium, rapidly replacing the parlor piano, and this show gave Art a wide audience. That audience was increased enormously when the Blue Network, the first nationwide network of radio stations, established in 1926, picked up his show for re-broadcast all across the country. Art was already being heard nationally before he ever tackled New York. Tape-recording too was still a distant possibility, so there is no permanent record of Art's playing in the studio of WSPD.

This radio spot may have made it possible for Tatum to buy his first car, and Art seems to have been crazy about that car. Eddie Barefield remembered a revealing incident concerning Tatum as a blind navigator: "One time when he first got the job at the radio station, he bought him a Ford, and got him a chauffeur." In these early Toledo days it was usually a friend or relative, such as his cousin Chauncey Long, who drove his Model A. "And we went one night down to a place called Dorothy's, just hanging out, drinking and playing. All of a sudden Art disappeared. Finally I went out looking for him, and he had gotten in the Ford and driven it right into a tree—it was steaming! We had to sort of pry him out." (Ray Charles, too, at least once demanded to drive his own car and ended by demolishing it, as his son related on a recent PBS TV program. For the visually handicapped to wish to be more mobile is certainly not surprising.)

John Sabry, a retired hotel manager, recalled that he hired Art, probably in the late 1920s, to play the intermissions for the name-bands that came into the hotel. He paid him a low weekly salary and all he could eat. "He was there for six weeks, and he outdrew the orchestras. He was the biggest musical bargain I ever got." Before New York, Art apparently never used an agent to negotiate his appearances, and as Rothman commented, "There is nothing to show that he ever refused a date because the money wasn't right."

Red Norvo was working with the Paul Whiteman Orchestra toward the end of the 1920s, when Roy Bargy, an outstanding pianist with the orchestra and another Toledoan, started telling him about Tatum.

> He said, "There's a guy in Toledo where I grew up who's one of the best I've ever heard." And this'd go on, we'd say, "Oh, yeah, Roy, we know, we know, Roy, yeah." We'd hear these stories all the time about other musicians. So we go on the road with Whiteman, go in the theaters, we were playing theaters like in St. Louis, all around, and we end up in Detroit. So, one day Roy came by, he said, "Hey, Red, would you like to go over and hear that piano player?" I said, "I'd love to." He said, "Maybe Mildred [Bailey] and some other guys would go, we'll drive over to Toledo after the show." So, we drove over to Toledo and went into this little joint—now this was after 10, 11 o'clock

when we finished in Detroit, we drove to Toledo, Roy went, he knew where Art was playing, we went into this little club, just an upright piano, and my!—we never heard anything like this in our lives. We just couldn't get over the way this man would play. We were just swooning, and Roy was laughing. He and Art grew up in the same town, and they went to the same piano teacher. That's how he knew about Tatum. So that was the first meeting with Tatum. And we stayed there all night—we stayed there even after all the people had left. He was so happy to see Roy, and he knew who I was and who the other people were. We just made that first show [back in Detroit], which is around noon. That's the first thing I heard of Tatum.

The young Count Basie, traveling with the Benny Moten band in the late 1920s, never forgot his first encounter on a Toledo stop-over:

We stopped off there and went into a bar where you could get sandwiches and cigarettes and candy and things like that, and they had a good piano in there. That's the part I will never forget, because I made the mistake of sitting down at that piano, and that's when I got my personal introduction to a keyboard monster by the name of Art Tatum.

I don't know why I sat down at that piano. We were all in there to get a little taste and a little snack, and the piano was there. But it was just sitting there. It wasn't bothering anybody. I just don't know what made me do what I went and did. I went over there and started bothering that piano. That was just asking for trouble, and that's just exactly what I got. Because somebody went out and found Art.

That was his *hangout*. He was just off somewhere waiting for somebody to come in there and start messing with that piano. Someone dumb enough to do something like that, somebody like Basie in there showing off because there were a couple of good-looking girls in the place or something like that. Oh, boy. They brought him in there, and I can still see him and that way he had of walking on his toes with his head kind of tilted.

I'm pretty sure I had already heard a lot of tales about old Art. But when I went over there and hopped on that innocent-looking piano, I didn't have any idea I was on his stomping ground.

"I could have told you," one of the girls at the bar said. "Why didn't you, baby? Why didn't you?"

[Crow, *Jazz Anecdotes*]

Earl Hines first heard him in 1931, when he (Hines) was already a big attraction with his band at the Grand Hotel in Chicago :

. . . he was already outplaying everybody, although he was not getting the attention he should have had. At that time he used to do imitations of Fats Waller, James P. Johnson, and me. He didn't know anything but playing the piano, and that's all he wanted to do. He lived with the piano, day and night. Every time he saw one, he was playing. I don't think he really knew how much he could play. . . . [he] could do as much with his left hand as most people could do with their right."

[Doerschuk, "Biography"]

Billy Fuster is a drummer from Cleveland who was working in Toledo in 1930–31, and he remembers two carloads of musicians, including Art, driving up to Chicago just to hear Hines:

A gang of us went up to Chicago, this little club on the South Side. Course the man then was Earl Hines, and of course he was the king. A couple of carloads, just drove up there, you know, trying to make contacts for future jobs. Earl was playing. So—I think Danny was the guy, Danny says, "Hey, we got a kid here we want you to listen to." Earl, being very gracious, said, "Sure." 'Cause he had no idea of Art's capabilities. Art started playing, and when we looked up Earl was going out the door!

Art's amazing style was not always appreciated by the singer or soloist who hoped Tatum would *accompany* him—or her. Ernestine Allen, a neighbor of the Tatums on City Park Avenue and an age-mate of Karl's, was a singing child prodigy, who like Art was asked to perform all around town (later she sang with Lucky Millander's popular band). She was perhaps the first of a very short list of people who actually complained about Art's style of backing a soloist: "They was wanting Art, you know, home-town talent, to perform at functions. But I would always tell 'em, I don't want Art Tatum to play for me. I wanted Earl Easterly. Art's playing, he was so advanced, you know, he was so far advanced, I'd say, he's featuring himself and not me. I was stubborn enough and cocky enough to know that. And I would tell 'em, as long as Art Tatum doesn't play for me." In spite of her resistance to having Art play with her, Ernestine still gives him credit for part of her education: "I think he taught me how to sing within a chord, because I had to sing between his fingerings. You just had to stay with him. So I taught myself, with him doing what he wanted, featuring himself."

Art and Teddy Wilson, two men who would dominate jazz piano playing for the next fifteen years, first met in 1931.[2] Wilson, three years younger than Tatum, had gone to Detroit to take his first professional job in 1929, with Speed Webb's band (other alumni of that band were Roy Eldridge and Vic Dickensen). In early 1931 he got a call from Milt Senior to come and replace Art Tatum on piano in the group with which Milt was appearing, at the Chateau La France in Toledo. It's not clear from Wilson's account why Tatum needed replacing, but Rudolph Perry thinks it was a rare instance of Art's having a disagreement with an owner: ". . . Art was at the Chateau, and Art got sore about something there, it didn't just suit him, and he walked off the job, right in the middle of the night. Teddy Wilson got here the next day. I never found out what was wrong—some kind of disagreement, I guess. Usually he was very dependable."

In Toledo, Tatum and Wilson became friends, and Wilson soon was joining Tatum every night, as soon as he finished at the Chateau, for a round of sessions in after-hours clubs and private homes that usually took them through to breakfast. Billy Fuster remembered at least one of these places:

> There was a joint in Toledo called Chicken Charlie's, oh it was about 30 feet wide, in the basement of a place, and maybe 100 feet deep. And they had a 15-piece band-stand, designed to hold 15 people up there. And all they served was hot biscuits and chicken, Chicken Charlie's, it was great. Art played there—everybody played there. They used to come in when they'd get off their jobs. That was a meeting place. Jam sessions—I don't know if you ever heard of Roy Bargy—he was Paul Whiteman's piano player, and anytime he was in town he'd come down, and if Art was there he'd sit under Art and just shake his head. Like José Iturbi said, "He can play what I can play but I cannot play what he can play."

Tatum and Wilson had a good chance to take in the other's style close-up. Years later Wilson said, "He is the one musician whose origin you cannot trace. Obviously Earl Hines was influenced by Louis Armstrong . . . but I've never been able to trace the influence in Tatum—where and how he evolved that way of playing in Toledo, Ohio" (Young, "Three Pianists"). Wilson has also said, however, that Tatum was much influenced by the recordings of Fats Waller, and years later Art said, in a rare bit of self-explanation, "Fats, man, that's where I come from" (Ulanov, *History*). But Teddy also claims that Art was much influenced by Earl Hines. Eddie Barefield, who knew Art before he left Toledo, has also testified to the role that Hines played in developing Tatum's style:

> His favorite jazz piano player was Earl Hines—used to buy all of Earl's records and he would improvise on em. Yeah, he'd play with the record but he'd improvise over what Earl was doing. Well, he was from a different school from Fats Waller. See, Earl Hines was the first, was really the change of the style of the piano players, modern piano players. Fats was from the old school. Course, when you heard him play you didn't hear nothing of anybody but Art.

But he got his ideas from Earl's style of playing. But Earl never knew that—'cause I worked with him 10 years ago in Canada, I told him this story, he said, "As well as I knew Art I didn't know that."

Tatum never publicly acknowledged any debt to Hines, and apparently he never admitted one in private to the Fatha, either.

With Wilson, as with many others in later years, Tatum was generous: "Art would show me anything I asked him to—he'd slow it right down, and let me stand behind his shoulder, and he would show me exactly what he did." Doc Cheatham passed through Toledo about this time and remembers the two of them:

Time I met Art Tatum and Teddy Wilson, both of 'em were there at the same time. I was in Europe in the late '20s, I didn't get back to America until 1930. Must have been in the '30s when I was with Cab Calloway, we played all those one-night stands down through Ohio, Michigan, everywhere. We would go out to hear Art Tatum, everyone was listening to Art Tatum, he was playing so well then. He was also a pool shark—he and I played pool a lot together. I never could understand how he could play pool so well, being blind, but we found out he could see a little bit. He was a good pool player. I was amazed but he had a little eyesight. We used to go hear Art, and Teddy Wilson—Teddy Wilson was on his tail all the time. Every time Art played down there Teddy was right there looking at him.

Years later, Teddy Wilson told his friend Milt Hinton, "Do you remember the grace with which he could shuffle a deck of cards? Just like a master card-dealer . . . In some ways, he was the most remarkable and phenomenal human being I had ever been around." Wilson ranked Waller and Hines as influences more important than Tatum in his own playing, and even told Hinton that his work with Louis Armstrong (in 1932) "was as influential in developing my music as the piano players that I used to listen to. . . ." But it's obvious that Wilson had the greatest respect and admiration for Tatum, and they were close friends the rest of their lives.

Wilson left Toledo later in 1931 for Chicago, to open at the new Gold Coast Club there with a band led by Milton Senior, possibly the same band that had been working at the Chateau (Chilton, *Who's Who*). Why did Senior take Wilson and not Tatum? Maybe Art didn't feel ready to leave home, or maybe Senior and the rest of the band found Wilson's style better suited to ensemble playing (which it most surely was).

In this period (1928 to 1932) Tatum was taking solo jobs in clubs, and playing all night in after-hours joints outside of Toledo as well, in Cleveland, Columbus, Detroit, perhaps Cincinnati. During the years of the Eighteenth Amendment (1920–33), usually referred to as Prohibition, after-hours clubs mushroomed and provided lots of employment opportunities for musicians. Jazz was not yet acceptable in legitimate restaurants and clubs, but the gangsters who ran the after-hours joints loved it and kept jazz musicians working even when many other skilled workers were unemployed. Jon Hendricks put it this way:

> If it had been left to the so-called decent people in this country there'd be no jazz. It was due to the Mafia, who liked the music and who ran the joints—Sicily you know is only 28 miles from Africa, so they have a great affinity. They're the ones who said, "Hey, you guys, come on and play in this joint." Those were the only places where we could play. So that's where the music had to grow. Now you can go into the big concert halls and so forth, but it's still on the part of a lot of people with a lot of reluctance. They still have a respect only for European music and they tended to stay only in their own art culture. This country still does that, it hasn't really grown past that. In Europe they look at jazz as one of the world's great art forms, which it is. But in this country they're so messed up by racism that they can see it as "those people's music," you know. So they deny themselves their own culture. It's the only country that does that. It's a drag!

One can get a snapshot-perspective on what kinds of fare the "respectable" clubs were offering in the early thirties from one Cleveland newspaper's weekly "Guide to Bright Lights," where the following talent was touted:

> *Chateau*—Jacqueline James dances a torrid "Passion Dance" and Ray Styles does magic tricks between Rod Lombardo's melodies. *Statler Pompeian Room*—Smooth New Yorkish rhythms by Stubby Gordon's lads, plus mint juleps made with applejack. *Torch Club*—Gene Beecher's tunesters and Leon LeVerde's female impersonators in a fantastic revue. *Airport Tavern*—Salome Fillen's dance with a black bull snake is good for a thrill, with fast frolic and Helen Dougherty's girl orchestra. *Alpine Shore Club*—A rollicking Tyrolean shindig by Herman Pichner with yodeling contests every Wednesday night. *Ohio Villa*—Paul Botta plays for Edith DeVand's exotic numbers while Henry Rich does things to a xylophone.

What a relief it would have been to push into one of Art's after-hours hangouts after a tour of that venue!

In spite of the growing power and influence of "the mobs," Toledo fortunately remained a quiet city. According to Fuster:

> It was not a tough town. We had one colored cop there, we used to call him Blue Steel. He knew all the musicians, the entertainers, he got along with people. Of course Toledo was a town that—the thugs would do a job in Chicago and then come back to Toledo and hide because they never pulled a job until later. They never did a stick-up there. As I said, Toledo was a clean town back in those years. They had no problems.

Alcohol was easily available—the whole point of the after-hours places was to make it available—and customers cheered performers on by buying them drinks. It was an occupational hazard that was almost unavoidable, the cost of doing business as a professional jazzman. Marijuana was a new thing, just coming north from the

South, and while lots of musicians were trying it, drug use was not at all the powerful accompaniment to jazz that it later became. Fuster says he never saw Tatum try marijuana and doubts that he ever did. No one I've talked to has ever connected Art to drug use except the guitarist, Steve Jordan, who told me he had heard that Art used to keep a cat, which he would sometimes put in a bag into which he had blown pot (marijuana) smoke: "The cat dug it, came out stoned!"

Accounts of Art's playing in those Ohio cities are not always clear about the year, but Tatum was now a professional and needed jobs, and with his growing visibility club owners would have found him an attractive performer. From all accounts the clubs in which he played (in or out of Toledo) were not always much to write home about (which Tatum never did anyway). This was especially true of the after-hours places where he spent most of his time. One can only marvel at Tatum's enduring the smoke, the noise, and the often abysmal pianos, all for the sheer love of playing—he may have gotten tips, and he was certainly fed and provided with beer, but he was rarely paid in cash for the hours after hours.

One such place which Tatum made famous (in a local sort of way) and which became a magnet for all the musicians in town, one of the few places where white and black could mix and play together, was Val's in the Alley, in Cleveland. Art appeared there frequently in his early years, and I believe returned there often even in his more successful years. He loved the food and Val apparently took good care of him in the kitchen department. Ed Ryan has described it (in a video-documentary on Tatum made for PBS-Toledo) as a tiny place, with a pot-bellied coal-stove and a single door which in the winter let the snow blow in whenever someone entered or left; and Billy Fuster remembered that orange crates served as both tables and chairs. Val's is where Sweets Edison first heard Tatum play:

> In Cleveland, Ohio, I was about 16 years old [this would make it 1931], I was working in a band in a nightclub, and he was working in a little place called Val's in the Alley. It was just one room, and they sold whisky in there, you know in those days they had speakeasys. And you couldn't

get in there, you had to stand on the outside, he was so popular. Especially all the musicians would take up most of the space in there 'cause they wanted to hear him play. Well, he was always friendly. I don't think I knew the importance of meeting him at that time, being a teenager. But in later life we began to run into each other, like in Chicago or NY.

Red Norvo heard him there a little later, sometime in the mid-1930s:

He was playing in Cleveland at a little rib joint, and I had a band that was playing at the Ball Room, and I used to go over and eat there, it was dark—it was an after-hours place, it was dark, you had to go in the parking lot and then go in the back, it was a house. So the first time I heard him there, I said hello to him and everything, and he made me come and sit by the piano. And we'd have a few drinks or something and I'd just listen. So I spent a lot of time in Cleveland there listening to him. Couple of months I played that ball room. And he was drinking those boiler-makers [rye whisky with a beer chaser]. Oh God, how many he could put away!

Art loved the atmosphere at Val's: good food, plenty of beer, the room filled with musicians who could really appreciate what he was doing, even on the old upright piano. Although the gig was after hours and Art did it mainly for fun, it did bring him some cash-paying gigs downtown. For example, Merle Jacobs was able to promote him:

Art Tatum was playing at a little place called Val's in the Alley. Someone told me about him, I went out to hear him, and of course I was astounded—being a musician and a former orchestra leader myself. So I made a deal to bring him down to a private club in the Hotel Hollenden where I was entertainment director. I think it was called the Artists and Writers Club. . . . later it became the 216 Club, it was located in suite 216. I brought Art Tatum down there to play, and he was a tremendous hit down there. . . . Probably 1932, something like that. I was in my late 20s. He was an awfully nice, easy-going fellow. He was almost totally blind, as you know. He had a little vision in one eye. And of course, he had indescribable talent. I don't believe there was ever a pianist his equal. From Toledo, Ohio. I was connected with the chain of hotels called the DeWitt Hotel Chain, and I was entertainment director for the whole chain, Cleveland, Columbus, Dayton, there were two hotels in the state of Georgia, one in Miami Beach. So I probably, it's possible that I sent him to—oh, and Akron, the Mayflower Hotel in Akron—I might have sent him to some of those hotels. It was a little unusual, but it was no problem. I think he was the first black artist to play the Hollenden Hotel.

Earle Warren is a reed player, later a regular with the Count Basie band, who still has fond memories of Art at Val's. In 1933 he had recently graduated from high school and had been leading his own band in Columbus, when he was recruited to join one of the big-time midwestern bands, that of Marion Sears, in Cleveland:

That was in 1933. I worked with Marion Sears—off and on, because work wasn't that heavy, and gangsters were quite bad. You had to work for nothing, you know. And so—I don't wanna talk about gangsters. Now, Art Tatum started to playing in a place called Val's in the Alley. That was just a house with sawdust on the floor, and an upright piano, and an old den-light over the piano, and Art used to play there. And I would finish playing where I was and I would run by to see him, and I would sing and split tips with him. I'd get $5, for "Body and Soul," "Once in a While," "I'm in the Mood for Love," tunes like that, maybe some women would like to hear. I'd keep $2.50 and I'd give Art $2.50. I swear to God this is the truth. If he was living he'd say that's right. Oh, I liked him very much, he was a fine man. He used to tickle me all the time. Any time I'd be playing in Cleveland with Marion Sears I'd always make it down to Val's. When Ben Bernie would come to town, and the Casa Loma Band, they'd have him come and play with 'em, on the radio. Yes, sir. And that wasn't heard of in those days. People would hear somebody playing piano, and they'd say, "Oh—I don't believe that!" You understand? I never knew where he lived. All I know is, we were playing little clubs on Cedar Ave., the colored street at that time, the black street, was Cedar Ave. down to 55th, and 55th to Scobel and Quincy. The Majestic Hotel was at 55th and Scobel, there wasn't no more hotels to give space to [black] people, you know. And down about a block and a half on Scobel, that's where Art Tatum used to work. He worked for a man named Jimmy Jones, it was an after-hours spot. Gangsters usually owned 'em. And you couldn't play two jobs, or gangsters would make you leave town. Paid us $10 a night. When I went to Cleveland I worked for $10 a night but I made a hundred-and-some dollars a week. I played for tap dancers, and women that picked the money off the table in those days, chorus girls—I called 'em chorus girls, they used to sing, get out on the floor and sing a couple of songs, pull their dress up and do a little dance and then start dancing around the tables, and singing the songs, and we'd split the tips. I sent so much money home to my mother she thought I was stealing. I never brought my horn to play with him, but he used to play so much piano when I would be singin', that it tickled me. I just couldn't imagine somebody playing that much piano and not getting in my way. And then when I would give him the $2.50, boy, he would like that. He liked me quite well, I got along with him fine.

I have never found a published clue as to how Art lived when he was away from Toledo in these early days, where he stayed, who were the friends who took care of him and got him wherever he needed to go. There appears to be nobody still alive who knows anything about it. But Tatum's independence, combined with his ability to make friends, makes his doing it less mysterious. One story about Art's independence comes from Harold Payne, who played banjo with him when both were very young; Harold said that Art didn't want to join the Musicians' Union, and put it off as long as he could, because if he joined the union they would have some control over him—could make him show up on time, or show up at a job he didn't want to do. In fact, it appears that he never did join the union local in Toledo. Bill Douglass, who in the 1950s used to drive him to work, do his banking and other errands for him, and who was one of the last musicians to record with him, told me more about Art's rather fierce independence. Bill could never guide him by taking his elbow because Art didn't like that. He was very touchy about his eyesight—it was never mentioned by anyone who knew him at all. Bill said that he learned to be tactful—if Art asked where something was, a telephone for example, Bill would feign not knowing himself, so as not to emphasize his sightedness, then appear to find out and tell him.

But if Art resisted help for the "handicapped," he also denied his blindness in ways that enhanced friendship. For example, Douglass said that often when riding in Bill's car Art would say, "Looks like you need some gas." Bill would reply, "No I don't," and Art would press him, "Well, you never know"—and insist on giving him some cash toward gas. Alongside his independence Art always looked out for people he worked with, gave them advances whether they wanted them or not, and in other ways impressed his friends with his generosity. His friend Billy Fuster told me, "He was very congenial. Easy to get along with. As long as you were a musician you were in his corner. Of course, he was well-liked, 'cause he always had a buck for somebody. He never was a tightwad." If he was making money he liked to spend it, even in his earliest days of making money out of music.

THE DECADE OF the 1920s was a decade of recovery from World War I, the rapid development of U.S. industry and wealth, mass production of the automobile with its enormous consequences for changing the American life style (it increased mobility for all and increased privacy for young people), the loosening of

Victorian standards for behavior and the spectacle of the "flapper" and shouts of "Twenty-three skidoo" (whatever that meant), and—what meant the most for Art Tatum—the tremendous growth of a new kind of music that somehow expressed all this. Jazz was a freer kind of music than had gone before, it was vigorous and joyful and optimistic, and it elevated individual spontaneity and improvisation to a moral imperative. It also generated a mighty resistance from conservative Americans who feared for "family values" and the established moral order, but jazz was part and parcel of the general rebellion against the established order and too much in tune with the spirit of the times to be suppressed.[3] The new music was spread across the nation through the technology of radio and recording, which in the 1920s replaced the piano in the parlor as our main home entertainment. Recordings played the role of teachers, as hundreds of future jazz musicians took their first steps by learning recorded solos, purely by listening.

This was the decade in which Tatum's powers first began to develop. It shaped him, it defined the playing field on which he had to make his runs, and it provided him with a base of operations, namely, jazz.

New York and Chicago

> *"It is no longer a question of this or that style of playing but the pure expression of a bold nature determined to conquer fate not with dangerous weapons but by the peaceful means of art."*
>
> **ROBERT SCHUMANN**, describing Franz Liszt

CLEARLY, ART KNEW from the beginning of his professional career—and there is no doubt that in 1928 he was already a professional—that New York was where the important action was. While Tatum was in grade school the dynamic center of jazz had moved from New Orleans to Chicago (not directly, or "up the river," but through many indirections), and then during Tatum's early 'teens New York became the center of most important musical activity (clubs featuring top musicians, musical theater, music publishing, the recording industry). In effect, until you had competed and succeeded in New York, you were still in the minor leagues.

There was a strong and advanced tradition of piano jazz in New York, and it was where several of Tatum's major influences were mainly to be found. Anyone who was anyone, and who didn't already live there, came to town frequently. Art was obviously thinking about going there to make a name for himself, and he was constantly encouraged by traveling musicians to do it; the only questions were how and when.

Dance bands, not solo pianists, were the rage in the late '20s and early '30s, and joining the right band was almost the only route to musical success on a national scale. I think all the band leaders who heard Tatum in Toledo recognized that he was not an ensemble musician, certainly not a candidate to play piano in a big dance band. Tatum however wasn't looking for a band to join. I believe his whole ambition was to succeed by himself, to get ahead with nothing but a piano as his tool. It may even be that "getting ahead" is a completely inaccurate term for what he wanted, that his ambition was not at all for fame and success, but only to play as well as he possibly could, to learn as much as he could from others, and to make a life out of music. It was the music, the substance of the playing itself, rather than being famous, that he concentrated on and lived for, at least early in his career.

The solution to the problem of when to head for New York came in 1932, with the arrival in Toledo of a young and popular singer called Adelaide Hall. She was touring the RKO theater circuit, with two pianists as her accompaniment, and was booked into Toledo's Rivoli Theater. Hall (who was born in 1904 but is not only still living, in London, but still performing and recording at this writing) had already been to Europe in 1925 with the *Chocolate Kiddies* revue, appeared in New York with the show *Desires of 1927,* and starred in *Blackbirds.* She also recorded with Duke Ellington in 1927 (the famous "Creole Love Call") and she was a regular at the Cotton Club in Harlem, its best-known showcase for top black musical talent. The two accompanists were Francis Carter and Joe Turner (who spent most of his later life playing in Paris and who died only recently, before I could reach him). Turner was another well-established performer who had already worked with Benny Carter (in 1929) and Louis Armstrong (in 1930). Adelaide's was a class act.

Hall's stint in Toledo became a landmark event in Art Tatum's life, but there are surprisingly different accounts of how Adelaide and

Art found themselves at a crossroads. I've decided to spell out several of the differing stories that have been told, if only as a warning to other amateur historians who may be thinking of writing a biography.

For starters, most writers have agreed the year was 1932, but Ray Spencer, co-author of the only available Tatum discography (Laubich and Spencer) and therefore not to be disregarded, once put the date as 1930 (Spencer, "Appreciation"), as did George Hoefer ("Tatum"). Whitney Balliett (in *American Musicians*) espoused 1931. The witnesses for 1932 (Chilton, Doerschuk, Howard, Keepnews, and Rothman) are the most compelling to me, although none has provided sources for his or her information.

As for how Tatum and Hall got together, there are two distinct versions. The first has differences in detail when told by the different actors in it, but it remains recognizable through the variations. The second version is simply a different story, which would be easy to disregard if it didn't come from Adelaide Hall herself.

(1) This is the way the incident has been recounted in the *Toledo Blade* (Rothman) and in a 1984 PBS television documentary on Tatum. When Adelaide Hall came to Toledo with her own show, including Turner and Carter as accompanists, she stayed with William and Ella Stewart, whose home at City Center Street and Indiana Avenue was a kind of social center for black Toledo. They often put up visiting black musicians, since access to decent hotels for them was limited or perhaps non-existent. The Stewarts lived near the Tatum house, and indeed they and the Tatums knew each other well. Turner turned up sick in Toledo (Mrs. Stewart says it was Carter who was sick) and it seemed likely he would be unable to work behind her, so when Hall mentioned her urgent need for an accompanist to fill in for Turner, Ella Stewart immediately urged her to try Arthur Tatum, Jr. An audition was arranged (the *Blade* says it was at the Grace Presbyterian Church, the one across from the Tatums' house on City Center, but Mrs. Stewart in the documentary says it was the All Saints Episcopal Church). According to the *Blade,* Art was hired on the spot to finish the Rivoli engagement and then went directly to New York with her. ("Art asked Mother Tatum. She

knew it was inevitable and she agreed—on condition that he write or call regularly.")

According to Harry Gregory's closely related account, Joe Turner was not sick but was looking for a way to leave Adelaide Hall's act so that he could join a big band. This version has it that Turner visited a bar on Pinewood Avenue late one night where he heard Art play, found out he wasn't regularly employed, and then proposed him as his own replacement. This account differs from the first only in that Art is taken to Miss Hall not by Ella Stewart but by Joe Turner.

Turner has given his own account of finding Art. It dovetails nicely with the Pinewood Avenue story, except that Turner fails to mention connecting Art and Adelaide Hall (so maybe it was the Stewarts after all):

> Benny Carter told me that when I reached Toledo I shouldn't play any piano because there was a blind boy there, named Art Tatum, and I would not be able to touch him. When the Adelaide Hall troupe finally got to Toledo, I asked where Tatum could be found, and I was given the address of a buffet flat [could it have been the one on Pinewood Avenue?] where he appeared every night at two o'clock sharp, after his work. After finishing at the theater at midnight, I went there and waited for Art to come. In the meantime I played some good stuff on the piano there, and two girls sitting near the piano started an argument over my playing in comparison with Art's. One girl said, "He'll wash Art away," while the other was insisting, "Just wait until Art gets here and you'll see how he will cut this boy." Art Tatum arrived at two o'clock sharp. I got up from the piano and greeted him. He asked me if I was the Joe Turner who had made a reputation with a fine arrangement of "Liza." I said it was me and begged him to play piano for me. After he had refused to play before hearing me (and, of course, with Art I lost the argument), I played first "Dinah" for warmin' up and then my "Liza." When I had finished, Art Tatum said, "Pretty good." I was offended because everywhere else I played "Liza" it was considered sensational, and there was Art Tatum saying,

"Pretty good." After that Art sat down and played "Three Little Words." Three thousand words would have been an understatement! I had never heard so much piano in my life. We became the best of friends after that. Art came to my home the next morning and, even before I left my bed, I heard him in the parlor play my arrangement of "Liza," note for note, after hearing it only once the night before.

There seemed no reason to doubt that something like the events of version (1) was a fair account of this milestone event for Art—until I communicated with Adelaide Hall herself in 1991, when she was eighty-seven. She complained that Turner had been taking credit for years for finding Tatum in Toledo in 1932, and said it wasn't so. She then gave me version two.

(2) Hall was performing in Cleveland (not Toledo) when Francis Carter (not Joe Turner) was called away on family business (not by illness). She had already heard about "this great young player" over in Toledo, so her husband drove to Toledo, picked up Art, and brought him back to the concert hall in Cleveland (not the church in Toledo) for an audition. There was a lot of work being done on the hall, lots of hammering and banging (no doubt Art could identify every note), but Art played through all this and they were sure he'd be great for the job. She made the offer, he accepted and went back to Toledo to pick up his things, and immediately began traveling on the road with the show. After about a month Art received a big-money offer from New York, and Hall encouraged him to take it. Hall's husband, Bert Hicks, later told Ray Spencer that it was he, not Art, who persuaded Mrs. Tatum to let him go. Spencer reported: "I was fortunate in meeting Adelaide Hall's husband, Bert Hicks, before he died. He talked to me about those days way back in 1930.[1] . . . Bert Hicks went on to tell me how he tried to persuade Art's mother to let him go on tour with them. 'Getting Tatum from Toledo to New York was like getting the Queen out of London,' commented Bert Hicks."

Whichever way it happened, and whenever Hall found him, Tatum definitely did make his way to New York with Adelaide Hall in 1932, just a year before Teddy Wilson first came to New York (with Benny Carter's band). The contract, dated 17 June, 1932, was drawn up by William Stewart and it names him as Tatum's manager for a period of five years ("Whereas William W. Stewart . . . has certain connections with musical organizations, entertainers, booking agencies, and the like; and Arthur Tatum . . . has certain talents as a pianist, which said talents he desires to turn to profit. . . .")[2] Stewart was to get any excess of Art's wages over $50 per week, unless his wages should exceed $65 per week in which case they would split the amount over $65. There is an interesting paragraph in the contract, which may or may not have been standard at the time but which sounds tailored to a contract with Art Tatum, which required Art to agree:

> That second party will at all times, as far as possible, keep himself in such physical condition that he will be able to proficiently play the piano and otherwise execute the contracts into which first party shall enter for and on behalf of second party, that he will refrain from the excessive use of alcoholic beverages, and will at all times conduct himself in a gentlemanly manner.

While Art may have failed the "refrain from excessive use" clause, he seems to have been true to the "gentlemanly manner" condition. In spite of his enormous consumption of alcoholic beverages it seems that Art never had any real trouble on a job because of his drinking, and all accounts agree that his behavior was almost always "gentlemanly."

Spencer says Tatum worked with Hall over a two-year period. This contradicts Hall's retrospective account in 1991 but if it's true it must have been off-and-on work, since we have pretty definite sightings of him at Val's in the Alley in 1933. These were deep Depression years and the work in New York was thin, so it's not surprising that he would have to travel a little to keep the cash flowing.

He definitely cut his first record before the end of 1932, playing behind Adelaide Hall. On August 5, a group which included not only Francis Carter and Art Tatum but also Charlie Teagarden (trumpet), possibly Jimmy Dorsey (clarinet), and Dick McDonough (guitar), recorded "Strange as It Seems" and "I'll Never Be the Same." On August 10, Adelaide and the two pianists recorded "You Gave Me Everything But Love" and "Tea for Two." Also on August 10, Tatum did a test-pressing of a one minute, 58-second solo version of "Tiger Rag" which has only recently been released.[3] Gunther Schuller says it contains "a number of note and rhythmic stumbles," and one wonders whether the recording studio was able briefly to shake his confidence, something neither audiences nor other piano giants could do. Certainly it never happened again.

Not surprisingly, he didn't stay entirely behind Miss Hall for long. According to one account (Doerschuk), Hall gave him his first solo spot during a show at the Palace Theater in New York; the applause was so great (so the report goes) that he was featured in a solo in all the shows from then on. Hall, by contrast, said in 1991 that he was given solos from the beginning since they were written into the arrangements. However he did it, he was able to make himself noticed, even as an accompanist, and that was the first step toward his leaving Adelaide Hall and appearing as a feature performer in night clubs. It's not clear how long Art worked for Adelaide Hall before he went to New York, nor after. He may have appeared with her off and on, joining her in different cities as needed, and as he had open slots in his calendar, which now began to fill up. Milt Hinton remembers seeing Art at the Regal Theater in Chicago with Adelaide Hall in the early 1930s; Joe Turner was then back on the other piano, as Milt recalls it. And Ernie Lewis, who knew Tatum well from the mid-'30s on, first heard Tatum with Adelaide in California:

> Adelaide Hall? Did you know that he went out on tour with her? He came to the Orpheum theater in Oakland. She had two piano players. He was the second player. That's when I picked up on him, the first time I ever heard a piano player play—really play any music. That's where I—all these years I remembered that name, Adelaide Hall. She was the only one on the show, she had these two piano players, and Art was one of 'em. She introduced him during the show as her second piano player. The other guy

did the solos, I guess he must have been an old man, during those times. Art played under this cat, but you could still hear him, he cut through. I picked up on it in a minute. Young as I was during that time. It had to be in the '30s, maybe in the early '30s, 1932? He and I are the same age. . . . You wasn't allowed to go backstage in those days. You went to see the show, and then he left, and you'd sit there and see the second show. I think that's what I did, 'cause I admired him so much. Would you believe that I could remember that woman's name, after all these years? It's because of Art! I don't remember the other guy, the other piano player.

The work with Adelaide Hall can hardly have been satisfying for Tatum. Even if he eventually got a solo spot in her shows, it looks like he played a number of concerts with her without soloing, and that couldn't have been easy for Art Tatum. On top of that, one person who knew him and many other musicians in the '30s claims that various people urged Art to leave Adelaide's show:

And she didn't pay him anything, he said—she paid him practically nothing, said she wasn't nice to him at all. And some of the musicians got mad with her one time, and said, "Art, what're you wasting your time for. Stop playing for her!" Some of his musician friends, and they got him a job somewhere else. . . . She just mistreated him when he was playing for her. He worked for her quite some time, I think he must have worked with her 2 or 3 years. She wasn't nice to him at all. Now, I don't know, that's what I've heard, I never have met the lady, I don't know her at all.

Soon after he arrived in New York Art started to show up at the after-hours places. It was time for the "Gladiator Scene" Ellington had anticipated. It began with a visit from Fats Waller:

Inevitably Art would have his baptism by fire at the hands of the New York jazz piano elite. His first contact with them was engineered by Fats Waller, who introduced himself backstage at the Lafayette, where Tatum was working with Hall. Fats, generally considered the city's keyboard kingpin at that time, was not terribly impressed with Art's playing at first, probably because Tatum was restricted that night to stock background chords for the singer, but nonetheless the two pianists agreed to get together the following night for some serious playing. [Doerschuk]

After his gig with Hall the next evening, Art was met by a welcoming committee from hell: Fats, Willie The Lion, James P. [Johnson], and Lippy Boyette, a pianist turned booking agent. Except for Lippy these were the very men who had been so significant in giving him a base from which to attack the jazz piano. Until now they had been merely names on recordings, something he could put on or take off the record player at will. If Tatum had not felt ready earlier, this is what he had not felt ready for. James P. and The Lion were the heart, soul, and brains of Harlem stride piano, which is to say of *jazz* piano, at that time. Waller, at twenty-eight the youngest of the Harlem big three that night, had already been a protégé of James P.'s, and may have studied both at Juilliard and with Leopold Godowsky in Chicago; he had been recording for ten years and had made several tours of the country with vaudeville groups and musical revues; he had appeared in New York with Duke Ellington and in Chicago with Louis Armstrong; and he had written not only more than a few popular songs but also two scores for all-black revues with Spencer Williams, one with James P. (*Hot Chocolates*), and one with Andy Razaf, who wrote the lyrics for many of Fats's best-known songs.

Art asked if they could pick up his friend Reuben Harris, at whose house he was then staying (Harris had been one of the earliest people to urge Tatum to come to New York); they roused Harris from his sleep and went off in search of a bar with a piano good enough for the first round of their get-acquainted duel. They settled on a place called Morgan's in Harlem. Naturally Tatum did not play first; it was simply something he didn't do. Someone else played a few numbers to break the ice, and then Tatum was talked into confronting the keyboard. The scene has been recounted in Maurice Waller's biography of his father, Fats Waller:

> Art played the main theme of Vincent Youmans' big hit, "Tea for Two," and introduced his inventive harmonies, slightly altering the melodic line. Good, but not very impressive. Then it happened. Tatum's left hand worked a strong, regular beat while his right hand played dazzling arpeggios in chords loaded with flatted fifths and ninths. Both his hands then raced toward each other in skips and runs that seemed impossible to master. Then they crossed each other. Tatum played the main theme again and soared to an exciting climax.

Robert Doerschuk has described events from there on:

> The entourage was stunned; lulled by Fats's preliminary assessment, they hadn't expected anything near Tatum's level of virtuosity. But gamely they tried to meet the challenge. James P. followed Tatum with "Carolina Shout," playing, Maurice Waller writes, "as if his hands were possessed by a demon. But it wasn't good enough." Waller then presented his showpiece, "A Handful of Keys," but Tatum still had the edge. Then Art came up once more and roared through "Tiger Rag." James P. tried one more time, with his version of Chopin's "Revolutionary Etude." "Dad told me he never heard Jimmy play so remarkably," Maurice Waller concludes, "but the performance fell short. Tatum was the undisputed king." Later on, James P. would admit, "When Tatum played "Tea for Two" that night, I guess that was the first time I ever heard it really *played.*" And in an interview with the *New York Times,* Fats capped his recollection of that night with this: "That Tatum, he was just too good . . . He had too much technique. When that man turns on the powerhouse, don't no one play him down. He sounds like a brass band."

From then on Tatum was in his element: playing all over town (all over Harlem, at least), on a spectrum of pianos, any of which he could make sound better than it was, staying up all night, consuming legendary quantities of beer, taking his place at the summit of jazz piano playing. Perhaps the first chance a wider group of New York jazz musicians had to see whether or not the rumors from Toledo were exaggerated was at Helbock's, on 52nd Street in Manhattan. During Prohibition, Joe Helbock ran an establishment in a brownstone apartment building where musicians and others from the nearby radio and recording studios could take their refreshment. Music was not a feature of the place, at least not until Willie The Lion started occasionally sitting down at the old upright in the back. Eventually Helbock started paying him to do it around five each evening (Willie and Joe may have invented the institution of the "cocktail pianist" here). After he had taken Tatum into the inner circle, Smith brought him around to Helbock's to show him off, with results that can easily be imagined. In any case, Helbock's business grew rapidly in the early 1930s, to the point where he felt he needed new quarters. He opened a night club across the street from the old place, probably in 1933, and called it the Onyx Club. The birth of the Onyx Club was the opening up of jazz on 52nd Street to the public, and the public would make 52nd Street one of the most famous street names in jazz. One of Helbock's first performers at the Onyx was Art Tatum, and the Onyx Club was Tatum's first solo professional appearance in New York. A first-hand account of hearing Art at the Onyx describes his repertoire at that point as "rags, one-steps, excerpts from the classics, and standard tunes, as well as frequent snatches of stride piano in the Waller-James P. Johnson manner" (Doerschuk).

From here on he was in some demand and made a number of solo club appearances, and he is alleged to have had two weeks playing with McKinney's Cotton Pickers, substituting for their regular but ailing piano player. Waller and Tatum became close friends, and a boisterous friendship it must have been. Waller's personality was probably the featured one, with Tatum's personality accompanying him, as in this anecdote: "On one occasion they appeared at a party dressed in women's clothing, with Tatum announcing himself as Mary Lou Williams and Waller taking the role of Bessie Smith, the fabulous 'Empress of the Blues.' While Tatum played, Waller sang, interrupting himself at one point to holler, 'Mary Lou, I'm really riding, and you're not doing so bad on the keys, either'" (Vance, *Fats Waller*, 111).

Tatum, I think, found a real soul-mate in Fats Waller, perhaps the only one he ever found. They lived alike (namely, as high as their income would allow), drank alike (almost constantly), and shared similar attitudes toward the piano (both had impeccable technique and a leaning toward more serious music that was largely suppressed by their need to make a career in jazz).

From Timme Rosenkrantz, a Danish baron who lived in New York in the 1930s and immersed himself in the jazz world there, we get a story that conveys very concretely what sort of impact Art had in New York in his early years there:

> One night I was sitting in a little bar in Harlem with some Negro men and women friends. A man burst into the place shouting, "Hey, Tatum is down at Basement Brown's getting his hands warmed up." It was almost 4. a.m. when we got to Basement Brown's. That's close to bedtime, but Basement Brown's had just opened. We stopped outside this ordinary brownstone house on 131st St., and one of my friends knocked three times on the door, blew his nose, and the door was opened [it may be necessary to remind readers that Prohibition was in effect and liquor-serving places like this were strictly illegal]. Basement Brown, an enormous man, filled the doorway. He must have weighed at least 300 pounds. But he had a kind face and a big smile. At first he looked at me a bit suspiciously, but my two friends explained to him that I came from Denmark where everyone is alike and that it was my greatest wish to meet Tatum. That did it. He led us through a long corridor, down dark steps, and into a large room. A dozen tables were scattered about, all filled with freshly homemade whisky and other delicacies. In a far corner was a broken-

down upright piano. A heavy-set man sat there, enjoying a bottle of beer, Art Tatum. Basement Brown introduced us. As practically everyone knows, Tatum was almost blind, but I never saw him miss his beer glass once. He was a wonderful, straightforward person with a great sense of humor. He said a couple of nice things about Denmark, a country he had heard about but just the same didn't want to visit, as he was mortally afraid of polar bears.[4] He put down his beer and let his fingers run over the piano keys. "Do you know this?," he asked, and then played "Tea for Two." It sounded like "Tea for Two Thousand." [This is a lot like Joe Turner's remark, "Three thousand words . . ."] What a fabulous technique! And what chords and melody. Never had I heard a jazz pianist with a touch such as this. It was absolutely overwhelming. Tatum was indeed the master. After he had played the melody a couple of times with both hands, he started playing it with just his left hand, while his right hand played "Hallelujah"—and he kept the two tunes going simultaneously while he drank his beer. Truly a feat, one must admit. . . . "Play this, play that," the customers at Basement Brown's shouted when he paused. And Tatum played so that, if the gods had been present in this basement, they would have wept. Then, with aplomb, he played Chopin as Brailowsky could never have done. Well, words are so inadequate. One must hear music.   [Rosenkrantz, "Reflections"]

Les Paul, the highly influential jazz guitarist, still playing once a week in New York at this writing, has a vivid memory of another one of those Harlem after-hours session, in what would have to be described as the ultimate after-hours place. The story goes a long way to explain how Tatum was able to make a hopeless piano sound acceptable.

I'll never forget this night, we were playing up in Harlem, and we took him up there, and he says, "What is that I smell?" I says, "We're in a mortuary." And we were down there and they had a guy on the drainboard. And we hadda walk through this, you know—where they do the work, go by him while he's being drained, and go in the next room where there's a jam session. And they had a washtub of beer. When you wanted a beer you threw a dime in the ice in the washtub and took a beer. And we had a can opener there, and you opened the beer, and that was it. So this night Tatum was playing the piano, Marlowe [Morris] was playing the piano, Billy Kyle, he was playing the piano, Teddy Wilson was there, there must have been about five piano players there, down in that funeral parlor. And when they were playing Art says to me, "Is that F# key stuck?" I says, "Yeah." And he says, "Is that E stuck?" I said, "Yeah, it's down, too." He said, "Any others down?" I said, "No, those are the only two." He says, "OK, get me another beer." So I got him another beer, and finally he says, "Well, I'm ready to go up there." So when he got up there, boy, he blew everybody away, and whenever he'd make a run down, he'd have those two keys pulled up. So with his other hand he'd pull those two keys up so they were ready to go down. And when he hit 'em and they were down, why, he'd pull 'em up again with his other hand. Which just stunned everybody, that this guy had it all worked out before he went up there, and he had two detours that he had to make sure were taken care of.

Art Tatum made his first solo record (aside from the test pressing of 1932) in 1933, for the Brunswick label. On March 21st he recorded "Tea for Two" and "Tiger Rag," the two tunes with which he had battered down the gates of the eastern piano establishment, as well as "The St. Louis Blues" and Duke Ellington's "Sophisticated Lady." On "Tiger Rag," an arrangement that had probably been in his repertoire for years, he showed the influence of his earlier listening; according to Felicity Howlett's analysis, Tatum's arrangement is taken directly from Duke Ellington's 1929 recording. Playing it, she writes, "Tatum becomes the Ellington band." When these recordings were shipped across the country he immediately gained a national reputation, at least among musicians, and set a new standard among jazz pianists for what could be done at a keyboard. That standard is still in effect, almost sixty years later: a recent computer search of contemporary newspaper files produced over 700 references to Art Tatum since 1977, most of them simple references to his work as an almost timeless standard (for jazz) for reviewing the work of current pianists.

Art also created his first and, I believe, his only child in 1933, a boy who was named Orlando. Art's father was not happy about this indiscretion, but I suspect it was nothing very unusual among musicians. As Ellis Larkins pointed out, "You know the piano player gets all the hottest chicks, the drummer gets the others, the bass player gets last. . . . The first thing the women see, 'Oh, don't the piano player play beautifully.' And that's it! Doors open!." Orlando's mother was a Toledo girl called Marnette Jackson, "a huge girl" according to a friend of Arline's. Rudolph Perry, who knew Tatum in his early years and did a little jamming on trumpet with him, told me most of what I know about Marnette. I asked him how they met:

> Well, just from going around places. They got together like young people do, you know. They used to go on rides together, Art bought a car, we used to ride around with him—1931 Ford. Used to take her on the boat, moonlight. We used to go out on the moonlight steamer, it went every Monday night—just for moonlight rides. They had a band on there, they used to wind up and then Art would play, and everybody would be standing there looking at Art. He didn't run too much with girls—not too much, Art was a quiet kind of fellow, you know. Art didn't talk too much, he mostly expressed hisself playing his music.

Steve Taylor, another acquaintance from the same era, told me: "Well, Marnette was his lady—that was his choice. I don't remember him wooing a whole lot of women. Women would chase after him, on account of his abilities, but he wasn't a woman chaser." And Harry Gregory confirmed the relationship:

> Yes—Art had at least one child. Marnette Jackson!— funny I remember that. It's been years ago. She was a

waitress at one of the bootleg joints. But they didn't stay together. Oh, no. He wanted his complete freedom, and he deserved it, for what he was giving to the public.

As for Orlando, Art's brother Karl suggested to me that Orlando and Art played almost no part in one another's lives.

> At the time when I was home, and things like that, I didn't see any indications that girls were important. Although later, when he became older, women were in his life. I know he and Marnette had a son, and he's now deceased. He died in Madrid, about a year or so ago [i.e., 1988]. When he was around Art would talk to him and things like that. . . . After Art's death he would come to see me practically every summer. We had a good relationship. He wasn't musical. He was a career serviceman, and had retired and was living in Madrid. He was in the Air Force. He was with the radio, what you called it, Radio Air Force or whatever they had. He was an announcer. Orlando didn't really play any part in Art's life. Neither did Marnette.

The way Arline tells it, however, Marnette and Orlando were accepted as family, Orlando was nicknamed Boobie and treated as any nephew would have been, and the family never lost contact with him, even though he spent most of his adult life in Europe in military service. Even after Art married his first wife Ruby, all three women often spent time together—Arline, Marnette, and Ruby.

Orlando was raised not by Marnette but by a friend who saw that Marnette "didn't have the time":

> When he was little growing up he went under the name of this lady that raised him. Marnette had a club here. She was married to—well, she wasn't married to this man, she had—this was before she got Collins—this white man, and he had a tavern, so he made everything over to Marnette. Marnette was gone most of the time down at her club. This lady knew Marnette, had known Marnette since she was small. And she was crazy about Boobie, she didn't have no

children, and she was crazy about him so she started to keep him. And then she finally put him in her name. See, I used to go, my husband and I used to drive up there to Columbus where they lived, oh, I'd say maybe once a month, to see about him. I'd go see Bubs, and this lady was crazy about me, you know, and I was crazy about her, I thought she was very nice. He was well taken care of. Oh, yeah, we was crazy about that boy.

It's not clear from all this how much contact Art had with Orlando, but it was apparently more than Karl had implied. Arline went on :

Art used to stop in Columbus and see him—Art bought him a beautiful piano. He's still got it, I think, in Spain.[5] Art bought him a piano when he started taking piano lessons. And anything that Orlando wanted he got it for him, when he was little. And Orlando used to come and spend weekends when his mother was living, used to spend weekends here, Saturday and Sunday, because my Dad made ponebread you know, like biscuits only they'd be larger.

IN 1934 AND 1935, Tatum was working mainly in Cleveland, at Val's, Jimmy Jones's, and the Greasy Spoon—not venues one might expect for a pianist of such a reputation, but times were definitely hard. In spite of this Tatum was in the recording studio in New York on four occasions in 1934, and was recorded live during a nation-wide NBC broadcast from Cleveland (during which as early as this he was described as "The blind king of the ivories"). The number of recording sessions dropped to one in 1935, plus one feature solo on another nationally broadcast radio program ("The Fleischmann Hour," hosted by Rudy Vallee), which was recorded and released much later.

Tatum's life style may already have been revealing its threats to his health in these early years. Luke Reed was a medical student in Cleveland in the early 1930s, playing sax and piano two nights a week for life-support. He discovered Tatum, followed him around from club to club, and established an acquaintance with him. Several years later (Luke's son, who told me this story, was unsure whether it was 1934 or '35), Luke, now an M.D., was on duty at the Lakeside Hospital around midnight one night, when a nurse called and told him there was a man in the Emergency Room asking for his friend, Dr. Reed. It was Tatum, severely sick with pneumonia. He had remembered his friend and somehow found him. Antibiotic drugs were still in the future and pneumonia was a life-threatening disease. Would Tatum have sought help if he hadn't remembered Luke Reed? In any case, he got the treatment he needed and a friendship was cemented. Long after this incident, perhaps in the early 1950s, and after they hadn't seen each other for at least 10 years, Reed found Art playing in Cleveland and after a set went up to him and said, "Art, that sounded wonderful." Immediately, Art responded, "Is that you, Luke?" The remarkable memory was still remarkable.

1935, the year in which Teddy Wilson first did some famous jamming at Mildred Bailey's house with Benny Goodman and Gene Krupa and in which the Goodman Trio made its first recordings, was by no means a lost year for Tatum. The owner of a well-known jazz club in Chicago, Sam Beers, heard Tatum at the Greasy Spoon in Cleveland and decided to import him for a steady job at his club, the Three Deuces at 222 North State Street. Like the Onyx Club in New York, the Three Deuces had been a well-known basement speakeasy and musicians' hang-out during Prohibition which turned into a legitimate night club and showcase for jazz when Prohibition was lifted. Art would make many appearances there over subsequent years, but his first residency began in September of 1935 and lasted perhaps a year. As far as I know this was Art's first billing in Chicago. He started by playing solo, behind the bar in the upstairs room, and he later moved to the basement, where he led a quartet which included John Collins on guitar, Bill Winston[6] on drums, and "Scoops" Carry, who later went on to become an important member of several Earl Hines bands in the 1940s, on alto saxophone. I talked with John Collins about this stint at the Three Deuces in 1935:

> We played with him for about a year. We had a few
> rehearsals, but the format was when he had his specialties

he did it alone, you know. It was an experience, you can believe that. And it was a school, you know, like going to school. No, he didn't take time to show us what he was doing, I don't think he had time. But, I was pretty apt, I guess. I spent quite a bit of time with him off the stand, going to afterhours spots. We'd go to afterhours spots and drink, some of 'em he played, you know, then, go home, go to sleep. Then we'd meet again the next night—we worked hard, you know, with the job, it was long hours. He was married to a lady, her name was Ruby. As a matter of fact she never came to work with him. We would pick him up and then take him home. He spent most of his time with us.[7]

As a matter of fact Art and his first wife, Ruby, were married on August 1, 1935, just a month before his stint at the Three Deuces began, so the observation that he spent most of his time with other musicians sounds a little ominous as far as the future of the marriage might be concerned.

Milt Hinton, the well-known bassist and excellent photographer, also got acquainted with Tatum at the Three Deuces, where he was in a group that traded sets with Tatum. Milt noted that Art made sure the waiters set up the tables the same way every night, so that he could make his entrance through them "with a bounce" (Arline said that he always walked on his toes) and as if he had no handicap—and indeed as long as the waiters remembered to set up the same way Tatum had no handicap. Tatum loved to play cards:

> So when we weren't playing we'd sit in the booths and have a drink and play pinochle. Most people didn't know Art could see some—he was only partially blind. His left eye was evidently the better one, because he used to put a light like this, right behind him. He'd deal the cards, pick up his cards and have the light right behind him, like this, and he'd put all his cards in their place. People would call their cards as they played them. If you'd call 10 of diamonds, and he'd have the jack, he wouldn't have to look at his hand again, he knew exactly what he had.

The Tatum memory banks again. He was as competitive about cards as he was about the piano; he won more often than not, and considered himself a champion among the people he played with—mostly other musicians or club owners. Joe Springer was a pianist who knew him in New York from the 1930s on and frequently toured the after-hours scene with him. Reuben's was a favorite hangout in the '30s, and when I asked Joe what Art was doing while all those other players were at the keyboard before him, Joe told me:

> See, Reuben's, it used to be mostly a piano players' hangout. Things would start moving around 3 in the morning, when the piano players would finish with their gigs. We'd go there and we'd take turns playing—when I say we, I didn't play often, I mean these other guys were better than I was. And then after everybody got finished playing then Art would be the last. Nobody would dare follow him. So once in a while he would show one or two things to the other piano players. But before that he was in the back room playing cards with Reuben himself, and I guess he would listen with one ear—you know, the music would still go back there. I guess he would hear some of it.

Milt Hinton talked about the difficulty of playing with him in those days:

> It was hard to play with him. . . . I know at the Three Deuces, 1935, '36, when I was out there, I just wasn't up to playing all those changes that he played. I was working with Zutty Singleton. Zutty had a quartet, no, five pieces. Lee Collins was his trumpet player, Everett Barksdale was the guitar player, and Cozy Cole's brother was the piano player. This was 1935, in Chicago. And Art Tatum was the relief piano player, he played the intermission. So we would play for an hour and then Art would come on for a half hour. For his last tune I was supposed to go up and take him out. Man, I was just like standing still there, on those wonderful things he was playing. I really wasn't capable of catching it. I don't think I got in his way. He was

awfully nice to me, but I didn't feel adequate playing with him. The changes he put in there, that just beat me to pieces. Every now and then, in every generation, someone like that comes along.

Art was also frequently in Toledo in the middle '30s. Jon Hendricks is the singer who was later famous as part of the Lambert, Hendricks, and Ross vocal trio which could do Tatum-like arranged scat singing, in three parts and at very high speed. His family lived just five houses from the Tatums. In 1935 he was fourteen years old and singing (as "The Sepia Bobby Breen") at the Waiters and Bellmen's Club in Toledo, and Art Tatum was his accompanist.

> The W&B was an afterhours club, but it was also a regular club. It was open all night. It had a restaurant next door. It was a regular club during the day, you see it was the Waiters & Bellmen's Club at night. Those were the two professions in which a Negro gentleman could engage with some dignity, waiter and bellman. . . . But it was open all night, and had jazz sessions. And because Art was playing between shows every band and musician that came to Toledo came there, to jam and to listen to him. And I was lucky because I was singing with him and I met all these people. I met Louis [Armstrong] when I was 14. And the whole Lunceford band came to my house to eat, 'cause my mother was the greatest cook in the world. Well, in those days they had shows, every club had a show, consisting of girls, you know—a chorus line. There was a featured singer, usually a man—that was me. And there was a girl singer, and there was a comedian. And we all used to dance at the finale, and there was a very hip band. In those days the music was jazz, it was the only music there was. There wasn't any line between jazz and pop and rock and all that stuff, there was just jazz music. So that was it. And Art did the intermissions. And then this lady that was playing piano in the band was so terrible that I asked her if she minded if I sang with Arthur—that's what we called him. So she said no. I asked him, and he was happy. So we

worked together for two years. It was great. That was my musical education.

It seems well established that Tatum's technique, in spite of his classical training, was very little like what one expects in such a pianist. A musician who saw Tatum at the Three Deuces in 1935 described how his hands looked at the keyboard: "The backs of his hands are fat and pudgy, but the fingers are long and taper to slender tips. Instead of the customary high wrists and curved fingers of the legitimate pianist, Tatum's hand is almost horizontal, and his fingers seem to actuate around a horizontal line drawn from wrist to finger-tip" (Hoefer, "The Hot Box," January 9, 1957). This observation needs a comment, because the assumption that the "legitimate pia-nist" works with "high wrists and curved fingers" is probably wrong. While tens of thousands of us, maybe hundreds of thousands, were trained in this hand position and led to believe that it was the only way to play properly, there is good evidence that many, if not most, great pianists—at least as far back as Chopin—have not used this position. John Eaton, the Washington pianist who called this to my attention, argues that the most accomplished keyboard artists have always discovered that flexibility, speed, and tone require flatter fingers and keeping the fingers closer to the keys. Certainly Horowitz failed to meet the "high wrist" criterion—at times his hands seemed to dangle from the keyboard with the wrists clearly lower than the keys themselves. Tatum had discovered independently what most other great pianists had found about how to accomplish great things at a keyboard.

In any case at the time this observation was made no one knew much of anything about Tatum's origins or training, so it must have been his playing itself that led to his being compared with the "legitimate" pianist rather than the "jazz pianist." From the begin-ning his playing evoked in listeners the whole classical tradition of the piano, in a way that Fats's or Teddy Wilson's or Earl Hines's did not, even though all of them were highly trained in the classical tradition. Tatum had a way of carrying an illusory concert hall around with him, and so long as "jazz" and "concert hall" were considered unbridgeable worlds it was probably inevitable that critics and reviewers would be confused by the question of whether or not to consider him a "jazz" pianist. His fellow musicians, from the down-and-dirty Jay McShann to the sophisticated André Previn, had no such confusion, but many critics found the question a hard one to decide.

He made no recordings in 1936 and his run at the Three Deuces came to an end. In spite of Sam Beers's enthusiasm (this was by no means Tatum's last appearance there), it was the musicians rather than the public who came to hear him. Whether Sam Beers felt that audiences in Chicago were losing interest, or Tatum made the decision on his own to try the waters elsewhere, the end result was the same. Some time in 1936, Tatum took the first of many long train trips to California. In spite of his reckless courage in automobiles he was afraid of flying.[8]

To California and Back

"Good God! This Tatum is the greatest! Thank God he's black—otherwise nobody's job would be safe." **ANONYMOUS**

TATUM WAS TWENTY-SIX when he made the long voyage to the West Coast. The movie industry was in high gear by the mid-1930s. It and the life that swirled around it attracted all kinds of creative people to Southern California. Fats Waller had gone out the year before, at age thirty-one, to appear in two movies. Among others, both George Gershwin and Nat Cole moved there the same year Art put in his first appearance in California (1936).

Art's reputation, which arrived in California before he did, was even larger (at least with musicians) than the one he had going when he first went to New York, and very little time passed before he began the familiar pattern of making large ripples with his paying engagements and tearing up the rest of the musicians after hours. He had engagements at the Paramount Theater, the Melody Grill, the Trocadero, and one of the favorite black haunts, the Club Alabam. He was soon in demand for parties given by Hollywood celebrities, such as Mary Pickford, and in November he appeared on Bing Crosby's radio show. It must have been a heady life.

Fortunately, there are still a number of people alive who remember how he inserted himself into the California scene. Bernice Lawson is a classical pianist who became a good friend of Tatum's when he came to Los Angeles, and shared her piano and her cooking with him:

> I first met Art—I was listening to a broadcast from Chicago, a radio broadcast, with some musicians, there used to be a musician here who was a violinist that I used to accompany, I like to accompany. And he said you should hear this man, oh you should hear him play. So—he came on early in the morning, he came on about 8 o'clock. And then one day, Richard called and he said, Art Tatum is in town, I'm going to meet him. So we met Art, and that was about the first week he came to Los Angeles. From then on we just listened to him play, oh he was just—and he liked my piano, I always had good pianos. He started coming to my house. And he brought his wife, we got along very well, she was very nice. And then she . . . became an alcoholic.
>
> I used to go hear him a lot, I had a friend who liked Art very much and he would drive for him—Art had to have somebody to drive for him, and he liked Art very much so he took plenty of time and he would just take him wherever he wanted to go. So we'd just go wherever he played. He had a lot of people that would help him, because he was a nice person, people would help him. He just drank too much beer, if it hadn't been for the beer he would probably still be living. He wasn't gonna try to control it. He drank beer by the case. Pabst Blue Ribbon, he'd buy it by the case, and he'd drink it all day long—and half the night, you know. Sometimes he'd come to my house because he liked the piano. Every once in a while he'd come and—not often, cause I was too busy, but he'd come and play after he got off from work, which was around 2 o'clock, 'til about 5 in the morning. And all my

neighbors would open all their doors and windows so they could hear him. So I'd go wherever he worked. He was a remarkable pianist, just remarkable. Stokowski [one of the preeminent symphony orchestra conductors of the time] used to come and listen to him, he'd come to the first show, and then leave. And he and Horowitz were good friends. I didn't see Horowitz here, but they say that in Chicago Horowitz would always go hear Art.

He liked sports, and he liked, you know, he was very good, he could go to a football game or a basketball game, and tell you everything that was going on. People with sight would miss half of it. And he could remember it. I had a friend who was gung-ho on football, and he would take Art to the football games, and they would have the biggest arguments about 'em—about the next year they would argue about 'em, and Art would know every play that went on on the field. He loved football. And he could play bridge, he played a good game of bridge. . . . He was a remarkable person. It's just too bad that he let liquor get a hold of him. He had a bad life, I guess, I don't know. . . . Yeah, I think he had a hard life. At 5 or 6 in the morning he'd go to somebody's house if they had a piano, and play and play and play, and then finally he'd get to the apartment or the house or wherever he was going around 9 or 10 o'clock, and then he'd sleep until time to go to work.

He did everything in cash. I remember that, 'cause when they [Art and Ruby] got ready to buy the house they didn't have any credit. They had money but they didn't have any credit, and they had a hard time. Seems to me that this friend of mine that used to drive for him—did he help them get that house? Somebody helped them. It was a very nice house. They had the money but they didn't have the credit.

What Tatum *did* have was diabetes, although it's not clear when he first knew about it. Since I've never heard it mentioned in connection with his childhood I assume it was type II, the kind that first shows up in adulthood. It is clear, though, that he never made any concessions to it in his life style. To be both diabetic and a beer-drinker on an Olympian scale is to invite disaster—or at least an early death, and the old saw comes to mind here, that Death is Nature's way of telling us to slow down. But making those concessions—drastically less beer, a controlled diet, more rest—would have taken away exactly the things that mattered most to him, and would have removed him from the night-life that he seemed to love more than almost anything (afternoon baseball or football games would probably come next). And it's easy to believe that even the strongest of men might not have been able to remove themselves from California night-life in the mid-1930s.

Ernie Lewis was a young pianist when Tatum first arrived in California. Lewis later moved to Oakland and after that Tatum stayed with him whenever he played in San Francisco. They were friends for the rest of Tatum's life.

> I was in Los Angeles when I first met him. It must have been the middle of the '30s, '36, somewhere around there. It was when he first came to Los Angeles. His manager brought him down on Central Ave., down there where they used to hang out at night, it was a club where they used to have shows in. And at 2 o'clock that was all over. But they had a bar upstairs, over the club, small club, and that's where all the musicians hung out, after they got off of their jobs. And that's when the music started. And the first night that he came in I happened to be in there. Art was very quiet, very unassuming, about his playing, you know. He liked to talk about baseball and football and all that. After he got through with his job, at one of those clubs out there in Hollywood, they'd bring him down there [to Central Ave.], he'd just sit there all night and play. All the other fellows would go up there and be playing, and he'd be back there talking and drinking—'cause they wouldn't dare get up there after him. So this would be about 4 o'clock in the morning, maybe a little earlier sometimes. And Art would get up there, after he got his share of booze, to get him started, and start playing. Don't say nothing to nobody, just go ahead and start playing. And

he played until daybreak, and this would go on day after day, long as he was in town. The musicians, there would be a few, quite a few present, to supply the booze. That would support the bar. . . . But that was his way, if he was in town that's where he would be. Club Alabam. They had other after-hours joints, too. About two blocks around the corner there was a fellow that had an after-hours joint where Nat Cole, and all the guys used to hang, too. And they took him around there. They'd go down there, eat, drink—in somebody's home. . . . That would go on for hours, until daybreak, sometimes until noon. When he was in town, that's what he would do. All he wanted to do. But he would drink that booze right along with his playing— and then, go on home. Go to bed, get up about 2 or 3 o'clock in the afternoon, get something to eat, lay there and rest until time to go to work that evening. That was his life. He followed the radio, I guess that's all there was in those days, and he talked a lot to a lot of very fine musicians, all the black musicians . . . they'd be right down in that room, listening to him. He was a great man to talk to. He was a very intelligent man.

Harold Brown, the brother of Duke Ellington's famous trombonist Lawrence Brown, was already a popular pianist when Art arrived in Los Angeles, and he continued to work in Los Angeles into the 1980s. (Brown was born the same year as Tatum, but oddly enough he had always believed Tatum was a lot older than he. I could hardly convince him otherwise. Maybe it comes from looking up to somebody.) I was able to ask him about Art's early days in California:

Well, I don't know too much about his life, I know he was a good friend of mine. He liked my piano playing. He used to come over to my home here, and the wife liked him, of course. We used to have friends over in the mornings. He got off from work—we used to have big kinds of parties. Yeah, when he got off at 2. My wife enjoyed cooking stuff up, you know, she enjoyed to entertain, and she was so elated that we were friends, you know. So he used to come over here after work, and he'd play for us, you know, it was such a pleasure, that was the greatest. Yeah, he loved to come over here. And he was very anxious about spilling food on his, you know, eating—he always worried about spilling food on himself. He drank a lot. That's what killed him, I think. He was a very nice guy. But he had to go, I guess. I got some records here, I play 'em every once in a while. He never gave me any lessons. Us piano players mostly copied from him, though, you know, like Louis Armstrong, trumpet players copied from him. I knew his wife Ruby, but I didn't know her very well. She was very jealous of him, though. She was a very kind of jealous woman. She didn't ever come to my house with him. I never was that close to her, never saw too much of her.

Eddie Barefield had first met Tatum in 1931 in Toledo, as we've seen, but he moved to California in 1935 and picked up with Art again when Art arrived in 1936. Prohibition had ended in 1933, but most states mandated closing times for liquor-serving establishments, and so a niche was created for the "after-hours" club which now meant open and serving after legal closing times. "Bootleg" took on the same meaning.

Helen was a lady that had a bootleg joint. She used to sell whisky, and Art used to go and have her stock up with Pabst, and that's where he would spend his nights. Spend the night there playing—'cause he always went from his job to some place like that and played all night. And all the piano players in town would congregate there. He and everybody else was out there in those days. Everybody hung out on Central Ave., Dunbar Hotel, Club Alabam— you could see everybody in show business there. Then they used to have a place about 2 blocks up . . . where everybody hung out. In LA you could buy your booze at a drug store. Everybody used to hang out, then they'd spread out to the different afterhours places. It was a lot of fun. It's not fun anymore. I used to play a town, and when you got off from work, whether you played theater or dances, there'd be a hundred places to go afterwards and hang out. But today, you go in all these towns and you play a 2-hour concert and by the time you get your instrument cleaned up and packed away everybody's gone home.

By 1937 "SWING" was in, Benny Goodman's star was rising fast, and Teddy Wilson had recorded his famous sides with the Benny Goodman Quartet (Goodman, Wilson, Krupa, and Lionel Hampton). Tatum made his first Los Angeles recordings in February of that year, as "Art Tatum and His Swingsters." (The term "swing" had an irresistible appeal in those years; "Nat Cole and His Swingsters" was the first version of the King Cole Trio.) The Tatum Swingsters were several musicians from the popular West Coast band of Les Hite: Bill Perkins (guitar), Joe Bailey (bass), Oscar Bradley (drums), Lloyd Reese (trumpet), and Marshall Royal (clarinet). Gunther Schuller comments (*Swing Era,* 482) about these four sides that "poor Lloyd Reese and Marshall Royal are constantly being swamped by Tatum." Marshall Royal, only three years younger than Tatum but still performing today, discussed that recording date with me, confirming the notion that as a group member Art was anything but easy and accommodating but, like almost everyone else, Royal expressed only pride at having played with him: "'Course, he was so great you didn't give a damn what he did, you just appreciated what he was doing." Marshall remembered that the studio (he thought it was Decca) had a giant picture of an Indian on the wall, staring out at the musicians, with the caption, "Where's the melody?"

Marshall's account of knowing Tatum at that time repeated the familiar elements of the marathon after-hours sessions running into the early morning, and also Art's intense interest in sports; Marshall recalled taking him to track-meets and finding that Art followed the action so closely it was hard to believe he wasn't actually seeing the events. But Marshall's most impressive story concerns the day he was able to introduce Art Tatum to Ignascz Paderewski, one of the most prominent concert piano virtuosi of the early twentieth century, and to be present when Tatum played for Paderewski in the virtuoso's private railroad car—a breathtaking moment for pianists to contemplate![1]

Besides being awed by his piano playing, Royal felt Tatum was a highly intelligent man. Most people I've talked to have shared that assessment, and certainly in his music one sees a monumental intelligence. But outside of his memory his intelligence almost never shines through in accounts of conversations with him. There have been a few glimmers. For example, the cornetist Jimmy McPartland gives a glimpse of a different Tatum from the after-hours marathon beer-drinker:

> I had a group at the Three Deuces in Chicago in the late thirties, and Art was the intermission pianist. We talked a lot, and I told him about a book I'd read on this German sea captain named von Luckner. He'd cruised all over the world during the First World War on an armed ship that was disguised as a neutral tramp steamer, and he'd sunk millions of dollars of Allied shipping. . . . Art was fascinated, so I started going to his hotel in the afternoon and reading it to him. We'd drink beer, and I'd read, and it was most delightful. He was a great listener. Sometimes when I'd get off the stand after a set, he'd sing phrases back to me that I'd played and that he particularly liked.
>
> [Quoted in Balliett, "Art Tatum"]

I doubt that Art knew very many book-readers, especially ones who would read out loud to him. Of course, this afternoon reading may not have been the purely contemplative pleasure that one imagines. Von Luckner may have been attractive to Tatum's competitive instinct; one can play with the idea of Tatum seeing himself in this sea captain—a blind, black tramp pianist, cruising around blowing everyone else out of the water. But the intelligence is still there, as it is in the story the concert pianist Steven Mayer has told me, about talking to a friend who said he had discussed Italian opera with Tatum and found him "very erudite." For me, and for Marshall Royal, one of the most poignant thoughts about Art Tatum is how much more he might have developed as a person if he had had access to a wider range of life's possibilities. Marshall said this better:

The only thing is, being a black dude, he didn't have the advantage of mingling with certain people who were knowledgeable in his particular thing. Because especially in those days he lived on the other side of the track. And there is a difference. I'm not one of those racial fighters, I try to accept things as they go, I don't hate nobody and no other kind of thing, but he had to do that mostly on his own, because he didn't have that many who could help him.

ART'S FIRST WIFE, Ruby, remains a shadowy figure in all the accounts I've been able to obtain, always so deep in the background she's almost impossible to see. She was Ruby Arnold, from Cleveland, where of course Art spent a great deal of time. They were married in 1935 and the marriage lasted until the early 1950s, although it's hard to see how. Art and Ruby established a base in Los Angeles and bought a house there, but he was probably gone from it more than he was home, and Ruby apparently rarely traveled with him or went out with him when he was in Los Angeles. Ruby eventually became an alcoholic, there was a nasty divorce (in which Ruby took Art's piano), and she died only a few years later.

Although Ruby had precious little of Art's time he was apparently very fond of her. Ruby stayed connected with the Tatum family, who liked her a lot; by way of Arline, Ruby's marriage with Art takes on a little more reality for us:

> Ruby was a good girl, the whole family was crazy about her. Oh yeah, there was nobody in the family that she didn't treat right. . . . We met her mother and her mother was just like Ruby. And, Ruby could play piano pretty good, too. And Art taught her quite a bit, you know. She was a good girl, though. And my Daddy, she'd come in, you know, "Poppa"—Poppa come in from work, you know, she'd come in, "Poppa, are you tired? Well come on and get some coffee"—she loved coffee, and everybody, you're gonna drink coffee! She used to come here and stay. Art used to get here and go to Cleveland, and get Ruby— like he had to go somewhere, bring Ruby on over here,

Ruby'd stay with us until he come back. She was a good girl, and my Mom and Dad was crazy about her because— they didn't have but me, and that made 'em feel a little better with another, you know.

Art did everything that he could for Ruby. 'Cause Ruby, she was a good girl. He did everything [for her]— he'd say hisself sometime, "Ruby's good"—he'd talk to Momma, you know, he'd tell Momma anything, and he'd talk to Momma and Momma'd say, "Yeah, Ruby's a good girl," you'd hear 'em sometime sittin' and talkin', Momma and Art.

Only months after his arrival in California, in 1936 Tatum was back in New York (another transcontinental journey by train), where he had a solo spot on the New Year's Eve "Kraft Phoenix Cheese Program," on NBC radio. On these trips he was often accompanied by a representative of the agency that handled his bookings, although he made the trip so often that later he could handle it by himself. Traveling alone, he required someone to meet him when he arrived. He usually depended on friends, who were not always reliable, and Bernice Lawson was often called into play:

For a long time my telephone number was the only one he could dial, 'cause he couldn't see, but he learned to dial my number. So whenever he came to town he would dial my number and I would either go get him or have somebody to go get him. Most of the time he knew, who was going to pick him up, but sometimes they didn't show up like they should. So—he knew he could count on me.

The coast-to-coast train trip took three days, which must have been highly stressful for Tatum, who for most of his life was never separated from a piano for more than a few hours at a time. Unlike Paderewski, he was unable to travel with his Bosendorfer (in Art's case it would have been a Steinway). Once again Art's talent for making friends came to his rescue and he found a way to break the trip. As Red Norvo explained to me,

There was a doctor that lived in Kansas City, a doctor, I
don't remember his name now, but Art stayed with him
when he was there, and he had a big family room like this
one. He had two grand pianos in this room. On his way to
or from New York he'd stop over for a few days. The
doctor was crazy about his playing and everything, they
had a good cook and everything, they'd fatten him up, they
said, they'd fatten him up for New York.

In early 1937 he traveled once more back to California, but the
engagements he was offered were apparently too few to support him,
and later the same year Art crossed the country once again, to return
to the Three Deuces in Chicago for another extended appearance
(six months this time), and then to New York to work at a club
which became one of the 52nd Street landmarks, the Famous Door
(the original Onyx by this time had burned down). The pattern of
Tatum's career was now well established. He would make frequent
appearances at well-known jazz clubs in New York, Chicago, and Los
Angeles, usually on a double bill with a jazz combo, and between
these he would fill in with jobs at lesser-known, often obscure clubs
where one would hardly expect to hear a performer of such stature.
Marian McPartland remembers one of these, in the late '40s or early
'50s, long after he had established his reputation on both sides of the
Atlantic: "I heard him once in Baltimore. I was playing at the Las
Vegas Club with my trio, while Art was across town at a place called
the Tiajuana. I would take a cab over there, between my sets, to hear
him. He was the most fantastic player, somebody I've always admired
and revered. We often chatted, but Art was not a big talker—he was
rather laconic, didn't have a lot to say. I guess everything went into
his playing." One almost gets the impression that Tatum didn't care
much where he played so long as he could stay active, and could keep
making the rounds of the after-hours joints, where his life seemed to
be centered and where he could keep up his extremely wide range of
friendships among musicians. He needed to keep playing, but it's not
clear how much of his need was for money and how much was for
the structure that piano playing gave to his life.

In November 1937 he recorded four tunes for Brunswick in New

York. Just as he had for his first solo recording session, he tapped into a variety of the streams of American popular music. "Stormy Weather" and "Chloe" were real pop songs, the kind anyone might whistle, sing or play; "Gone with the Wind" was a much more sophisticated song, with harmonic changes the living-room pianist would not be likely to try without the sheet music, and "The Sheik of Araby" was a tribute to another era and a tune usually requiring a five- or six-piece band, a companion to his earlier "Tiger Rag."

BY 1938 THERE had developed in Europe a signifi-cant audience for jazz, an audience which many musicians, especially blacks, found much more appreciative than those in the U.S., and there was a steady stream of prominent jazz musicians making Euro-pean tours. The trend was so pronounced that in 1938 *Down Beat* ran a series of articles on American musicians appearing and working in Europe. Fats Waller, who gave his first European performance in 1935, made another trip in 1938. Tatum was usually not involved with trends and developments in mainstream jazz, but this one caught him up. He and Ruby (together for once) left New York on the *Queen Mary* in March of 1938. Art, now twenty-nine, was headed for a three-month series of engagements in England—Ciro's, the Paradise Club, and a number of other venues, where he was im-pressed by British audiences who listened to him quietly and without the background chatter he detested in American audiences. A num-ber of stories exist showing his irritability, at least in the posh clubs, with people who talked over his performance. My favorite is one in which he says to a tableful near the piano, "You played the last three numbers, how about if I play the next three?" Art's appearances in England were not concerts, but the audiences made them something closer to concerts than anything Tatum had experienced at home. He also appeared on the BBC and at the Aston Hippodrome in Bir-mingham, and he later told an American interviewer, "Sundays when everything was closed there [in England] we'd fly to Paris for $15. The Champs-Elysées was jumping in those days" (Bower, "Star Gazing"). According to Doerschuk, he went on to play "at the Café de Paris and concerts on the Continent," but Doerschuk is the only author who has mentioned appearances outside of England.

For all his towering talent and especially his harmonic daring, Tatum composed almost nothing. However, his trip to England stimulated some small effort at composition and resulted in the British publication (by the Peter Maurice Music Co., Ltd.) of four piano pieces attributed to Art (the parallels between Tatum and Waller assert themselves again here, and one is reminded of Waller's "London Suite," which he too wrote in 1938). Tatum's four pieces were given the titles of gem stones: "Sapphire," "Amethyst," "Turquoise," and "Jade." These sound like wonderful mood pieces— imagine a sapphire polished by Art Tatum! I have not heard the pieces played nor seen the transcriptions, but I believe the titles are misleading about the flavor of the music. The fact is that "Amethyst" is basically the same composition as a tune he wrote and recorded in 1934, which he then called "The Shout"; and "Jade," according to Arnold Laubich, "seems related to 'Gang O' Nothin'." This was no explosion of creativity nor tapping of new resources, and the idea for doing the pieces may even have come from the British publisher.

On his return he could once more be found playing solo at the Three Deuces, where it seems the news of a successful European tour created a new ambience for Tatum. Fame is strange in what it feeds on. Europeans were impressed by the American successes of jazzmen, while many white Americans were not impressed until they noticed the Europeans applauding. It was now the case, according to the Chicago writer Sharon Pease, that "When he approached the piano, a hush fell over the capacity-jammed place. Not a murmur, not a cough. When he cut loose, there wasn't one in the place who didn't experience that goose pimply feeling down the spine"(Spellman). Now Tatum began getting some attention not just from musicians but from the night-club-going white public too. This included the affluent and newsworthy, who were often to be found not only in night clubs ("downtown") but in previously all-black after-hours clubs ("uptown").

For example, it was actually the white debutante Tallulah Bankhead, socially prominent and famous in her time, who brought the two blind blacks Art Tatum and Al Hibbler together, around 1941 or '42. As Hibbler tells it:

> The first time I met Art was here in New York. First time I met him I was working with [Jay] McShann, and there was a afterhours place—Clark Monroe, Monroe's Uptown House, and—so I'm singing over at Monroe's—Tallullah heard about me, I was singin' blues then—she sent somebody over to Monroe's and said, "Bring Al over, I wanna hear him sing "Outskirts of Town," and I wanna hear him sing it with Art Tatum." I said, Art Tatum? I went over there and sang, and she gave me my first hundred dollar bill. Tallullah and—I'm trying to think of this other girl that was there—Barbara Hutton [another equally well-known society girl]. "Poor little rich girl." See, that's when New York was New York, you know. All them big stars, Lana Turner, Carol Landis, Paulette Goddard, all them people was hanging in them afterhours joints. Tatum made me acquainted with all the afterhours joints. I quit Mac [McShann]—I wasn't gonna leave NY. I had me a thing going, I still got the silver dollar. See, I put this silver dollar in my sleeve, and I'd get out on the floor and start singin'. And I'd hit some real groovy notes, and I'd drop my arm, like that, and that silver dollar would hit the floor, make somebody think somebody was throwin' silver dollars. Shoot, I made so much money—So Art and I hired a little white girl named Phyllis Martin. And he said, "Now you keep her with you." She had a little whisk broom, she'd go around and sweep this money up, put it in her purse. She and I would get together and count this money. Art wouldn't take none of it—he'd say, "You keep it, man, I'm makin big money." See, I didn't have no contract with nobody. He said, "You hustlin, I'm not."

Al strongly reminded me of how aggressively independent both he and Art were, when I asked him whether Karl was driving them around in 1941:

Didn't need no car in New York. Get in a cab and ride all over New York for fifty cents. We just jump in them cabs, man. Yeah! And Art could see a little. 'Cause I can't see at all, but Art could see a little bit. I never used a cane, man. Shoot, I'd walk all over New York without a cane. You wanna make me and Art Tatum mad, you put a cane— Shoot, we the forerunners of blind people out here. We didn't hang out with no blind people. They too slow. Bring us down. . . .

By 1938 Art began to get another kind of attention reserved for major figures. He had enough visibility that publishers began trying to transcribe some of his recorded performances, to make them available to other pianists—for most of us, hearing him or even watching him still failed to make the blizzard of notes he was playing accessible. As the radio and television personality Steve Allen once commented, "Listening to Tatum is like riding past a DaVinci painting on a fast bicycle"; or Buddy DeFranco, the clarinetist who played on some of Tatum's last recordings: "Playing with Tatum is like chasing a train and never catching it" (quoted in Gitler, *Swing*). In 1938 the magazine *Orchestral World* published a transcription of "a simple chorus by Tatum." In 1939 the English transcriptions appeared; Sharon Pease, Chicago teacher and critic, published his transcription of Tatum's 1938 recording of "Royal Garden Blues" in *Down Beat;* the Robbins Music Corporation got out Volume 1 of its *Art Tatum Improvisations.* None was very accurate or successful as transcription, but some of them could at least make you feel heroic as you tried to come to grips with Tatum.

From his return from Europe until 1943, a five-year period, Tatum's bookings were mainly "residencies" (several weeks or more) in New York (Cafe Society, Kelly's Stables, and other well-known clubs) with occasional short trips to other parts of the country for brief appearances. At Cafe Society the owner, Barney Josephson, like Sam Beers an ardent fan of Tatum's, had a policy that allowed no serving of food or drink while Tatum played. This was, no doubt, not only what Josephson wanted, but also what Tatum wanted. I have never heard that he wanted this kind of setting from his mainly black, after-hours listeners, but with mainly white audiences his performances were now beginning to take on the character of concerts. Once when Art played the Latin Club in Toledo (a club situated just above the Rivoli Theater, where Adelaide Hall had appeared when she first came to Toledo), Art's agent insisted that the cash register not be used. Cash registers were mechanical and noisy in those pre-electronic days, and the cashier at that time recalled that while Tatum was playing they had to work out of cigar boxes (Roberts). In fact, the Tatum arrangements—and this is something one can easily hear in the recordings—had always had the character of concert pieces, in their overall structure, in their use of sophisticated impressionist harmonies, and in their bravura technique. Many of his better-educated listeners could easily bring the standards of the concert hall to bear when listening to Tatum. They readily recognized the concert-like qualities in his playing and were a willing audience for them, and Tatum arguably wanted to show these audiences that he was a master of the qualities they appreciated. Given that, he could only be frustrated by patrons who came only for the alcohol and some background music, and so we get the stories about his irritation with noisy club patrons. It is certainly worth mentioning here that Tatum (like several others, including Duke Ellington and Miles Davis) was not fond of being called a jazz musician. Tom Tilghman, owner of the Hollywood Bar in Harlem, where Tatum spent a great deal of time even when he wasn't playing, said once, "You could always get his goat by calling him a *jazz* piano player. He didn't like to be called that; said he was a *piano* player, a *musician*" (Keepnews, "Art Tatum").

In an era when jazz and the individual jazz soloist were not at all associated with the concert hall, it's interesting that together Tatum and his white audiences colluded, meshed their expectations, to create the aura of a concert-like performance. At the same time, black after-hours places remained the setting where Tatum could let his hair down and play king-of-the-hill with his peers, and the workshops where everyone learned from everyone else, but especially from Tatum. In a way Art was having his cake and eating it, too—"having it" in the form of maintaining and displaying his extraordinary level of pianistic performance in a concert-like show-case, and "eating it" in the sense of giving away his performances night after night in a vibrant, boozy atmosphere, in endless variations on whatever tune he might be challenged on. How many people could put a Lippizaner horse through its paces in the morning, and ride bareback in a rodeo in the afternoon?

In August of 1938 Tatum had an extended recording session (or possibly two separate sessions) during which he did sixteen tunes, including his first of many recordings of "Sweet Lorraine" and his famous version of Jules Massenet's "Élégie." None of these tracks was ever released on 78 rpm pressings but were made available only ten or more years later when material was needed for the new "long-playing" records. The first versions of "Sweet Lorraine" (which André Previn could still play note for note thirty years later) and "Élégie" to be available on 78s were recorded in 1940.

Tatum has taken a certain amount of critical heat for drawing on classical compositions for material, but in "swinging" a light classic Tatum wasn't doing anything unusual; stride pianists from James P. Johnson on had considerable respect for classical or non-jazz works and loved to give them their own treatment. In fact, Billy Taylor (quoted in Gitler, *Swing*) has claimed that Tatum recorded "Élégie" as a sort of reply to the stride pianist Donald Lambert, who used to do a lot of classical pieces in stride style; if that's true, then Tatum was extending his "cutting session" tactics into the domain of re-cordings. Jim Maher (collaborator with Alec Wilder on *American Popular Song*) remembered this about the ragtime and stride pianists of the late 1920s and early '30s:

> I can remember going out to New Jersey to hear Donald Lambert with either Lennie Kunstadt or maybe Rudi Blesch. You'd ask for something, say, "Twelfth Street Rag," and instead Donald would launch into "The Bells of St. Mary's" and he'd go on and on through one variation after another. And, when Alec Wilder and I interviewed Eubie Blake for our research into *American Popular Song*, all Eubie wanted to play for the first half-hour was Victor Herbert. And he'd say, "Now listen to the harmoniza-

tion—this man really knew harmony. We all learned from him, you know." And he played Herbert's music with such meticulous care. Sometimes I think about Art Tatum and Eubie Blake and Donald Lambert, and the common thread of their virtuosity. But that was an essential part of the ragtime tradition—pure showmanship and entertainment. They really loved to enthrall you. Oh my God, Donald Lambert could do "The Bells of St. Mary's" until you'd have bells in your head for two weeks.

There is, incidentally, a lovely story about Tatum and Lambert. Lambert traveled in to Harlem to challenge Tatum. As Dick Wellstood tells it, "He found Tatum and Marlowe Morris (considered second only to Tatum) sitting in the back room of some bar [shades of "Gunsmoke"!]. Lambert flung himself at the piano, crying, 'I've come for you, Tatum!,' and things of that nature, and launched into some blistering stride. Tatum heard him out. When it was all over and Lambert stood up, defiant, Tatum said quietly, 'Take him, Marlowe'" (Giddins, *Riding*). In spite of the flavor of such a story, Lambert apparently became a favorite of Art's and a good friend.

IT OCCURS TO me that I haven't said enough about "cutting" sessions. They have long since disappeared from the scene, but they were such an important and characteristic feature of the early years of jazz that I wonder whether jazz would have evolved as it did without them. Competition and more or less unspoken ambitions to outdo someone else have probably always been part of the performing artist's life; even Mozart once wrote to his father while on a concert tour, comparing himself with a local pianist: "Count Wolfeck and several others who are very enthusiastic for Beecke said recently at the concert that I can play Beecke into a bag" (Loesser, *Pianos*, 104). But cutting sessions went far beyond covert ambitions. It's impossible for me to imagine a "hotter," more intense climate for learning than those late-night and all-night sessions provided, and without them younger jazz musicians may have lost a powerful stimulus for growth and especially for creativity. They were tough and competitive, with all the sharp edges left on, and all the language that goes with them comes from combat and conflict ("cutting," "carving up," "blowing away," "wiping out," and all the rest). Egos got bruised and even damaged, and there was sometimes the spirit of the gladiator arena about them. As Orrin Keepnews put it, "The first thing to do on arriving in any town was to look up the best players in town and have at them" (Keepnews, "Art Tatum"). Or the other way around: if word got out that a famous player was in town, a local gang would surround him or her. For example, Mary Lou Williams, an exceptional pianist, tells a story about Coleman Hawkins coming to Kansas City:

> Fletcher Henderson came to town with Hawkins on tenor, and after the dance the band cruised round until they fell into the Cherry Blossom where Count Basie worked. . . . The word went round that Hawkins was in the Cherry Blossom, and within about half an hour there were Lester Young, Ben Webster, Herschel Evans, Herman Walder, and one or two unknown tenors piling in the club to blow. Bean [Hawkins] didn't know the Kaycee tenor men were so terrific, and he couldn't get himself together though he played all morning. I happened to be nodding that night, and around four a.m. I awoke to hear someone pecking on my screen. I opened the window on Ben Webster. He was saying, "Get up pussycat, we're jammin' and all the pianists are tired out now. Hawkins has got his shirt off and is still blowing. You got to come down." . . . The Henderson band was playing in St. Louis that evening, and Bean knew he ought to be on the way. But he kept trying to blow something to beat Ben and Herschel and Lester. When at last he gave up, he got straight in his car and drove to St. Louis. I heard he'd just bought a new Cadillac and that he burnt it out trying to make the job on time.
> [Shapiro and Hentoff, Hear Me, 292–93]

But such sessions were not only competitive; they were also intimate and personal, and powerfully supportive and encouraging if you weren't too vulnerable to damage. And they were dedicated to excellence—playing at the top of your form was what it was all about, and there are many stories about performers in these sessions reaching heights they never could on a regular paying job. Certainly people went to them to play for fun, and they were anything but "recitals." But at the same time it was definitely a chance to show off skills you were proud of, to try out new ideas you had been working on and get immediate feedback, or to get new ideas from what other people did. As Jo Jones, the drummer, said about the Hawkins incident in Kansas City, ". . . most of the time at sessions guys would just be trying to show Hawkins how they had improved since he had last heard them." It was a chance to measure one's own progress and development against a range of other talents, to learn what they were up to and to see where you might fit in—and in Harlem in the '30s a pianist could measure himself against the best there was—*and* to have a ball while doing it. Talk about your mentoring—and it was available every night!

Jam sessions, or cutting sessions, were filled with the profound pleasure of being with people who shared one's deepest interests (passions would be more accurate), and with the more sensual pleasure that alcohol (and sometimes marijuana) bring. But what really made these sessions so attractive was the way in which musical interests and passions were not just talked about, but were alive and aroused and even whipped up into a frenzy. The story may be dubious, and is certainly not typical, but you get the flavor of what could happen from hearing Tom Tilghman's story about the time Tatum battled a pianist (unnamed) for twenty-four hours (2 a.m. to 2 a.m.) in his back room. Everett Barksdale, the guitarist, is a little more believable with his story, that "young Art was once involved in an argument with a drummer who felt he could keep playing longer than any pianist. They decided to battle it out, each using only one hand, and according to Barksdale, it was five hours before the drummer quit" (Keepnews, "Art Tatum"). Oscar Peterson tells a somewhat similar story, of watching five consecutive bass players try to play with Tatum at a party, only to fall one by one by the wayside. (Ray Brown was one of the bass players at that party, and he described it slightly differently: "Well, everybody was supposed to play, you know. A bunch of us played, and then we just sat on the floor like a nice bunch of little kids and let Tatum play for the next couple of hours. And that finished off the party. And that's exactly the way it should have been." These dramatic accounts reek more of a pure gladiatorial spirit than was usual—even though that spirit was commonly there it was usually in the background. More typical is Billy Taylor's account, in *Jazz Piano,* of how Tatum and Clarence Profit liked to challenge each other by playing chorus after chorus using the identical melody but varying the harmonic progressions each time—incidentally, the reverse of what jazz musicians usually do (p. 20). This is surely the kind of training that made it easy for Tatum to delight George Gershwin by playing "virtually the equivalent of Beethoven's thirty-two variations on his tune 'Liza'" when Gershwin went to hear him in California (Levant, *Smattering,* 196).

All this was going on long before Tatum hit New York, of course; James P. Johnson, Willie Smith, Clarence Profit, Donald Lambert, and a number of others were masters of this form of musical combat, which had a lot to do with the growth and development of the New York, or stride, piano tradition. Smith has described the early days:

> Sometimes we got carving battles going that would last for four or five hours . . . We would embroider the melodies with our own original ideas and try to develop patterns that had more originality than those played before us. Sometimes it was just a question as to who could think up the most patterns within a given tune. It was pure improvisation. You had to have your own individual style and be able to play in all the keys. In those days we could all copy each other's shouts [a form of composition] by learning them by ear. Sometimes in order to keep the others from picking up too much of my stuff I'd perform in the hard keys, B major and E major."
>
> [Quoted in Nanry and Berger, *Jazz Text,* 126]

For that matter, one finds something resembling cutting sessions even in New Orleans, in the earliest days of jazz. Before there were individual gladiators there were collective ones, the spontaneous predecessors of those engineered and over-hyped "battle of the bands" that entrepreneurs were so fond of in the 1930s and '40s. Sidney Bechet once talked about the truly early days:

> Sometimes we'd have what they called in those days "bucking contests"; that was long before they talked about "cutting contests." One band, it would come right up in front of the other and play at it, and the first band it would play right back, until finally one band just had to give in. And the one that didn't give in, all the people, they'd rush up to it and give it drinks and food and holler for more, wanting more, not having enough.   [*Treat It Gentle*, 62]

After Tatum arrived in New York, and immediately "blew away" the top-seeded players (Johnson, Smith, Waller), he had no further need to challenge others. Everyone understood that he was the ultimate man to beat, but it took some years before everyone around was smart enough to stop trying. In the meanwhile he had to endure such scenes as the one with Donald Lambert. He had some rather cutting ways of dealing with it, such as disdaining personal combat and letting a lieutenant (Marlowe Morris in this case) respond for him. On another occasion he expressed his sardonic wit through a song title. A number of people told me essentially the same story as Red Norvo gave me:

> A bunch of guys, piano players, were playing, see, and Oscar Peterson was there, and they got him to play, too. So Art came in, very quietly, with somebody, and he was sitting at the bar drinking, see. So some of the guys saw Art, and they said, "Art, you gotta play!" And he'd listened to all these three or four piano players play, see, so he didn't want to play. So finally, he sat down and started to play, and he played, I don't know, just zooom, cut the whole thing—this was right after Oscar played—and then he went into, "Little Man, You've Had a Busy Day."

Art was apparently very fond of Oscar and the musical humor in that would have taken the sting out of any possible insult to him. I've never heard that Art directly insulted anyone.

From my conversations with people who knew him, I get the impression that Tatum didn't actually savor or have an appetite for the king-of-the-hill struggles that after-hours jam sessions often became. It was the piano and the structure of music and his own limitations that challenged him, and his best energy went into pushing his technical facility to impossible heights and into finding amazing new ways to re-structure popular songs. The fact that by doing this he made himself into the target that everyone else had to shoot for seems to have become a bore for him. He knew early on that he played the piano better than anyone else, and while challenging him might be extremely meaningful and adventurous for the challenger, for Tatum the outcome was never in doubt. One night he was driving through New York with Les Paul:

> And I remember one time we were driving down, well, where Madison Square Garden used to be, and he says, "Where are we now?" I said in front of Madison Square Garden, Joe Louis is fighting, and we got to talking about that. And he says, "You know, I'd like to rent that place, I'd like to rent Madison Square Garden, and I'd like to take on all the piano players and for once and for all settle it. Rather than me go around from nightclub to nightclub to beat these guys, I'd like to get 'em all in one place and knock 'em all off."

As a matter of fact the old Madison Square Garden used to be the site of important ragtime piano playing contests, and Tatum might very well have known that.

THERE IS A curse the Chinese use against an enemy: "May your children be born in an interesting time." The 1930s certainly qualify as an interesting time. When the decade started, the Eighteenth Amendment Act was still part of the Constitution and jazz musicians found their most secure employment in those spinoffs of Prohibition, the speakeasy and the after-hours club. The speakeasies, like the earlier brothels in New Orleans, with all the undesirable characteristics they undoubtedly had, were oases of employment for musicians and important sites where a great deal of jazz development went on. They were often if not usually run by organized crime, which made (and spent) a lot of money. This was especially important for musicians since the decade also started during the Great Depression, with Wall Street stock brokers jumping out of Manhattan skyscrapers or reduced to selling apples on the street, masses of Americans out of work, droughts making a dustbowl out of some of the midwestern states and driving their farmers (the "Okies") in despair to California with everything they owned piled on their cars. The early years were the years of *Tobacco Road* and *Cannery Row,* and songs like "Brother, Can You Spare a Dime" and "Side by Side" ("We ain't got a barrel of money . . ."). The nation needed entertainment that could counter the economic gloom, and it got it in the form of the great radio comedians (e.g., Jack Benny and Fred Allen), movies full of laughs (the Marx Brothers, the Three Stooges) and happy endings and images of elegance and sparkle (Fred Astaire and Ginger Rogers), and ever more dance bands playing swing music (Benny Goodman formed his first band in 1934 and became a national phenomenon in 1935). Franklin Roosevelt was elected to the first of four terms as President on the basis of his powerful image of strength and confidence ("We have nothing to fear but fear itself"), and addressed the Depression with a wide range of programs collectively known as the New Deal. Scholars are still trying to establish whether or not these programs actually worked to heal the very sick economy, or whether the real healing force was the threat of World War II in Europe which was developing in the later years of the decade, only twenty years or so after "the war to end all wars."

Art Tatum, aged twenty-one at the beginning of the decade, as well as all those other musicians born in the first fifteen years of the twentieth century, had to take the leap into his career under these interesting conditions. Music was the obvious, if not the inevitable, career for him, and it was lucky that the jazz bandwagon was there for him to climb on, whether or not it was what he most wanted to do. He did climb on, and not only found a safe haven for weathering what turned out to be a disastrously difficult time for millions of

Americans, but came into his own as a performer of the very first rank, at least in the eyes of fellow musicians. It was a decade in which music was overwhelmingly important to Americans, and Art Tatum made profoundly significant contributions to it. He devoted himself, however, to the mastery of solo piano playing, and so remained outside of the mainstream of jazz, which lay with swing and the big band, at least until the bebop movement came along.

The Mind of a Pianist

"I think it is infinitely more difficult to play solo jazz piano than to play serious classical music."　　**MEL POWELL**

THIS SEEMS LIKE a good point at which to take time out from Tatum's life story and consider him simply as a professional pianist. What exactly was Art Tatum doing at the piano, and how did he arrive at doing it? A technical answer to that question will come only from a patient reading of Schuller, Howlett, Howard, and a few others who have tried to analyze what went into a Tatum performance. Readers who are interested in the question, but who may not have the time to find and study those sources, deserve at least a sketch of an answer.

First a few words about forces and trends that were part of the sea into which Tatum sailed. He was born into a world in which the piano had become a very important part of the American scene. Pianos were almost everywhere (one piano for every fifteen people in 1920), and they had a dual existence, first as an important tool of recreation and second as a social symbol of their owners' cultural sophistication. Almost everyone had some kind of experience with it and could appreciate it when it was played well. There was even a general agreement as to what playing well meant: a whole tradition and set of standards for how a piano should properly be played was established and in place when Tatum arrived. This was a result of more than a century of study of its possibilities, culminating in the achievements of such virtuosi as Chopin and Liszt, to name only the most widely known.

The piano as a physical instrument presents a formidable range of possibilities as to what can be done with it, and in dealing with that challenge a long line of European composers and performers had set a really demanding standard of excellence. The teaching of piano playing was based on the European tradition and anyone who took lessons was thereby exposed to the tradition. Most, of course, learned just enough to be able to play simple sheet music and entertain themselves and others at home. Others felt the excitement of the challenges and the opportunities of the keyboard, and whether they knew it or not set out to follow the paths of the European leaders, trying to achieve excellence on their terms.

Tatum did more than simply follow, of course, but he was one of those who accepted the tradition. He took in more than most of us possibly could from his lessons and his listening, discovering what a difference touch can make, the importance of the pedals, the emotional appeals of different ways of voicing a chord, the heights to which technique can take you. And further, with what appears to be an absolute minimum of formal instruction, he listened to various kinds of music and grasped the logic of Western harmony, developed an awareness of the structure of compositions. By all the criteria of the nineteenth-century piano tradition, he made himself into a piano virtuoso worthy to be compared to the best who have ever played.

This achievement certainly did not come from years of hard labor under European-trained teachers, which is the usual route for concert pianists. It seems instead to have come from a very fine match between the opportunities the piano offers, on the one hand, and Tatum's innate sensitivities and gifts of coordination, on the other. Once he had been exposed to it and his mind had gotten its teeth into it, he was launched into a search for higher and higher levels of achievement, in the same way the great European artists had been. He responded sensitively to the nature of the piano, as they had, and he arrived, probably independently, at many of the same ways of dealing with it as they had. His basic gifts, in other words, were world-class, and his gifts drove him to be the pianist he was. Tatum wove the virtuoso tradition and the jazz idiom together in his playing, from the early days of his development, and brought a previously unimagined level of playing into jazz.

The jazz that he started with must have been ragtime, which was still a national craze when he was born. Ragtime started in a fairly simple way but it went through a hot-house kind of development and evolved into a highly technical kind of music in a short time. By Tatum's teens the level of difficulty was at least up to Zez Confrey's "Kitten on the Keys" (1921) and his later "Dizzy Fingers" (1923), which other composers followed up with such titles as "Fine Feathers," "Feather Fingers," "Fidgety Fingers," "Fancy Fingers," and "Hot Fingers"—all of which were beyond the reach of the casual tinkler. The whole thing smacks of the popularity of the more and more difficult *études* that famous pianists turned out in the early 1800s. In listening to ragtime and novelty music Art Tatum would have been absorbing quite difficult and sophisticated material, built on the basics of the virtuoso tradition even if it was considerably behind its leading edge.

As he developed he took the complexities of the ragtime music that he heard on player pianos and on early recordings and pushed them to unheard-of heights in his improvising and arranging. His listening was as good as his playing, and his huge innate talent practically forced him to explore and expand on anything he heard.

The particular strain of ragtime that Art Tatum seems to have incorporated and built upon to the greatest degree was Stride Ragtime. Stride was an eastern version of early jazz piano, developed by players from Baltimore, Philadelphia, and most importantly New York. Contemporary piano players often look down on the stride style as something primitive, but in fact a number of extremely talented if not always tutored men worked the style into something exceptionally complex.[1] The earliest well-known figures connected with the style, if it's fair to identify only a few, were Luckey Roberts and Richard McLean (better known at the time as Abba Labba). There was also One-Leg Willie Joseph, and Jack the Bear, and Paul Seminole, who apparently had a left hand that left others in the dust (and who for a specialty often played piano with his right hand and guitar with his left), and troops of others who had a hand in creating "stride" piano. But all are agreed that the person who put the stride style together and passed it on was James P. Johnson. He and Willie (The Lion) Smith trained Fats Waller, and it was Fats whom Tatum most publicly claimed as his own model.

James P. was an amazing phenomenon. His influence was enormous and so must have been his raw talent. He began making piano rolls in 1917 and recordings in 1921. Before his career was over he had made 55 piano rolls, cut more than 400 record sides, written some 230 popular songs (including "If I Could Be with You," "Old Fashioned Love," and the music that still triggers some odd behavior on the dance floor, "The Charleston"), scored eleven musicals for the stage as well as contributed numbers to more shows than even he could recall, and created nineteen symphonic works. Stride piano, as Tatum would have received it via James P. and other New York pianists, was nothing frivolous, trivial, or primitive. They were serious in New York, and there was a concentration of disciplined talent and technique there that established a very different standard for performance than was typical in the honky-tonks of the American Midwest and Southwest. It was the virtuoso standard again, although in a very different context from that of the concert hall.

James P. always told interviewers that the rest of the country was behind New York pianistically: "New York piano was developed by the European method, system and style. The ragtime player had to live up to the standard" (quoted in the booklet accompanying the *Time-Life* boxed set of Johnson recordings). Not only were the performance standards high, but there was a constant pressure for innovation. The New York pianists competed vigorously with each other in nightly "cutting-sessions," constantly raising the stakes on each other in a way not possible where pianists were dispersed widely over a geographical area such as the Midwest. Pianists had reached a critical mass in New York and the heat went up considerably, but always controlled by those European standards of discipline and mastery. The pressure was on to come up with new tricks every week, in every encounter, and improvising became the norm. The practice of spontaneously inventing variations on a theme, once a skill limited to concert artists, was being re-invented in a new context. Even here James P. drew on his classical training: "I did double glissandos in sixths, and double tremolos. These would run other ticklers out of the place at cutting sessions. They wouldn't play after me. I would put these tricks on the breaks and I could think of a trick a minute." "Playing a heavy stomp, I'd soften it right down—then I'd make an abrupt change like I heard Beethoven do in a sonata. Once I used Liszt's "Rigoletto Concert Paraphrase" as an introduction to a stomp" (*Time-Life* record set booklet, 13–14). Eubie Blake referred to the tricks he learned, too: "I don't play any better than any real pianist, but it's the tricks I know. I know tricks that the average guy don't know. Because I've been playing all this time, I had to play against this guy, that guy—the finest pianists, see?" (Jasen and Tichenor, 241). The standard of excellence was very high indeed.

All this was not lost on Art Tatum, even though he was not part of the New York scene as he developed. I think the technical complexity of stride piano must have attracted him; it was certainly the most advanced school of jazz playing that he encountered. Incidentally, in spite of Tatum's remark about coming from Waller I cannot hear any more of Waller than of any other stride pianist in Tatum's playing, and I think he drew from all of the great ones. My guess is that what he found in Waller was a total life style that appealed to him, more than a musical mentor, and that his remark came more from the psychological than from the musical bonding between them. And as for his not having grown up on the East Coast, all who treasure Tatum should probably be grateful that Art was not born in New York. (The story is that James P. never forgave Joe Turner for even bringing Tatum to New York.) There's no way of knowing, of course, but he might never have developed his unique blend of musical trends if he had been swimming in that stream only, doing hand-to-hand combat with the stride giants every night. Instead he had his own scene in Toledo and he drew on everything that interested him.

Earl Hines was a pianist outside the stride school who is often mentioned as an influence on Tatum. Tatum never acknowledged the influence, and the argument for this notion has to come from tracing similarities in their styles. Hines, six years older than Art, was active professionally before Art was, so if there was any influence one might argue that it flowed from Hines to Tatum. Hines's first recording was in 1923, and I've been told that Tatum used to improvise along with Hines's recordings (this report came from Eddie Barefield but he was unsure about the time period; it may have been well after Art had developed his basic style). Also, Hines was broadcasting from Chicago at least as early as 1928, another source from which Tatum could have absorbed Hines. It seems entirely plausible to me that any similarity in their styles was a result of highly comparable talents making independent discoveries—although once Tatum discovered Hines I don't doubt that he paid attention. Whether Earl influenced Art, or both had similar sensitivities and drives, they were alike in ways that set them apart from most of their contemporaries.

Perhaps the most striking of these was the way in which they frequently abandoned the steady rhythmic beat of most 1920s piano playing. Hines broke up the beat with "amazing, swirling, careening" rushes of notes in the right hand and with delayed rhythmic accents in the left, sometimes seeming to lose the beat entirely but always turning out to be right on target. The same feature has often been noted in Tatum's playing. He would turn his back on the clear rhythmic pulse for measures on end, using both hands to carry the arpeggios up and down the keyboard and then picking up the beat again with great precision, like a trapeze artist catching his partner out of the air. But the ways in which they were alike seem to me more a matter of temperament than influence. Gunther Schuller has written a passage which, although it is about Earl Hines, seems to me to define Tatum's playing very well indeed:

> As in a perfectly trained race horse, Hines's capacities are
> at all times working at maximum speed, double that of

most musicians of his generation. This is true not only in horizontal (linear) runs, but vertically as well. For Hines solos are generally operating on several linear—one could almost say contrapuntal—tracks simultaneously. Melodies and themes, counter melodies, harmonies, and of course rhythm, are all amalgamated in a unique symbiosis that sometimes defies belief. . . . ultimately it is his mind which is to be revered, a mind whose imagination and fertility are seemingly boundless. . . .

Hines is one of those jazz artists for whom slowing down is next to impossible. His razor-sharp mind and nimble fingers function best at high velocity. Like many major jazz virtuosos—Milt Jackson, Parker, Gillespie (in his early days)—Hines creates with the fastest rhythmic units available in a given situation. . . . Such players will rarely slow down to quarter notes or sustained melodic ideas. It is a certain restlessness (and virtuosity) which they, unlike "classical" players who have to play whatever the composer has written down, can exploit and use creatively. . . . With the total independence of both hands at his command, Hines is constantly engaging both hands in competitive exchanges or langorous dialogues. His mind (*and* fingers) are continually driven towards complexity—rhythmic and contrapuntal complexity. His mind works so fast and deeply creatively that the "simple" musical statement bores him, leaves him unsatisfied, unchallenged—all this often to the consternation of his listeners."

[Schuller, *Swing Era*, 279–80]

One more important thread in the fabric that Tatum wove was Lee Sims, a white pianist entirely outside the realm of jazz. James Maher (Alec Wilder's collaborator on *American Popular Song*) recalls once sparking real animation in a conversation with Tatum when he mentioned Sims. Maher was in Chicago after his discharge from the army in 1945:

So, while I was there, I went to dinner one night. I can't remember the name of the restaurant, it was probably on the near North side. It was a very nice restaurant—possibly the London House—and I was absolutely astonished when I walked in and there was a little sign about Art Tatum. That was a treat, you know. So, I sat down, had a drink, and listened to the end of his set. And I said to the waiter, "Would you ask Mr. Tatum if he would kindly stop over, and we could have a drink together," something like that. So, he brought Tatum over, we shook hands and he sat down, and he said, "Listen, first of all I've got to tell you there's some friends of mine waiting at another table, we had made this plan and I'm gonna have dinner with them. But let's talk for a minute." So I told him, "I've got something to tell you that happened to me when I was just a high school boy in Cleveland. I used to listen to you on the radio, 15 minutes, before dinner. You know, one of those sustaining programs—you didn't get any dough." And he started to laugh, and he said, "Oh, yeah." And I said, "And the odd thing was then that during the evening, I think it was on CBS, I would hear Lee Sims. And Lee Sims would be on, maybe for 15 minutes, possibly for a half-hour, but it was a regularly scheduled sponsored broadcast." So, when I told Art Tatum about listening to Lee Sims, boy, he grabbed my arm and he said, "You listened to Lee Sims?" He said, "I always listened to Lee Sims," and he was so enthusiastic about it, he talked on about him for a few minutes, and he said, "When I go back to start the next set I've got a treat for you. I'm going to play two or three of Lee Sims' piano compositions." These are not "songs," these are piano compositions, instrumental pieces. So he went away and sat down, and I ordered—I wasn't too far away from the piano, and when he came back to play he turned over in my direction, and he just started playing. And he played two, maybe three pieces, and I want to tell you, they were absolutely extraordinary.

Sims was more than a decade older than Tatum. He made his first recordings in 1927 and turned out ten more sides in 1928. Most of these were sentimental popular songs ("Adorable," "Are You Think-

ing of Me Tonight?," "When Summer Is Gone"), but he had his eye
on something more serious. We find Lee Sims linking himself with
the concert world by recording something of his own in 1928 called
"Improvisation from *Five Piano Rhapsodies*" on one side of a 12-inch
78 rpm record, and "Contrasts from *Five Piano Rhapsodies*" on the
other. Sims was deeply imbued with the nineteenth-century European tradition and especially interested in the newer, impressionist
harmonies of Debussy and Ravel. He went on to compose a number
of pieces the publisher (Robbins Music Corporation, which also
published the first Tatum transcriptions) called "novelty piano
solos." It must have been several of these that Tatum played for
Maher. With titles like "Meditation," "Retrospection," and "Simili-
tude," these have the full flavor of romanticism in them and are
drawn from the same sources as Bix Beiderbecke's "In a Mist." Bix's
pieces in this mode were clearly written for the piano, but Sims
thought orchestrally and his pieces were more like piano reductions
of larger scores; even his treatments of popular songs had this flavor.
Eventually this yearning toward larger forms expressed itself in the
writing of background music and two scores for movies (*Drums* and
Alexander Korda's *Dinner at the Ritz*), as well as a symphonic tone
poem he called "Blythewood," which had the distinction of receiving
a performance by the London Symphony Orchestra in an orchestra-
tion made by Ferde Grofé, who had earlier orchestrated Gershwin's
"Rhapsody in Blue."

With most of Sims's recordings already available before Tatum
went to New York, and with his considerable exposure on the air, the
Sims style (a discographer referred to him as a "piano stylist" rather
than as a "pianist") was readily available to Art, and we have Maher's
and others' testimony that Art was enthusiastic about Lee Sims's
playing. The appeal was almost certainly in the scope of his conception (orchestral and richly textured for the time) and in the coloration
of his chord voicings, both features that characterized Tatum's playing. The difference of course is that Sims never attempted to enter the
world of jazz, and jazz influences were minimal in his playing. But the
attraction of Sims for Tatum reminds me of Eubie Blake's great
admiration for the harmonies of Victor Herbert. As Jim Maher

remarked when he told me about Eubie, musicians don't necessarily draw the same boundaries that musical fans do.

MOVING BEYOND HIS own influences, Tatum incorporated all these ways of playing into a style with his own stamp on it. No one ever confuses him with James P. or Fats or Earl Hines or Lee Sims. He pulled together a variety of approaches to the piano, starting with ragtime and stride but expanding beyond those styles to include elements from both the early and late nineteenth-century classical traditions. Johnson, The Lion, Don Lambert and others tried to do this, too, but their efforts seem weak and piecemeal next to Tatum's. Great as they were, Tatum simply transcended them; he had achieved a level of technique equal, many think, to that of the great European pianists who defined the word *excellence* as it applied to piano playing. The phrase "organic whole" has been used almost to death in recent years, but it still seems the best way to characterize Tatum's integration of different approaches to piano performance. In his playing the varying elements became, not so much pieces of a quilt patched together, but threads almost inseparably inter-woven, working as smoothly as the human body itself.

It was his mind, of course, that accomplished this. We're not talking now about his technical facility or power, which put him in a class with the best pianists of all time. We're talking about the brain power that controlled his technical gifts, about the strategy with which he deployed his troops, about how he *perceived* music, *remembered* music, found *relationships,* and explored hidden *implications* of music. These are the things that fed into his improvisation. Every jazz musician does those things, to a greater or lesser degree. Tatum's mind did them, not only far faster than anyone else's, but on different levels at the same time—and then subordinated all the material that his musical intelligence was turning up for him to the requirements of a particular performance, fitting it to an individual song, or keeping it to a certain length, or even adapting it to a specific piano with its own peculiarities. Felicity Howlett once likened him to a hawk going after a fish, adjusting to the wind, judging the waves, and predicting the fish's turns and dives—an attractive image. Of course he was the fish, too, and the wind and the waves, setting the problems for the hawk.

His was anything but a one-track mind. It was restless, combinatorial, continually furnished and maybe over-furnished with musical material, and naturally he wanted to express it, to get it all into a performance. As Billy Taylor put it, "There was always a desire to fill in all the other things he could hear besides just a normal piano part" (quoted in Keepnews). For Schuller he had "an unquenchable desire to compress musical ideas," to get as many as possible into a given space. His mind, Balliett said, "abhored a vacuum."

As jazz moved beyond ragtime it took as its main subject the popular song. This was a new situation: "the major new problem that faced the creative jazz musician from the late twenties onward [was] that of making good music out of the popular ballad and diatonic, major-minor harmonic system" (Finklestein). At their best such songs can be superb music, but there are not enough superb songs to go around and jazz musicians have often applied superior talent to inferior material. The results often were musical triumphs (Louis Armstrong springs quickly to mind here), but they were triumphs that arose "out of a fierce struggle, between the performer and his material, a struggle to give the material a distinction it lacks in the original." Musicians tried to develop individual styles that would make their renditions of this common material distinctive. For the most part they accepted the published chord patterns for a song and created variations by changing the melody line. Tatum was up to something different. You see it in Billy Taylor's description of Art's sessions with Clarence Profit: "They often jammed together, and one significant feature of their piano exchanges was that they liked to play chorus after chorus of the same melody, each time with a different set of harmonic progressions" (Taylor, *Jazz Piano,* 20). One-Leg Willie Joseph, back in the beginnings of the stride tradition, used to do this, too, according to The Lion. Here the standard jazz approach of the time is turned upside down: the melody is accepted as a given and improvisation is applied to the harmonization. Mait Edey ("Tatum: The Last Years") has provided the best short description I have seen of what Tatum was up to:

> It was his totally different approach to improvisation
> . . . which set Tatum apart from the stream of modern
> jazz. Unlike most players, his aim was not to construct new
> lines over a given [chord] progression, but to play or
> suggest the melody of the tune chorus after chorus, erect-
> ing a massive structure of countermelodies, fluid voic-
> ings, substitute chords, and sometimes whole substitute
> progressions, beneath it. . . . At worst, the melody
> would be adorned with cascades of runs, at best it would
> serve as a mere framework, becoming fragmented into
> essential motifs which would constantly recur altered and
> revoiced.

The complexity of things going on when Tatum played, and the speed at which they went on, could have been more baffling than dazzling to listeners, but Tatum's material—basically, the American popular song—was so familiar that it provided listeners with a road map, and gave him a free hand to "tantalize the ear with new combinations and challenge the perceptions of his listeners." Tatum never lost sight of the melodies of the songs he played no matter how much he varied their surroundings, so listeners seldom felt lost. More often, they just felt played with, as Tatum teased them, led them down paths that seemed familiar, gave them glimpses of pictures on the wall (his little quotations from other music), and then swept them around amazing corners into unfamiliar spaces.

Compression may be the key to understanding an Art Tatum performance. "Tatum," Edey wrote, "packs into a few dense bars the content a lesser pianist would spread over a long solo." Whether or not you like this, or find it admirable, may depend on how closely you are willing to listen. Tatum, in his own time, made far more demands on his listeners than anyone in jazz had ever done, and even ardent admirers might have trouble with it. I suspect many listeners have had an experience something like the one Les Paul described to me:

> We're sitting there listening, and all of a sudden I got up
> and walked out. And so Vern [a friend who idolized

Tatum] came out and said, "What's the matter, Les? Are you sick?" I says, "No, no, no." And he says, "What's the matter?" And I says, "I had enough." And he says, "Enough what?" And I says, "I just can't handle any more." I said, "It's just too much for my head." I said, "He just plays so much it's just time for me to get outta there, and take it home and digest it."

The problem Tatum was continually trying to solve was not just how to entertain an audience, but how to use, in a few tiny moments, all the enormous skills with which he had been endowed. Burt Korall put it this way ("Tatum . . . Like the Wind"):

> Like a big man in a suit too small for him, Tatum literally burst out of songs, bringing to them the entire history of jazz piano, his classical training—a vast universe of sounds and ideas he could so easily translate into music. His basic area of endeavor was jazz. But the voice and pulse of his people could only be considered a foundation of his restless, thrusting, eclectic style, which went beyond idioms and the piano itself.

A composer, working by himself and in whatever musical form he chooses, has plenty of time in which to think, to select ideas, to shape them and harmonize them, and to develop them into variations. A jazz musician, who may start with a mind full of similar material to work with, has almost no time to carry out those operations and has to do it under an array of pressures unknown to the composer. Classically trained pianists are usually in awe of the "jazzer's" ability to improvise, and it's no wonder that Mel Powell has said he would rather perform a classical concert than a jazz one anytime. A jazz performance by someone with a really musical mind has to be a small miracle of both generation and compression of ideas, compared with formal composition, and Art Tatum's was one of the most musical minds America has known. His problem, working within the confines of the three-minute 78-rpm recording, was a little like that of the man trying to do an Olympic dive from a three-foot high board, and the resulting gyrations were not always admired. Some critics were tempted to echo Dr. Johnson's remark on hearing a violin solo: "Difficult do you call it, sir? I wish it were impossible!"

For such critics Tatum is "garrulous," "congested," full of "a disarray of flourishes," constantly working with "a predictable bag of tricks."

> The enormous esteem in which Tatum is held by nearly all jazz pianists has not been unreservedly healthy. At his best, Tatum fused complexity and musical imagination with compelling success; but the seeds of degeneracy lay at the heart of his style. And its worst effect may be seen in the way in which his followers, [Oscar] Peterson foremost among them, forget the imagination for the technique. I admire Tatum enormously, but I remain persuaded that much of his influence has been fundamentally unhealthy and devitalizing. [James, *Essays in Jazz*, 135]

It is certainly interesting to put these criticisms side-by-side with the scathing criticisms endured by Franz Liszt, the nineteenth-century composer/virtuoso who is often cited as the creator of modern concert piano playing, the man about whom Berlioz said, "There is a god of pianists . . ." (prefiguring Waller's praise of Tatum). Like Tatum a figure of towering capabilities, he was accused of giving the public "glib concoctions," "circus tricks," and "artificial playing mannerisms." The pianist Clara Weick expressed the "seeds of degeneracy" notion when she said that Liszt "has the downfall of piano playing on his conscience" (quoted in Fisher, *Musical Prodigies*, 48–49). Liszt's reputation, we note, survived these blows, and Art Tatum's may, too.

What cannot be apparent to a casual listener, in fact may only become apparent to really intensive analysis, is the extent to which Tatum thought musically like a composer, even within the short time-spans available to him as a jazz player. His performance of any tune was like a small piece of architecture, with structures and designs used over and over with variations, with large thought-out patterns giving coherence to details that might seem fragmentary. If the reader should think here of the similarity to the sentence diagramming Art liked to do in school, then we are thinking along similar lines. Those runs that are so prominent in his playing—that sometimes seem like "mere" decoration, and that may remind the reader of little Art who "loved to fill the blackboard with his work"—those runs always have a place in the architecture. Most often they are like arches, connecting different parts of a structure, providing vistas down long hallways. Minute examination of his performances, according to Felicity Howlett who has done more of this than anyone, reveals complex processes occurring on a highly compressed scale, giving an effect like looking at a cell through a microscope. Commenting on one of Tatum's earliest recordings, "Tiger Rag," Howlett writes:

> The study of a transcription of the performance helped this listener begin to understand how Tatum thought as a composer while working actively as an improviser. Working in layers of thought, he was able to retain large frameworks while manipulating small details and/or simultaneously reworking larger phrases or sections. . . . Anyone who listens many times to the recording will gradually absorb the relationships of these internal structures which provide such coherence underneath the shimmer of surface sound. . . . The "Tiger Rag" performance may be enjoyed and appreciated on many levels. One of its most fascinating characteristics is that the more closely one looks at what may appear to be frivolous decoration or detail, the more obvious is its significance in terms of the total structure and continuity of the performance.

Of course, and obviously, a tremendous amount of preparation went into what Tatum did. There are many identifiable patterns in what Tatum does with a song: runs to which one can almost give names and recognize them when they come around, harmonic progressions that he uses often; favorite keyboard intervals that predictably turn up for different kinds of emphasis. All these things were on the shelf, as it were, ready to be put together into a performance.

And many of Tatum's arrangements of songs had a general structure that remained the same through many performances, so that his "Sweet Lorraine," for example, is recognizably *his*, in spite of the many variations he introduced into each playing of it.

There are those for whom any thought-out design in a performance disqualifies it as "jazz," because they understand *jazz* to be synonymous with *spontaneity*, and *thought* as the enemy of *spontaneity*. That I think is simply a misconception, but an understandable one. Jazz has an indelible American stamp on it, and through most of its short history it has been associated with ideas of freedom and release, of escape from tradition and rules, and in that spirit "spontaneous" improvisation has been, as I said earlier, a moral imperative. There is an inherent tension in the history of jazz, as in Western music in general, as each new generation tries to escape from the predictability of the previous one, finding new ways and its own identity. Improvising, however, cannot mean a complete absence of rule or pattern or structure; that would be pure randomness, which is probably impossible for the human mind and in any case the result would be unacceptable to almost every ear. What jazz musicians are doing when they improvise is not spontaneous randomness, but the invention of *variations* on forms and patterns that they accept as their raw material. There are wild differences among musicians as to what raw material they are willing to start from, but it seems to me psychological bedrock that they have to start *somewhere,* and achieve their freedom and individuality through their own way of creating variations—which, once established, will be recognizable and even predictable. There simply is not, in the last analysis, any absolute and uncrossable border between improvising and composing, or between musical spontaneity and musical thought. Tatum's creativity was not only in his overall style and conception, which is so recognizably his, but also in the incredible speed with which he could vary his patterns and materials and remain recognizably himself. His improvising, like that of all great musicians, is really high-speed composition.

The base from which Tatum operated, the element around which he organized his talents, was harmony. He had, as Gunther Schuller put it, "an uncanny ear for adventurous harmonizations." The simple triads of ragtime, and even the slightly expanded chordal language of stride, were simply not enough. His understanding of harmonic conventions, as well as of alternative ways of harmonizing melodies and unusual harmonic routes from one spot to another, operated so rapidly in Tatum as an adult that it seemed to be automatic, spontaneous, without the intermediate stage of thought. He had such an easy grasp of the logic of harmony that as soon as a given harmony was suggested to his mind he immediately understood the available alternatives, took into account where his hands happened to be at the moment, where he had just been and where he wanted to go, and put this all together into something his listeners might have trouble following—or believing. Lizst, Rachmaninoff, Debussy, Fats Waller, Earl Hines, Lee Sims, all became grist for the mill of his harmony processor and increased the alternatives at his fingertips. He loved to find new paths for modulation, or to move quickly in and out of other keys than the one he was playing in. But he always knew exactly where he was, and all his split-second choices were under the strict control of a firm logic. To quote Howlett again:

> The imagination, flexibility and ease with which Tatum created new approaches within established, accepted harmonic structures is one of his magical qualities, and one of the slyest methods by which he could retire his competition in a "cutting contest." Many of these choices are barely audible: there is often a variety of musical activity taking place simultaneously much of which may attract attention away from the subtle but continual process of variation in the approach to the progressions of the bass lines. [p. 236]

Rhythm and the patterns of accents imposed on a series of notes was another musical element in which Tatum's control and imagination were far superior to anyone else's (with the possible exception of Earl Hines). Ragtime had added syncopation to the regular and march-like rhythms of early jazz, and the stride school had found ways to introduce surprise but without breaking out of the basic pattern. Tatum mastered the stride style, but quickly found ways to break up the rhythms he inherited in unique and always interesting ways—and ways so stamped with the signature of his own mind that no school of piano playing ever developed out of them. He teased the listener who was expecting a steady, swinging beat, buried it under an avalanche of runs or arpeggios, traded it back and forth between hands, pitted two rhythms against each other, and persuaded some listeners that he was unable to keep a beat. Measuring a Tatum performance against a metronome proves that to be completely false. Instead he was a total master of rhythmic complexities and, again, always knew where he was even if the listener did not. He could swing with great effect, but as a soloist he seldom stayed in a clear swing mode for very long. "Swinging," Schuller commented, "was generally not Tatum's primary concern" (480). A simple swing approach was too confining for what he had to express. Rhythm instead was simply another element in his compositional approach to improvisation, and like harmony a subject for continual variation.

TATUM, FOR ALL his immersion in jazz, was playing a kind of concert music, a music designed for serious listening and not for dancing or conversation. He was in a way an alien in jazz, he was something like "news from a distant star." His playing had more to do with intellect, or with refined craftmanship, than with providing a simple accompaniment to fellowship and good times—although he certainly accommodated himself to that in the after-hours places he practically lived in. He loved that, too. He was a remarkable combination of imagination ("a great soaring thing with wings") and power ("a member of the reptile family"). He drew on jazz influences, but he had to stretch them, find possibilities that were only implied and then realize them, push forms and devices to their outer limits. He could not do otherwise, and he had to do it within the confines of a career in jazz. He was an early but a towering manifestation of that drive toward complexity and the exploration of new possibilities that has always been inherent in Western music, and that jazz was not about to escape.

8

1939–1945

IN THE CLOSING months of 1939, James P. Johnson, only forty-eight years old but now referred to as "the old master" and "the gargoyle of the keyboard," was still appearing in New York and "still rules at the keyboard."[1] He had a week's solo spot at Cafe Society, where he was followed by Stuff Smith and the Slam Stewart Trio. Marlowe Morris was playing piano at Kelly's. Clarence Profit was working with his own trio and in September was rumored to be Goodman's choice to replace Teddy Wilson with the Goodman Trio. Wilson had recently left Goodman to organize his own big band. A week later it was Mary Lou Williams who was "slated to join the Goodman Quartet," but only a week after that she was criticized for the fact that she "like Teddy Wilson—perhaps following him—has given up that simple, powerful style, in favor of a characteristically delicate, decorative way of playing." ("Delicate" and "decorative" were negative terms for some jazz critics, as Bill Evans was to discover later.) Joe Bushkin and Billy Kyle were noted as talented young pianists, but Kyle was categorized as "a young man with a great deal of technique and nothing to say." In late September 1939 the Onyx Club ("cradle of swing") folded "for good"; in early October it opened again, only to close once more toward the end of the month.

In 1939, *Jazzmen,* edited by C. E. Smith and Fred Ramsey, was published and reviewed as "the first good book about jazz"; but Winthrop Sargeant's *Jazz, Hot and Hybrid* also received kudos. Arguments raged, especially among white intellectuals, over the timeless question of what jazz really is, set off by the revival of interest in the traditional New Orleans style of playing—some felt it was the only authentic, living jazz and others felt it was long dead and should have been left resting in its grave.

Dizzie Gillespie was twenty-two and had just joined Cab Calloway's band. Thelonious Monk was also twenty-two, and after several years of touring with a traveling evangelist's show was beginning to take jobs around New York. Charlie Parker out in Kansas City was nineteen, Bud Powell was fifteen and had just dropped out of high school to start gigging around Greater New York. Unaffected by the intellectual arguments the forces of be-bop, like the forces of war in Europe, were gathering.

In January 1940 it was reported that the Three Deuces in Chicago had burned down. Tatum was identified as the first in a line of famous musicians who had played there, and characterized as "a pianist who seemed to know every note on the piano and to feel every chord, who played Bach all afternoon, and the blues at night." (It seems clear the reporter was uneasy about how to position Tatum in the jazz field.) In January, Tatum was working at the Swanee Inn in Los Angeles, where a reporter wrote: "Unfortunately, Tatum seems to get more technical as the time goes on. He is highly regarded by many musicians who even affect his style on other instruments." To balance this faint praise he went on, "This writer is one of the few who have heard him really swing on occasion. It was on the blues— he played Pine Top's Boogie-Woogie and worked in some of his own improvisations—the place really jumped." This reporter sounds suspiciously like another someone who might be wary of delicate and decorative playing. He would have been happy if he could have heard

Tatum playing stride piano back in Harlem, as Billy Taylor has described it:

> Stride is a very difficult style to play. It wasn't just *oom-pah;* in the work of the masters . . . there were extremely subtle rhythmic devices. Art had all those subtleties under control . . . This brings to mind many Monday nights up at Tom Tillman's (*sic*) Hollywood Bar in Harlem, where I heard Art Tatum play stuff he never did record. Once some of the guys there went over to New Jersey and came back with this old-time stride player named Don Lambert, whose speciality was playing stride versions of classical pieces. When Lambert finally showed up, he and Tatum talked for a while, and then someone twisted Don's arm to go to the piano . . . He sat down and played, and then Tatum took his turn. The only things Art played that night were right out of the stride repertoire, requiring a back bass, hitting the top of the tenth first, and playing that kind of three-against-four syncopation that Willie the Lion used to do. . . . The point is that Don Lambert was one of the great stride players, but Tatum could restrict himself to just that one style, never go outside of it, and more than hold his own, even though that was only one small aspect of what Art could—and did—do. [Taylor, "Recollection"]

Lambert was only five years older than Tatum, but in jazz the generations seem to turn over faster than elsewhere.

Billy Taylor was one of a number of younger pianists who moved into Tatum's circle and influence in the 1940s: Billy Kyle, Bud Powell, Gerald Wiggins, Jimmy Rowles, Ellis Larkins, Hank Jones, Dorothy Donegan, André Previn, George Shearing, Oscar Peterson. One simply cannot find a significant jazz pianist over a certain age who doesn't recall the first time he heard or met Art. Wiggins, for example:

> The first time was an after-hours place in Harlem, where everybody gathered, named Reuben's—it was a hang-out for all the piano players. I forget what street it was on,

132nd, 133rd?—one of them brownstone houses, you walk in, go down a flight, open the door and you hit the piano, it was right by the door, an old upright. At that time most of us were working in the Village, you go to work at 8 o'clock and get off at 4 in the morning, 8 hours, just one group, you know . . . —but that was normal. Salary was like $3 a night. This was late '39, '40. Anyhow, so everyone would grab the A-train and come on uptown, to Reuben's. And that's where all the piano players would be. They'd all take their turn to play until Tatum walked in, then everybody got away from the piano. He'd sit down with his big quart of Pabst Blue Ribbon. Yeh, they used to buy a case of quarts for him. Even when he came out to Los Angeles here, he used to go by a place called Lovejoy's, Lovejoy always had a case of quarts of Pabst Blue Ribbon beer for him. . . . Art got me my first really big-time gig. He got me a job with Stepin Fetchit.[2] Stepin Fetchit was on tour, you know. All he did was carry a piano player, I helped him with his act, a little playing, help him with his costume. We did theaters. Step was looking for a piano player, Art said, here's a young man, take him with you. It was summer vacation, I was out of school, so I went along. I think I was making the enormous sum of $50 a week, and that was a princely sum in those days.

André Previn, who started life as a child prodigy on the piano and who had a long love affair with jazz on the way to becoming one of the leading symphony conductors in the Western world, once thought with disdain that a jazz musician was "a guy in a hotel dance band with a white tuxedo and a funny hat" (Bookspan and Yockey, *André Previn*, 103). Previn sounds here like someone whose mother might have been frightened by Cab Calloway. What turned him around was the 1940 Tatum recording of "Sweet Lorraine." Like Mel Powell, whose beginnings were similar to his, Andre had never imagined that such virtuosic technique could be put to jazz use. At first Previn assumed, like Horowitz, that what he heard Tatum doing was a highly arranged, almost a composed, variation on the simple tune of "Sweet Lorraine." It took him a long time, and months of learning to play note for note pieces Tatum had recorded, to realize that "the trick was not to *play* this stuff but to make it up as Tatum had done. . . . Improvisation. *That's* what jazz was all about."

It was about the same time, 1941, that Jimmy Rowles had his first exposure to Tatum:

> I met him first, before I heard him. I was playing at a place called the Latin Quarter on Vermont and 8th St., in LA. And Art had worked there in the past. The same fella owned the club, and somehow he hired me to play solo piano in there. There was no business. The piano was up on a pedestal in the middle of the room, a grand piano, and there was hardly any business. This one night I was sitting up there playing, I heard the front door open, and close. I looked toward the door, it was very dark, and I couldn't see anything. Tiny the boss went down and started talking to whoever had come in, and I started getting a funny feeling, I said, I think I'll get off the piano. So Tiny says, "Come on down here, I want you to meet a friend of mine, this is Art Tatum." Then after that he went to work for a few days up the street at the 331 Club, and my wife and I went down to hear him, we got a ringside seat, we sat and watched him play, the first time. That was around '41. I heard him, and then the guy that owned the club wanted me to play intermission piano [alternating with Tatum], and I didn't have very big eyes to do that. I was out sitting on the street, waiting for the bus to go home, and he dragged me in there. And I played a couple of nights and then I got out of that. No, no, I didn't feel like getting up there and playing the piano after him. I just felt paralyzed around him. I mean, anybody that would disagree with me would be crazy. Anyway, then I got to finding out where he was playing, got to know him, you know. And finally I got acquainted with his chauffeur guy, and the chauffeur would come over where I was working, like if I was work- ing at Billy Berg's and Art was working in town, he'd come and get me and we'd all go out, he'd have three or four guys, maybe Gerald Wiggins or something, we'd all go out to some afterhours place and sit around and listen to Art

play. But of course nobody felt like playing when Art was there. You know, why play when God's in the house? He played all kinds of stuff, he'd play songs that you didn't think that anybody knew. He knew everything from "Mighty Lak' a Rose" to "Rose Marie," and he'd turn 'em into crazy things and play them. He was just unbelievable. Oh, I loved it. Most of the stuff he played was clear over my head. There was too much going on—both hands were impossible to believe. You couldn't pick out what he was doing because his fingers were so smooth and soft, and the way he did it—it was like camouflage. Bobby Tucker and I were working at Billy Berg's, and we'd meet him at this one place, clear up by the Dunbar Hotel, we'd meet there and there wasn't anybody around very much, not crowded and all that, and he would talk to us, and say, "Well, if one of you guys ain't gonna play I'm gonna play." He made us play, and we used to stand over him and ask him to repeat things, you know—And he was so nice, he was really a wonderful person.

George Shearing, in England, first heard him on records in 1937 when he was playing with an orchestra made up entirely of blind musicians. He didn't actually meet him until 1946:

> I remember the first time I met him, I've seen fans that do that to me, come up and you know, their heart's in the right place, they're very sincere, but they proceed to tell me who was in my first quintet, when they first heard "September in the Rain," and this whole thing. And I was just as guilty, I said, "Mr Tatum, I've been listening to you for years, I have a lot of your records"—and he let me talk for about three minutes, and then he said, "Glad to meet you, sir, you gonna buy me a beer?"

Although it takes us a little ahead of the story, one of the most interesting first encounters was that of Stanley Cowell, a very contemporary pianist.

My first contact, even ever hearing of the man, I guess, was in 1947. I was six years old. My father had a hamburger grill, a little restaurant, it was on Indiana Ave. in Toledo, Ohio, across from a club called the M and L Club. Art Tatum and his manager—I think it was his manager—anyway, this was a white man that brought Tatum by the restaurant to see my father. My father was interested in having Tatum play for me, play the piano at our house—we had a Storey & Clarke studio upright. I have two older sisters that played, took lessons, and they taught me—already by this time I was taking lessons for two years. I started lessons at 4 and they taught me to read notes at 3. Anyway, my father plied Art Tatum with a drink. They grew up together. He used to shoot marbles with Tatum and with Francis X. Williams, trumpet player that died a few years ago, used to be with Ellington. He was from Toledo also. That's all I ever knew, that's all my father ever told me, that they used to shoot marbles together. Art shot great marbles, so evidently he was not totally blind, as some people have implied. He could hear the marbles, the inertia of the marbles—I don't know. So, my father succeeded in having Tatum play. First Tatum asked me to play. I played for him out of John Thompson, book 3. I don't know what I played for him, but some piece, I can't remember. So I played, then he sat down and played so brilliantly that I never heard anything like it. The only other thing I can remember about that is that Tatum played so brilliantly and so much, played for five or six minutes on that piece, you know, stretched out on it, he played so much that I thought the piano was gonna break. My mother left the room, and started washing dishes, and she was very nervous, so I said, "What's wrong, Mama?" and she said, "Oh, that man plays too much piano." She was really upset by it. I even remember the piece. Subconsciously the piece stayed in my mind. I never did hear a recording of it. He played "You Took Advantage of Me," a piece that I still play. He was probably, tongue-in-cheek, talking through the title. Talking through the title, probably to my father, about making him play. And much later I started playing it, made a few mistakes, played it in the wrong key. And sort of on a whim I recorded it on the first album I ever made.

IN 1939 TATUM recorded eighteen tunes, including his first recordings of "Get Happy" and "Humoresque." However only two tunes from these sessions ("Tea for Two" and "Deep Purple") were issued on 78s, and the now-famous versions of "Get Happy," "Sweet Lorraine," "Cocktails for Two," "Élégie," and "Humoresque" were actually recorded in February of 1940. These were the first Tatum recordings I ever heard, and I'll never forget the liberating effect of "Humoresque" (I was taking "serious" lessons at the time). First he plays the melody in an out-of-rhythm style, much like the original, evoking a proper, salon-like atmosphere. Some of the chord voicings seem to be slightly creamier than Dvořák wrote them, but clearly Tatum is saying, "Here's a picture that was painted by connecting dots, but I can fix that." Then comes a short transition, obviously not Dvořák's idea, setting up an exquisite rhythmic tension (Oh God, what is he going to do to it?). Then instead of tearing it off he saunters away at a light and easy tempo, as if out to enjoy a walk down the street on a glorious day with a pair of Reeboks on his feet and not a care in the world. Tatum discovers in "Humoresque" a melody that could easily have been written as a popular song in the 1920s or '30s, no better and no worse than a lot of the other melodies he recorded. With this as a vehicle he generates the same feeling of light, effortless intricacy, perfectly controlled, that one gets from watching Fred Astaire. I know that Gunther Schuller has little use for this kind of thing and puts it in the same drawer with Tatum's "irritating" quotations from outside jazz. But it still makes me feel good, for reasons that have nothing to do with "jazzing the classics," but only with his phenomenal touch and rhythmic feeling, which is easier to appreciate on a light swinging number than on one of his flying tours de force.

I know now that I was not alone. When Itzhak Perlman, the

concert violinist, heard this recording he "absolutely fell in love with Art Tatum," and on another occasion Perlman said this particular Tatum recording was what first seriously interested him in jazz. Marian McPartland said, "The first inkling I had of Art Tatum was his recording of Dvořák's "Humoresque," which I heard when I was still in England. I couldn't believe it" (quoted in Balliett, *Musicians,* 206). The jazz singer Mark Murphy got his first introduction to jazz when an uncle played Tatum's recording of "Humoresque" for him, and he testified: "I've been hooked ever since" (Stokes, *The Jazz Scene,* 173). Incidentally, in 1925 Zez Confrey, a composer of ragtime novelties, had published a treatment of Dvořák's piece, calling it "Humorestless," which included a section putting Dvořák in counterpoint with "Swanee River." Knowing Tatum's listening habits it would be hard to believe that he had not heard Confrey's version and found it worth improving upon.

In spite of such testimonials Tatum's appeal was in fact limited. He was practically alone among jazz artists in making solo piano recordings, and only those of us deeply interested in piano playing were likely to buy them. Even Fats Waller was recording mainly with a small group all through the 1930s, and was probably more widely loved for his singing than for his superb piano playing. Big-band swing was the thing, and big bands were spawning the vocalists who would soon be the big record sellers. Recordings had become very big business, but Tatum had to rely on night-club bookings for his living. It was apparently not a bad living—by the 1940s his name was very well known to the supporters of jazz clubs, and when he appeared in his home town, Toledo, in 1942 his going rate has been reported as at least $2000 a week.[3]

In January of 1941 he made one of his few big-selling records— not as a soloist, needless to say, but as a member of a group (Art Tatum and His Band) that included bass, drums, and guitar (a four-man rhythm section, completely uncharacteristic for him), a two-man front line, Joe Thomas on trumpet and Edmond Hall on clarinet, and Big Joe Turner, a well-known blues singer. Ernie Lewis estimates that the 78-single of "Wee Baby Blues" may have sold as many as 500,000 copies. This popularity led to two transcriptions of

Tatum's playing on "Wee Baby Blues," one by Sharon Pease in *Down Beat* and another by Frank Papparelli.

I don't know how much money Tatum made from this recording—his contract probably paid him only for the session and may not have included royalties—or from the transcriptions (probably nothing). But in any case this recording session, which included two other atypical tunes ("Last Goodbye Blues" and "Battery Bounce"), in the words of Gunther Schuller, "showed that Tatum *could* simplify and deepen the expression of his playing when he cared to. Indeed, his performances here seem to pay tribute to the superb Kansas City blues pianist Pete Johnson . . ." (486). In June the same group (minus Hall) recorded more blues-oriented tunes: "Rock Me Mama," "Corrine, Corrina," and "Lonesome Graveyard Blues." Two of these (again according to Schuller):

> . . . feature a number of moving Tatum solos, all the more expressive for the radiant beauty of his tone. In one section of "Rock Me Mama" the usually irrepressible Tatum even lays out completely. At the same time he seems no less inventive harmonically when given the opportunity. In "Lonesome Graveyard," for example, Tatum pits some astonishing, gently clashing bitonal harmonies against Oscar Moore's guitar in what was undoubtedly meant to be the latter's solo chorus, but which Tatum deftly turned into a fascinating piano-guitar duet.

Perhaps at the urging of some record producer, Tatum had acquiesced to the re-discovery of the blues and of boogie-woogie taking place in America in the late '30s and early '40s, as well as to the interest in ensembles over soloists. However it happened it paid off.

The only other recordings from 1941 were made live, and privately, and not released until many years later. Jerry Newman. then a student at Columbia University, had begun using his own portable equipment to capture live jazz in New York clubs, and he recorded Tatum at Reuben's, at the Gee-Haw Stables, and at Clark Monroe's Uptown House, all Harlem clubs. Schuller was particularly struck with Tatum's mellowness on "Mighty Lak' a Rose" and with other features which remind him of some of Thelonious Monk's "suspended-time improvisations of the mid-fifties" and which lead him to speculate that Monk could very well have absorbed many of Tatum's after-hours appearances.

One of the performances preserved by Newman and later released on various LPs, including the Time-Life series, is "Toledo Blues." This one is especially treasured by some, not only because it's rare to find Tatum playing the blues but even more so because on it we have the sound of Tatum *singing* the blues. Felicity Howlett calls it "enlightening and revealing," "an intimate and fond caress of the blues tradition" (Howlett, "Foreword," xiii). Indeed it is revealing—so much so that the pianist/writer Dick Katz felt strongly that it shouldn't be released at all: "My view was probably a minority one but it goes something like this—If Tatum heard it he'd roll over in his grave!" Katz's opinion was that Tatum's every recorded performance, excepting this one, showed him to be an "absolute perfectionist—every hair in place, not even a hint of a mistake." When Newman captured this recording Art was not at his best and clearly had a fairly high blood-alcohol level (toward the end he inserts the line, "My damn drinks ain't comin' fast enough"). Even here there aren't any mistakes, but neither is there any brilliance, and Katz felt, as I now do, that Tatum would never have chosen to include this in his recorded output. But the argument was that because such informality was rarely caught on record it was therefore especially valuable and Tatum's fans ought to have it. One might dimly perceive here a hint of the attitude that a bluesy, not-entirely-in-control-Tatum is closer to the "real" Tatum, but I suspect the opposite is the case. What he gave us time and time again is probably the real Tatum, and he might well have felt this one was just for the friends who were around him when he played it.

Somehow, in spite of all this activity, Art managed to avoid joining the New York Musicians' Union until November, 1941, even though he had been working around town since 1932. Harold Payne has explained that Art was reluctant to join the union even back in Toledo, out of a dislike for anyone telling him when and where and how long he could play, so his late affiliation with the union is no surprise. He was in good company when he did finally join: the next new member to sign on with Local 802, after Art, was Béla Bartók, just newly arrived from Europe.

The war in Europe was now on and perhaps related to that there was no recording for Tatum in 1942. Where 1941 was spent largely in the East (away from Ruby?), in 1942 he was back in California for much of the time. Joe Bushkin was one of those who spent some time with him that year. Many musicians had enlisted or been drafted into the service, and Joe had just finished basic training:

> It was very early in '42, he was appearing at a place called The Streets of Paris, on Hollywood Blvd, it was a saloon, down in the basement. And as I recall, it was Coleman Hawkins and a quartet or quintet, and Art Tatum. We used to shoot crap while the band group was on, with the waiters, Tatum, too—I gotta tell you, he was very trust-worthy of the guys, as far as calling the numbers, along with the fact that he always carried one of those little pin-light flash-lights, you know, that you carry in your pocket. And he did have sight, I think it was his left eye, I'm not sure. In one of the eyes, he had a pin-point vision, you know, not totally blind. He could also count the money that was being paid—with the little flashlight, you know—and keep check on that shit. I just went out and hung out with him all night. He had a car and driver—took us to the south side to an afterhours joint where he just sat down and played the piano until about seven in the morning. On the corner there was a furniture store, I was always tempted to go in there and lay down on one of the couches. But, Art immediately dropped me off at a board-ing house, 'cause I was off, on a pass, I had a three-day weekend pass from March Field Air Base. He stopped at a boarding house where he knew the madam, one of those rent-party joints, they put me in a room, I flopped out—I was drunk. And he made sure I was taken care of. He was always very protective.

Art Tatum, Sr.
(*Courtesy Arline Taylor*)

Mildred Tatum, Art's mother
(*Courtesy Arline Taylor*)

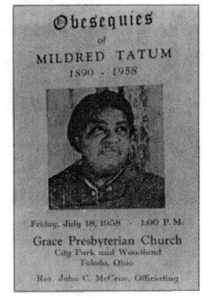

Obsequies
of
MILDRED TATUM
1890 - 1958

Friday, July 18, 1958 - 1:00 P. M.

Grace Presbyterian Church
City Park and Woodland
Toledo, Ohio

Rev. John C. McCrae, Officiating

ABOVE: Tatum in a radio studio, early in his career. (*Frank Driggs Collection*) BELOW: Tatum performing, probably in the late 1940s. (*Frank Driggs Collection*)

A posed portrait
of Tatum in his 20s.
(*Courtesy Dave Reed*)

Orlando Tatum Jackson,
Art Tatum's son.
(*Courtesy Arline Taylor*)

Tatum at the piano (*RCA Victor photo*)

Latin Quarter advertisement. (*Frank Driggs Collection*)

From left to right: Elmer Snowden, Fats Waller, Art Tatum, 1943. (*Frank Driggs Collection*)

Tatum Trio with Billie Holiday. (*Photographer unknown*)

Beryle Booker in the middle, with Tatum to the right, then Marlowe Morris (with glasses), Philadelphia c. 1947. (*Frank Driggs Collection*)

Meade Lux Lewis, Art Tatum, Pete Johnson, Errol Garner, "Piano Parade," photo by Dorothy Siegel. (*Frank Driggs Collection*)

ABOVE: The Art
Tatum Trio playing at
the Three Deuces,
52nd St., N.Y., 1944.
Slam Stewart on bass;
Tiny Grimes on guitar;
Art Tatum on the
piano. (*Frank Driggs
Collection*)

RIGHT: Tatum and
Oscar Peterson
laughing together.
(*Photo courtesy of
the Toledo Lucas
County Public
Library*)

Tatum playing cards backstage. (*Photo by Duncan P. Schiedt*)

Art Tatum, 1944.
(*Frank Driggs Collection*)

Some time in the 1940s we get another glimpse, this time from Al Hibbler, of Art still fighting with his inability to drive a car:

> It was in Los Angeles. It was hot that day and we'd been hanging out—high noon, one of these kind of things. Art was sittin' up there—we was at Stuff Crouch's place—so I said, "Well, I'm going home, man." And Art said, "I'll drop you off." Me not thinking about him, you know, I figured I'm going to get in his car and he's going to have somebody drive us home. And I get in the car, just sit there, and he gets in the car, and—before he got in the car, I'd reached over there, saw the keys was in the car, he got in the car in the driver's seat and was fooling around over there, he say, "I can't find the keys." And I thought, "Man, I'm crazy sittin' up here and I'm goin' let this blind fool drive me? I'm a fool—and the keys were in the ignition! I'm gettin' out of here—he ain't driving me. I can see better 'n you can! I ain't goin' to let you drive me all over." He got real mad about it. Yeh. But it passed over, you know. Yeh, but he was really goin' to try—he's drunk, and I'm drunk. We both drunk as fools! Sittin' up there drinkin' all night, and singin'. He wasn't goin' try it with me! Art could see just a little bit—but not well enough to drive no car. And I knew it, and he knew it.

IN 1943 THE combination of a happy accident and Tatum's difficulty in finding enough work led to the formation of the Art Tatum Trio—a move that surprised everyone since Art was so thoroughly established as a soloist. Perhaps most people were unaware of his problems with cash flow—he was such a paragon that it would have been hard to believe he wasn't working as much as he wanted to. Tiny Grimes and Slam Stewart, guitar and bass, were working around New York as a duo, and sometime in early 1943 they found themselves together with Tatum at an after-hours spot, where they "fell in with what he was doing." They started in the usual after-hours way, jamming for fun and food and alcohol. But, "First thing you know there were large crowds" (Spellman, p. 19). Grimes went on, "Tatum had been catching it pretty hard himself. There was so much in his playing that people couldn't dig, and he wasn't getting too many jobs." Selling the Trio to club owners was an obvious step to take under these circumstances, and critics who felt it was the wrong move for Tatum to make artistically were simply beside the point.

There were at least two strong precedents for the Trio. Clarence Profit, a pianist who had been playing around New York since the middle 1920s, had formed a trio in 1937 which was a commercial success and worked continuously through 1944. And in California, also in 1937, Nat "King" Cole gave up being a band pianist and started working with a trio which became very popular. Like Tatum's, both these earlier trios consisted of piano, bass, and guitar (instead of drums, which might seem more likely and which indeed became the format among the many trios that followed the Tatum Trio).

The amazing thing is that Tatum was able to find two other rhythm section players who were willing to play with him. His speed and advanced harmonies were admitted by most to be beyond their capacities. If Art had held auditions I doubt many would have shown up; it is probably no accident that the Trio came together in the relaxed and casual atmosphere of the jam session. Slam Stewart was a highly competent and respected bassist. Milt Hinton said of him, "I marveled at what Slam did with him . . . I know at the Three Deuces, 1935, '36, when I was out there, I just wasn't up to playing all those changes that he [Art] played, you know. " Grimes remembered, "The arguments he [Art] and Slam had were funny to me. They both had perfect pitch. You could hit on a glass, and they'd tell you what note it was, or what notes it was between. They'd get into arguments about things like that, but all in fun. Because Slam had that perfect ear, Tatum couldn't lose him." Red Norvo also could testify to Slam's ability:

> See, Slam Stewart was the only guy that could ever play with Art. He had the ears to play with him, he could do it. Art tried to break in [Charlie] Mingus out here. Mingus

could never do it. 'Cause I had Mingus, I knew exactly how much he knew and how well he played. There was no comparison between Art and Mingus. He couldn't hear exactly the tonic which Art wanted. See, now Slam Stewart, Art could play all those difficult atonal things, and he'd hear the boom, the tonic. He'd just, boom, he'd hit that tonic note every time.

Slam could coordinate his ensemble playing well with Tatum, but solos were another matter. Like so many others Slam felt run over by Art on his solos: ". . . here's a point I'd like to bring out. When I was taking a solo, a bass solo, at times Tatum would, not knowingly, possibly he would kind of drown me out, not meaningly, but [it was] his style of playing the piano. I'd be trying to take a solo and Tatum would be soloing also, along with me, and at times that was a little bit perturbing to me, you know, until I got used to it . . ." (Slam Stewart interview, IJS).

That same competitiveness (if that's what it was) could show up off the bandstand, and Slam was able to describe still another encounter with Art's automotive ambitions:

. . . we had asked Al [Hibbler] to come with us up to Lovejoy's on this particular night to jam a little while, you know, to a session. So one word led to to another between Al and Art and somehow, they started arguing amongst themself—I don't know how it started—they started arguing, friendly-like, about who could drive a car, you know? And this thing went on and Art would say to Al, "Oh, I can drive better than you, man. You can't drive no car." And the same, vice versa, Al would holler over to Art that he could drive better than he. In fact, the argument started as we started—when I started the car to take us all up to the session, you know. They were in the back seat of the car. The guitar player and myself—I was driving, you know, up front. All this argument was going on and I had just started out, we hadn't gone a block. Art would holler out, "Stop the car, Slam. Stop the car. I'm going to show this cat who's the better driver," you know. So I don't know what he was getting at. I stopped the car, pulled over and stopped the car, and Art said to Al, "Well, I tell you what, Al. Here's your chance to drive the car because I can drive better than you, I'm sure." So Al backed down. Al said to Art, "Well, man, you know I can't drive." But anyway, one word led on to another and Art said, "Well, I can drive." And Al wanted to disprove him. So he said, "Slam, let me get over to the wheel," which I did. Al was in the back seat laughing and Art—I started the car up for Art and let him get behind the wheel and do you know that Art drove at least a block down the street? Somehow this particular street, he must have known how the situation was, because he kept a straight line right down the street. Fortunately, there wasn't much traffic. He pulled over to the curb after a while and stopped. So that was one of the—I was so frightened, everybody was, you know. But this was one of the experiences that I never will forget, that Art Tatum actually drove a block down the street.

[Slam Stewart interview, IJS].

Tiny Grimes was more of a long shot for a Trio member, but it paid off. He had played drums in high school, and after his drum set was washed away in a flood at a beach resort, he turned to piano, without instruction, and finally got together a vocal trio that was good enough to appear several times on the Major Bowes Amateur Hour (a major institution on national radio in the '30s), and later to get small-time work in Alexandria, Virginia, and then Philadelphia. As he told Stanley Dance, "I didn't start playing guitar till I was very old. It must have been '37 or '38, after I hit New York" (Grimes was then twenty). The interview went on:

I've learned everything I know by *myself*. No one ever learned me *nothing!* I never could read too much. The way I did my chords, I used to find sheet music with ukulele diagrams on them. I got my own little system going, found out how to make certain things, and just translated the music my way. It took a lot of practice. After I got inter-

> ested in it, I used to lock myself in my room all day, every day, because there was no piano and I had nothing else to do. After three months of sitting up in that room day in and day out, I could make little gigs.   [*World of Swing*]

He took the place in the Slam Stewart duo of the guitar player who had been drafted (Slim Gaillard), and soon afterwards he and Slam "fell in" with Tatum, at Lovejoy's Chicken Shack in Los Angeles.

> Now I had only been playing guitar two years, but I had quick ears, the desire to play and be in the fast crowd. We played every night, and the word got around. When we went outside, we saw long lines of people and a chain across the door. We never paid it any mind at first. He was making thousands of dollars off of us, and we didn't even know. We were just having fun! After a time, we said, "Man, look at all these people in here! Do you think they have come to see us?" A fellow at the Streets of Paris heard about us and suggested to Tatum that he form a regular trio with Slam and me, and that he would pay whatever extra money was necessary. I think Tatum was to get between $150 and $175 a week.   [*World of Swing*, 361–62]

The Trio was probably Tatum's best commercial success to this point in his career, and it was soon a bigger drawing card on 52nd Street than anyone but perhaps Billie Holiday. It was even featured briefly (33 seconds) in a "March of Time" film, part of a series on Music in America. Art allegedly told an interviewer that the key to the Trio's success was in keeping the melody simple and not losing it in a flurry of abstract improvisations. "If we make arrangements difficult, people won't understand what we're playing. We keep it melodic. That's not my idea to have all the technique in the world and not be able to play the nice basic harmonies and nicer things about the piano" (Doerschuk). This I think is Tatum selling his act, and presenting a necessity as a virtue. He needed work and the public needed understandable music, and that I suspect will account for any approach he may have made to "nice basic harmonies," from which he usually ran as fast as he could.

The public and the critics had changed positions, however, and the Trio was generally disappointing to reviewers. One writer called it "frankly, a mistake" (Gibson); and Gunther Schuller said, "Many of the trio's recordings are flawed and except for Tatum's own playing do not even measure up as trio/ensemble performances to the best work of the Nat "King" Cole or Clarence Profit trios." And further, "Tatum himself confined his playing to a much simplified style, limiting particularly his harmonic imagination. Moreover, most of the Trio's repertory was pre-arranged, leaving very little room for real improvisation, with the result that most of its recordings have a calculated feeling. They remind us of a kind of musical façade with not very much depth behind it" (489).

Slam later confirmed that maybe three-fourths of what the Trio did was arranged, which called for considerable rehearsing. Oddly, Tiny Grimes, who liked to refer to himself as "the bottom man on the Tatum pole," remembered it differently:

> We never rehearsed. Everything was made up on the band-stand. Why in the world did those two guys keep *me?* I know I was the weakest thing in there, but after we started working I'd go downstairs during every intermission with my guitar and work on whatever song we'd been playing, trying to catch up with them as best I could. I did that every set, every intermission, and they would have to come and get me. I think that's the only thing that kept me with them. They knew I was trying so hard. . . . I tell you it was an honor playing with them, but playing wasn't too much enjoyment. It was a struggle, because nobody would learn me nothing, and I had to catch it as it went by, and it was so fast all the time.   [*World of Swing,* 362]

For Tiny, more than for Slam, playing in the trio with Art was "no picnic." Slam commented later that "He [Tiny] possibly couldn't hear as well as I could. He wouldn't be keeping up with it, you know.

He laid out quite a few times . . . just lay out 'til he got himself together." Tiny claimed in retrospect, "We were never a nervous group," and he described what went on during a typical set: "[Maybe we'd be playing] "I Got Rhythm" way up in tempo, and we'd talk about baseball or football, you know, like there was nothin' happening, like we were holding a conversation."[4] To have been challenged the way Tiny was in the Trio, and also to have had to act "like there was nothin' happening" must have doubled the stress. Personally I think the valiant Tiny Grimes should have been given a medal for bravery.

It seems likely to me that Tatum, the Ultimate Solo Pianist, had little real interest in the Trio and no real artistic ambition for it. For whatever reason, he simply went with "the flow," capitalizing on the surprise popularity that this accidental trio generated. He seems to have had no vision of the real commercial and artistic possibilities he might have realized if he had brought together and rehearsed with musicians who could think alike and play at somewhere near his high level. In other words, what Oscar Peterson accomplished later with Ray Brown and Herb Ellis could have been his. Perhaps it was a matter of loyalty to friends, or maybe he lacked judgment and especially the ability to imagine the future, simply taking everything as it came. (In the second incarnation of the Trio, Tiny was replaced by Everett Barksdale, the guitarist who much earlier had given up piano after hearing Tatum, but we don't know how this replacement came about.)

Nevertheless the Tatum Trio was almost surely the model for a number of trios born after his, most notably the Lennie Tristano trio of 1946 and the later Oscar Peterson trio, in which Schuller says he can hear specific musical ideas and devices borrowed directly from Tatum. And the Trio work was not all under par. Schuller has commented that in the early 1940s Tatum's style was developing "a propensity for longer lines and more continuous phrases." His earlier style was directly related to the form of the typical popular song, which was usually two bars of active melody followed by two relatively stationary bars, and it was those second two-bar phrases that Tatum used for his stunning runs. In the '40s, however, Tatum began to expand the runs beyond those open two bars, to lengths of eight or more bars, and sometimes crossing over the natural eight-bar segments of the song. It was as if he were trying to turn the runs so often condemned as merely decorative into melodic or linear improvisation, which had never been one of his strong points. This development reached a peak in one of the Trio recordings, "Exactly Like You," where Tatum's right hand plays an entire chorus in this linear, straight eighth-note style, and in this chorus, Schuller comments, Tatum "comes quite close to the kind of modern jazz conception then emerging with the younger players like Peterson, and Bud Powell" (*Swing Era, 490*).

IN DECEMBER OF 1943 Art's close personal friend and possibly his own strongest influence, Fats Waller, died. He was only thirty-nine, but he had seemed even less concerned with taking care of himself than Art was. I got a glimpse of Fats in action from talking to Joe Bushkin:

> I had the greatest time with Fats. I was playing with Muggsy Spanier's band and we played back-to-back with Fats' band on the vaudeville tour. It was a hell of a show, sort of like too good for the time. Chicago was swingin' for me. I used to hang out with him, you know, after the show, he used to stay up most of the time, hardly got any sleep. Well, we did it somehow. We'd sort of nap off while the movie was on, with the stage shows—we did 4 or 5 a day, you know. One night I finally quit, I couldn't make it. We were on the south side at the Regal, and I remember we were staying at the same hotel I said, "Hey Fats, I can't make it"—young as I was, so much younger than him, you know—what the hell, in '38 I was 21 or so. And Fats said, "You'd better hang out with us tonight, we got a lot of action going"—you know, there was always the chorus girls or something, he had a whole scene going. And I said, "No, man, I'm falling apart," and I went to sleep. And when I arrived at the theater at 11:30 for a 12:15 show, the noon show, there was Fats, he'd been up all night, drinking

like crazy. And I passed his dressing room and he said, "Hey, boy, hey, Jo-see-phus," that was a name that both Louis Armstrong and Fats referred to me as, Joe-see-phus. And he said, "Joe-see-phus, come in here." And I said, "Hi, Fats, how you feeling, you look terrible." He was drinking, and he filled a water glass half full of gin. He said, "Down that and [let's] even up." So—I had some wonderful moments, you know.

Fats's engagement schedule had for years comprised what one writer (Machlin) called "perpetual performance" and "feverish activity." He shuttled constantly around the country from one night club to another, also doing radio shows and an average of six recording sessions per year, composing not only songs but a whole show (*Early to Bed*, an ironic title for him), and generally extracting as much fun out of all this as he could. He was enormously cheerful publicly, and his humor, his vigor, and his very high level of musicianship could make almost any song worth listening to. In his later years he had been giving more and more expression to his interest in serious music: he experimented with writing a piano suite in a jazz idiom, and recorded spirituals, folk songs, and excerpts from well-known operas, giving them jazz interpretations (another echo from the virtuoso century). Harry Gregory, Art's old friend in Toledo who seems to have known everybody in jazz at one time, said, "I once asked Fats—we drank a lot together—where did he experience his greatest thrill? He thought for a moment, then he said it was in Paris—I forget this guy's name, the black composer who wrote "Sweet Georgia Brown," they were in a show together, and he said that he asked for the chance to play on the great organ in Notre Dame, and they consented. And that was his greatest thrill."

Fats died on a train, en route from Los Angeles to New York, the same trip which Art had to make so many times. His corpse was discovered in Kansas City, the town Art used as a stop-over on his own trips.

Bill Douglass, the drummer, says he has seen tears in Tatum's eyes when he was playing one of Waller's tunes. And there was the following vignette which I would like to believe is authentic, behind its fairly purple prose, but on which there is no way to check so many years later:

The walls and the ceiling looked like a kid's first grade painting, a disharmony of colors and shades that were gaudy and unreal. It was a step-down New York bar on 52nd St. in the mid-1940s and it was a center of jazz. At night low lights played against these walls and they were warmer and more subdued, but, when daylight sneaked through the narrow front door beneath a canopy, they looked thoughtless, expressionless, and macabre. The place was small. A long narrow bar stretched like a lead pencil just left of the door. The rest of the room was a checker board of chairs and tables, with a tiny stage, like a king's throne room, looking down upon them.

On the stage, night after night, the greatest jazz pianist of all time sat and played, Art Tatum, heavy set, nearly blind, wet-faced, sat hunched on his bench and played and played and played from nine until two. But it was noon now and there was no music, save the playing of a tiny radio behind the bar as a 'tender wiped glasses and hummed. The door was open to let out the smoke and dust and staleness of the night before and a stranger wandered in. He sat there talking to the bartender when Tatum walked in. He was led, one hand gently on his arm, by a friend or a manager.

He came to the bar and said hello and leaned against it and drank a glass of cold water. His face was limp and tired, his eyes weighed by rolls of heavy flesh, his hands nimble even as they foundled [sic] a glass.

Then he heard the music. "And we continue with the music of the late, great Fats Waller," an announcer was saying through the radio and Tatum listened. And a record was spinning and it played "Confessin" and Waller was singing, the sound came from somewhere deep in his breast, and one great musician listened in admiration to another. Waller had only recently died and Tatum listened reverently. . . . Waller was playing "Keepin' Out of Mischief Now" and Tatum swayed back and forth with the tune. Then he began to talk. He looked at the radio and talked to Fats Waller. . . . "Fats, play, Fats," Tatum was saying, his hands mechanically drumming on imaginary keys.

And then he left the bar. "Take me up there," he said to his friend, pointing to the piano on the stage. He was led to the piano, felt for the bench and sat very still for a long time. Then he started playing, tears streaming down his face and falling like dew on the black and white blur before him. The bartender shut off the radio, and Tatum's hands moved like a ballerina's toes, gently and lightly, across the keys. He hummed to himself and played for a long time—playing to Fats. . . .   [Scheer]

AROUND 1943, THE noted jazz writer Leonard Feather organized a panel of experts on jazz for *Esquire* and started polling them for their most-admired musicians on each instrument. Tatum never fared very well in polls that tapped the general public, but was usually near the top when leading musicians were asked their opinions. For example, *Down Beat,* the leading jazz publication at the time, started polling readers about their favorite players in 1942; in that year as well as in 1943 *Down Beat* readers' favorite pianist was Jess Stacy, and from 1944 through 1948 it was Mel Powell (both played primarily with Benny Goodman, who was very well known to the general public and through whom they had considerable visibility). In fact Tatum never won a *Down Beat* readers' poll. However the *Esquire* experts in their first year[5] gave Tatum their gold medal (and in 1945 and '47, the silver).

The Esquire gold medal winners of 1944 gave a concert at the Metropolitan Opera House in New York in January of that year, and one enthusiastic writer called it "probably the greatest jazz concert in history" (Spencer, "Recordings," 32). The rhythm section included Tatum, Sid Catlett (drums), Oscar Pettiford (bass), and Al Casey (guitar), and featured as front-line soloists Louis Armstrong, Roy Eldridge, and Jack Teagarden (all fans of Tatum's since the early '30s), Barney Bigard, Coleman Hawkins (who had changed his style after first hearing Tatum sixteen years earlier) , Lionel Hampton, and

Red Norvo (another old friend, as we have seen). Billie Holiday sang. Oddly, Decca Records, who recorded the concert, never released any of the recordings and all of the published pressings were taken from unofficial and presumably unauthorized tapes. These recordings are certainly valuable, in that they show Art Tatum bending his more heroic impulses into submission and playing, far more than just satisfactorily, as a member of a *section* and an ensemble. Whitney Balliett remarked, "He had his solo outings that evening, but for most of it he was just a member of possibly the most sensitive and powerful rhythm section ever assembled . . . the four men developed a cyclonic propulsion" (*Ecstasy,* 112).

The month before this concert Feather had organized a studio recording session involving the concert's rhythm section, but with a front line consisting of Cootie Williams (trumpet), Coleman Hawkins, and Edmond Hall. A number of the tunes planned for the concert were recorded on this earlier session (e.g., "Esquire Bounce" and "Mop-Mop"), which was released on Commodore Records, and it almost looks as if Feather was putting something in the bank in case the Decca recordings failed to materialize (as they did). In Schuller's opinion of the Leonard Feather All-Stars' playing, "To the extent that it succeeds, it does so because of the rhythm section, including Tatum, somehow holding the diverse strands of musical styles together." And further, "The strong rhythm section, particularly Pettiford's vigorous bass walking, spurred Tatum on to some of his most swinging playing" (p. 489). It seems odd that it was the polling process that put Tatum on a stage with stronger musicians than he usually played with in jamming sessions, where by this point musicians usually stopped to listen when Tatum got up to the piano. His playing with the *Esquire* All-Stars poignantly suggests another direction his career might have taken if he had been willing to play more in such groups—or if someone had taken time to point him in that direction.

Tatum's studio recordings in 1944 were entirely with the Trio and this is the year that produced the bulk of their output.[6] He also recorded for the Armed Forces Recording Service, which issued the wartime V-discs for broadcast only to servicemen, and made a number of radio appearances: the Philco Hall of Fame, the Mildred Bailey Show, the Chamber Music Society of Lower Basin Street, and a number of live broadcasts from locations where he was playing, again mainly with the Trio. One can see how important the Trio was to his livelihood that year, even without knowing the details of his club appearances around the country. He was recorded with the Trio, privately, at Frenchie's Pink Pig in Milwaukee, and both Gunther Schuller and Stanley Cowell have singled out one performance ("Exactly Like You") from that evening as especially worth noting, both because it revealed the kind of "treacherous harmonic waters" into which Tatum could sail if he chose to, and because his playing on it was so similar to the more modern conceptions of such young giants as Bud Powell. In his playing on this cut Tatum's improvising was "harmonically quite advanced, often related bitonally to the underlying changes [that is, it was as if he were playing in two keys at the same time], thus using the kind of oblique substitutions that musicians like [Thelonious] Monk and Eric Dolphy were to develop into a whole new language years later" (Schuller).

Hank Jones had his first close-up of Tatum in 1944, and in his account one can see that there was still plenty of power in the Tatum presence:

> I was working in Buffalo at a place called the Anchor Bar, and Art Tatum was working at another nightclub in town. His last show was later than ours. And our little group, we'd all go out and listen to Art play his last set. After Art finished his last set, he would go down to a club in the downtown section of Buffalo where there was, I guess you could call it, an after-hours spot. . . . And Art loves nothing better than to sit down at the piano and play until the wee hours of the morning—actually the mid-hours of the day, I should say, because he'd get off at 2 o'clock and then he would sit down and play until 10 or 11 o'clock. See, he had boundless energy, you know. And many times I'd get to talk with him, ask him various questions about various things and so forth. But actually he was playing so much, you never got much of a chance to talk with him. I

was very fortunate to be able to listen to him play close at hand—I mean just to sit two feet away from him and listen to this man play, which really was something rather unusual. I'm grateful that I was able to do that, because he's not around today, and this will never happen again.

[Jones, 12]

Unfortunately Art was still drinking heavily. Most of the people I've talked to who heard him play in after-hours clubs maintain stoutly that his drinking never showed in his playing. Unless Tatum's nervous system was made of different material from the rest of us that "never" just doesn't seem likely, so I was almost relieved to hear of at least one time when he seemed less than superhuman. Ernie Lewis described the incident for me, when I asked him whether anyone ever tried to tell Art to cut down on his drinking:

No! They wouldn't dare. I didn't, even. Well, I did once. He got upset about me doing it. He was playing in 'Frisco. I was to wake him up at a certain time, which I did. But he wouldn't wake up. So I think I went and—I washed his face, with cold water, a cold towel. And he was late. So he said to me, "I'm going to have to show you how to wake me up." That's the way he put it to me, but I knew what that meant. He was mad—that I woke him up. But he had been drinking too much. And he was late on his job. Well, me being a union man as well, I know what they do to him, what they would do to him. So I said, "Art, you're late. Let's go!" So he struggled up, and when he got down there, the guy gave him hell. But he was still drunk. They noticed his piano playing. Man, he was going off, his thumbs were all over the piano. I was embarrassed. It was in a joint downtown in San Francisco. He shouldn't have been working the joint to start with. But he had to work. If he didn't like the joint, then he really didn't—now this was before going to a joint after he gets off, that's where he would really play. But he was too drunk, out all night and the night before. The doorman was a young kid—he was a smart-ass to start with, and he told him when he first got there, when he got off his first set or something, "Yeah, I know you been drinking. You're drunk now." Right out loud where the boss could hear him. Nobody said nothing else. Art just looked at him, and walked off, went back upstairs. That's the only time I've seen Art act like he acted. He could sit there and drink, he could hold it pretty good. But this time he'd gone a little too far. I could always tell if he'd been drinking too much. I knew every move he made on that piano.

NO ONE TELLS ANY stories about Art Tatum's relationships with women. He certainly didn't chase them, and from what I've heard it's easy to believe that he rarely or never took advantage of any of the openings that inevitably come, especially to itinerant musicians. Billie Holiday loved him but no one has ever hinted at a relationship; she called him "The Banker," probably because he always wore a three-piece suit and was, as Sylvia Syms said, "a very dignified gent," a fastidious man who "spoke impeccable English," was very articulate and "very, very intellectual." Maybe it was also because of his generosity. Sylvia Syms, a popular nightclub singer in the 1940s, is the only woman who opened a window for me on Tatum's tenderness, his ways of being affectionate. I had heard a private tape-recording of her and Art together, Art trying to teach Sylvia a new song—no tenderness there. But it came through when Sylvia talked to me about him:

> I had those big long braids wrapped around my head, for which he named me Moonbeam Moskowitz. I had very long, long hair and it had never been cut, and I guess the first time Arthur ever met me he pulled my braid and said, "Are you an Indian?" I said, "No, I'm from Brooklyn," and he said, "Oh, you're a Jewish Indian," and he named me Moonbeam Moskowitz. This of course was in the very beginning, I had not yet even gone to work, I was just coming around 52nd St., hanging around there. There was something about him that was very conservative. I guess you could not, I at least could not get inside of Arthur. But I know he adored me, and I know he adored the fact that

in my own virtue I was great, greatly innocent. That's the only way that I can describe it. I think he kind of got a kick out of how crazy I was, and how not having very much knowledge as far as the profession was concerned, never having studied music or not knowing what keys I sang in or whatever, I guess maybe it was kind of refreshing to him. He was extremely generous. And he loved limousines, which of course were not all that expensive in those days. I used to go home to Brooklyn in a limousine all the time. Arthur never really made passes at me. I don't know what would have happened if he had—but I think he was more amused by me than in love with me. That is not to say that he didn't want to, because he would allude to them, he made passes but they were very verbal, and he was very amused by me. But I think—I think he thought better of getting involved with a crazy girl. But he was very kind and very generous to me, very gentle. You know, he had some sight. He could see—he always knew when I wore blue.

A whole new side of Art appeared when Sylvia talked about presents he had given her.

But Arthur always gave me these—they used to make these little pianos then, see he had a friend who was a glass-spinner, whatever they call that, do you know what they call that? They used to spin things out of glass, they would make it and weave it into various shapes and things. He knew somebody who did that, and he gave me one once and then it got broken. Erroll [Garner] was very upset because Erroll wanted that, 'cause it said "ATSS." The next thing that Arthur gave me, for my birthday, was a kind of a charm, a gold piano, from Van Cleef—Oh, God, it was so many years ago. Pearls and little sapphires, and a keyboard, and the top of the piano opened up, it was a grand piano. When Arthur died, I finally gave that little piano to Erroll, right in that little pouch that it came in. I don't know what happened to it on Erroll's death. Erroll and I were very good friends, and Arthur was the one who made us good friends.

Garner, like so many other pianists, was under Tatum's wing from his earliest appearances on 52nd Street, where he started as an intermission player, often near where Tatum was playing. It almost seems he replaced Marlowe Morris at Art's side, as driver-courier-helper and as respected colleague, and there was lots of mutual affection. Sylvia described it:

> Erroll would come and get me and take me uptown if I had to meet Arthur. Arthur really adored him. As a matter of fact, Arthur at that particular time thought he was the best of the young pianists around. Erroll adored him and he adored Erroll, and he thought that Erroll was some day going to be very big stuff. It used to make him crazy, because people thought at the time—Erroll was an inter-missionist, just beginning—and people used to say that Erroll played very well but Erroll couldn't keep time. And Arthur used to think that was ridiculous, because his time was a special kind of time, that was very unusual, and would come to find its way into everyone's life. And it did. I was so dumb I didn't know, all I knew was that he was funny, he used to make me laugh. As a matter of fact, I know nothing about the piano—I know nothing clinical or studied about the rights or the wrongs, I can't even read music. But I know Arthur was a very gifted man.

IN 1945 TATUM could be heard on the radio, if briefly, on average every other month. There were only two studio sessions, however. In January in New York he made four songs with the Barney Bigard Sextet, including the un-Tatum-esque title of "Sweet Marijuana Brown," sung by Joe Thomas. In May in Los Angeles he recorded nine solos; he had been persuaded by an agent (according to Tiny Grimes) to give up the trio format, and he made no more recordings with a trio until 1952. In fact, from 1945 until 1952 he made very few studio recordings at all.

Tiny Grimes was not only a hard worker but he thought about what was going on around him, and he had an insight into Art Tatum:

. . . the most underrated person—I mean, too much talent, they hurt theirselves, it look like. That kind of thing is possible, you know. You can be too good for your own self. To me, if Tatum just had a little flash, a little jive, a little whatever. But that wasn't him. . . . He was serious. When he sat down to the piano he played—there was no clownin'. A little gimmick, you might say, is the only thing in my eyesight that held him back. . . . The man never got the right PR [public relations].[7]

THE YEAR 1945 SAW the ending of World War II and the beginning of a prosperous postwar period for America. But it also marked the beginning of a significant eclipse of Art Tatum on the jazz scene. His standing and his reputation were established beyond challenge, but his popularity, such as it was, faded seriously in the remainder of the 1940s. What cast its shadow on him—it was not a total eclipse—was the latest development in jazz, which had been taking over the minds of emerging musicians since the early '40s and which now began to take over the night clubs and the recording studios. The new style was called be-bop. Fifty-second Street, which itself would suffer a decline toward the end of the 1940s, began to showcase some new names: Dizzy Gillespie, Thelonious Monk, Charlie Parker, Bud Powell, Al Haig, Max Roach, Kenny Clarke, and a host of others who responded in the 1940s to what these leaders were doing. The generational struggle was catching up with God.

9

1945–1949: The Be-Bop Years

"First you speak of Art Tatum, then take a long deep breath, and you speak of the other pianists." **DIZZY GILLESPIE**

HENRY MINTON HAD once been a sax player himself but had moved from music-making to a job as a union administrator, the first black delegate to New York Local 802. Devoted to jazz, he converted a dilapidated room in the old Hotel Cecil, on W. 118th Street, into a club and, according to Leonard Feather, "made the place an open house for musicians, where jam sessions were practically a nightly event" (*Inside Be-Bop*). The now legendary Minton's Playhouse became another hothouse, in which young plants could grow fast. Among established musicians, Marlowe Morris, who played more like Tatum than anyone else according to some, was almost always there on piano. He was joined by whoever showed up, and in the early 1940s that regularly included all the stars: Lester Young, Ben Webster, Rex Stewart, Roy Eldridge, Clark Terry, Milt Hinton, Jo Jones, and the rest, creating a brew almost beyond imagining for a jazz fan. And to hear the stars, maybe to play with them, a lot of younger musicians hung out there, including Thelonious Monk, who eventually became the house pianist at Minton's, Dizzy, Bud Powell, and other future be-boppers who were going to turn jazz into a different kind of music and leave Art Tatum further away from the mainstream than he had ever been. But in the early 1940s Tatum still was on his throne, even at Minton's. Drummer Louie Bellson told me, "I used to go up quite a bit to Minton's in Harlem. They had some classic jam sessions there like you never heard before, by so many giants. And when all these people finished playing they'd put about 3 or 4 bottles of beer on the piano, and here comes Tatum. And when Tatum finished playing, nobody played. Nobody wanted to follow him."

Les Paul, with his flair for description, almost made me feel I'd been there:

> I remember one night that Charlie Christian and I were up there battling on guitar, with Leonard Ware. There were three guitar players in this town that were good. There was Leonard Ware who played 4-string guitar and he played damn good, real good. And they had Charlie Christian who I knew from Oklahoma 'cause that's where I met him, out in Oklahoma before he ever joined Benny, and the other one, myself, the three of us, we'd go up there and we'd battle it out. And after that a guy came up to me and he says, "Do you mind if I play your guitar?" And I says, "No, not at all." It was Floyd Smith, with Andy Kirk, and he got up there and he broke off the neck of a bottle, and he played slide stick-fingered guitar, and he blew us all away, playing slide guitar. He played real dirty blues and he wiped us all out. And then when that got done it would be three drummers and when it finished three drummers, why, it would be three piano players, or five.
>
> Roy Eldridge was up there playing one night, and he's going like a bat outta hell, up there screaming and he's way up there, and he has got the audience goin' crazy. Everybody in the joint's goin' crazy. And when he took the horn away from his lips when he was done, the people applauded and when they stopped applauding the note con-

tinued on—and he didn't have the horn up to his mouth! He had the horn by his side. And we looked down, and standing down there at the bottom of the bandstand was Dizzy Gillespie. And Dizzy was sleeping in Central Park and borrowing fifty cents so he could get something to eat. I gave him fifty cents and my bass player gave him fifty cents. And he come in there to knock off Roy and Roy blew him away, but then he got up there and really challenged him, and again there was a fiasco. And it was a dynamite night, because this kid come in, and finally Roy whipped him. And he says, "Well, I guess I'm not ready yet." And he went back into his hole.

At places like Minton's nobody served as a gatekeeper, and anybody with courage (or a lack of perspective on what was going on) might try to join in. Monk has said that one of the sources of what came to be called be-bop was the desire of his and some of his friends, e.g., Dizzy, to create a new ball game for themselves instead of always chasing after established musicians, and to keep uninspiring and inadequate musicians off the stand at Minton's. Dizzy and Monk figured out that if the group on the stand was playing material that was unfamiliar, not only in its content but even in the musical language it used, and if on top of that it was also technically difficult, then half-baked musicians who wanted to play "Indiana" wouldn't even think of joining in. Probably Roy Eldridge wouldn't either. Milt Hinton has reported that Dizzy used to take him up onto the roof, probably at Minton's, and show him the alternate chord changes he wanted to use—without knowledge of those chord changes, conventional or limited musicians would make fools of themselves playing with Dizzy and Monk.

Whether or not that story is true, what Dizzy and his coterie developed was indeed forbidding to players strongly rooted in the 1930s and in the language of swing. The tempos got faster and faster, the musical bars that went speeding by were crammed full with more and more eighth- and sixteenth-notes, and the improvising strove for longer lines, longer continuous threads of notes, with only a distant relationship to the basic underlying chords supporting them. A casual relationship with one's instrument simply wouldn't do. Bop called for a kind of virtuosity, whether intentionally, as Dizzy allegedly said, or simply because it took virtuosity to play what the bop musicians were hearing (as seemed to be the case with Charlie Parker). Judged by the criteria of "swing" the tempos were frantic, the beat was buried, the melodic lines were harsh and jagged (one hostile critic said that he could always make his infant cry by playing Charlie Parker recordings to it, and another likened Monk's playing to a "faux-naif elephant dance")—but it was certainly new and different, it brought an excitement that the familiar no longer could do, and it was claimed by a new generation as "their" music.

While some of Tatum's playing, as the 1940s progressed, shows a certain similarity with the features of be-bop—the longer lines and the advanced harmonic ideas, not to mention the virtuosity and the speed which had always characterized his playing—Tatum made no effort to follow where the "boppers" were going. They did take some inspiration from him, however, before they moved on to the beat of their own drummer, and even when he wasn't a source of their ideas a number of be-bop musicians were able to recognize that he had been there before them. Charlie Mingus (whom Art once considered for his trio but found wanting) once said, "Tatum taught me a lesson. The hippies were so proud of themselves, making minor ninths and going through a cycle of fourths on a song like "I Can't Get Started." Tatum has been doing it all the time, sometimes so fast you weren't even conscious of it" (Horricks, *These Jazzmen,* 181).

Ellington believed that the seeds of be-bop were in the piano playing of Earl Hines, and certainly Hines was highly receptive to the new style and encouraging of it—his was the first of the big bands to try to translate the idiom into that medium. Tatum, too, with his overpowering presence in the late '30s and early '40s, must have had at least an indirect influence on such innovators as Dizzy Gillespie, suggesting to them the harmonic complexities and the virtuoso technique on which they would build be-bop as a style. But he had an undeniably direct influence on two of be-bop's heroes: Charlie Parker and the leading be-bop pianist Bud Powell.

Not a lot is known about contact between Parker and Tatum.

Sometime in the late 1930s, according to Red Norvo, Tatum met Charlie Parker on one of his stays in Kansas City. As Norvo tells it, both he and Tatum were present on one of those early nights, before Parker had mastered his instrument, when he tried to sit in with a band and was rebuffed, and then again on a later night when Parker had improved.

> And one night I met him [Tatum] at the Kentucky Club, and while we were there, see, this kid came in, and sat in with the band. And they kicked him off the bandstand. So about a year or so later I was back at the Muhlback Hotel, and Art was coming back from New York. See, he took the train from New York to Kansas City, and then from Kansas City here [California]. I went down to Texas and I played Texas, and came back up to Wichita—we played a lotta college dates, like Georgia Tech—I came back about a year later, still on the road . . . and here's Art. Gives me a call. He saw the advertisement that I was in town—and I met him at the Kentucky Club. This guy that was running the place was a saxophone player, at the Kentucky Club. The guy that had the band there came over and said, "Hey, Art, you remember that kid who was here about a year and a half ago that I threw out? Well, he's here in town. You should hear him. He's gonna come in tonight. Stay here." You probably know who I'm talkin' about. I was sitting with Art, see, and the guy brought him over to meet Art, and he met me with Art.

Parker, unlike Art Tatum, seems to have been a slow starter on his instrument, and maybe a poor judge of when to stick his neck out. He himself tells of his first attempt to sit in with a group: "I knew a little of "Lazy River" and "Honeysuckle Rose" and played what I could. I was doing all right until I tried doing double tempo on "Body and Soul." Everybody fell out laughing. I went home and cried and didn't play again for three months" (Gitler, *Jazz Masters,* 18). On another night, when Parker was jamming with members of Count Basie's band, drummer Jo Jones announced his opinion of Bird's playing by sailing a cymbal out across the dance floor.

Perhaps as a direct result of this incident, in the summer of 1937, when Parker went off to play at resorts in the Ozark Mountains not far from Kansas City, he took with him all of Count Basie's recordings, from which he learned Lester Young's solos note for note.[1] (Gitler notes that "Years later, in the fifties, Lee Konitz walked into Bird's dressing room during the course of a tour and heard him play Young's solo from "Shoe Shine Boy" at twice the tempo of the original.") That summer made a huge difference in Parker's playing: he learned about chord progressions, he started to practice long hours, and he returned to Kansas City a different musician. It may have been in the fall of 1938 that Norvo and Tatum were back in the Kentucky Club for the second time, when the band leader told them they ought to stay and hear the difference. (Not surprisingly after all these years Norvo couldn't recall whether or not they stayed.)

Parker may or may not have heard Tatum play in Kansas City. Of course Tatum in the late 1930s was simply part of the musical air that jazz musicians breathed in. Many Tatum recordings were available, and Parker had learned how to listen closely, so he could have been studying Tatum whether he heard him in person or not. He probably heard him in late 1938 or early 1939 when he traveled to Chicago. From Chicago, Parker went to New York, where for a while he took a job as a dishwasher at the Chicken Shack in Harlem, where Tatum was playing, so that he could immerse himself in Tatum's flow of notes. By this point in time Parker, the soon-to-be legendary hero of the be-bop movement, had identified Tatum's playing as having many of the features he wanted to master. At some point, reflecting on Tatum, he is reported to have said. "Tatum—he's like Beethoven" (Teddy Wilson, liner notes).

As far as I can tell Parker and Tatum never played together on a club date, nor even jammed together. As late as 1950 or '51, when Bird was well established, he tried (according to Al Levitt) to sit in with Art. It was in New York, at Cafe Society Downtown. Bird's quintet had been hired as the house band, and it was his opening night. And the second Art Tatum Trio (with Everett Barksdale instead of Tiny Grimes) was the feature attraction. The quintet played several tunes from Bird's recent album *Bird with Strings*. And then:

> When Art Tatum came on, the trio opened with Tatum's famous version of "Tea for Two" [still an important number in the Tatum repertoire almost twenty years after the original recording]. Bird was standing off stage with a big smile on his face, obviously enjoying what he was hearing. Before you know it, Bird picked up his horn, waited until the end of a chorus, then started playing and walking to the center of the stage at the same time. Art Tatum was shocked for a split second and then angrily said, "No, no, no, no." Bird looked a little disappointed, stopped playing, turned around and walked off stage. After the show, the quintet was supposed to play for dancing. Bird pulled up a chair and sat right in the middle of the dance floor and played all the bebop you wanted to hear. The audience loved it . . .   [Levitt, quoted in Gitler, *Swing to Bop*]

Would Tatum have rejected Parker in an after-hours setting (and why, one wonders, did they apparently never meet at such a session)? Did he feel he was concertizing at Cafe Society Downtown? Was he now using arrangements with the Trio which he felt Bird would disrupt? Did he feel Parker's bebop style was too far away from his own? Was it simply ego? Whatever the reason, all the musicians who had come to hear these two giants that night were deprived of a possibly mind-blowing conjunction, two musicians in complete control of their instruments, and both playing way over the heads of their peers.

If Tatum was the culmination of the major developments in jazz piano that had gone before him, Bud Powell was to be the leading light for several generations of jazz pianists to follow in the 1940s and '50s. He was, Gary Giddins has said, "the most brilliant pianist of the modern jazz movement in the forties, and the most influential," and, "if one were to reduce the history of jazz piano to those quintessential figures whose innovations shaped the course of the music, then

Powell would stand foursquare between Art Tatum . . . and Cecil Taylor . . . whose galvanized keyboard assaults are kin to Powell's electrifying improvisations" (liner notes).

Powell was more deeply engaged with Tatum than was Parker, even to the point of near hand-to-hand keyboard combat. Bud himself sometimes referred to Billy Kyle as his idol (at least according to Billy's widow), and other observers have cited Clyde Hart and Thelonious Monk as his mentors and models. But there is strong reason to believe that in certain ways Tatum was his major influence. Raymond Horricks says of Powell that "the major admiration of his life has been for Art Tatum," and in 1963 when an interviewer asked Powell who his piano teacher had been, Bud responded, "Art Tatum."[2] Some writers have suggested that musicians of the bebop school simply ignored Tatum, feeling that they were leaving him and the rest of his generation behind, but we have it from Miles Davis that "all the bebop piano players were crazy about Art" (*Autobiography*, 79), and perhaps none more than Bud Powell.

POWELL WAS BORN in 1924 and so was fifteen years younger than Tatum. His grandfather had learned some Flamenco guitar while in Cuba during the Spanish-American War, and his father was a stride pianist who got him started. His older brother played violin and trumpet, and his younger brother, Richie, was well on his way to a career in jazz when he was killed in an automobile accident (together with the famous trumpet player Clifford Brown, with whom he was playing at the time). Like Tatum and so many others, Bud's talent drove an interest in music to the surface very early on. His father once said, "I tell you when Bud was seven, the musicians would come and actually steal him, take him from place to place playing music. Nobody had ever seen a jazz musician that young or heard one play like Bud. He was a li'l old chubby fellow, and by the time he was 10 he could play everything he'd heard by Fats Waller and Art Tatum." (One can forgive a father a little exaggeration.)

He had classical training for something like nine years, but he was hell-bent for jazz. He quit high school at fifteen (the year would have been 1939) and began working small clubs at Coney Island, after which, like so many others, he would tour the Harlem bars. He was befriended by Monk, who introduced him to Minton's and protected him from others who didn't like what he was doing in the beginning and wanted him off the stand. Before he was eighteen he was under Monk's influence and had already played, at Minton's, with such giants as Parker and Charlie Christian, the seminal guitar player. He went on to make important recordings with groups led by both Charlie Parker and Miles Davis, as well as many trend-setting solo efforts.

Powell had tremendous technical facility. What he absorbed from Monk was primarily Monk's compositional ideas, while in his desire to master the keyboard and play the piano in a comprehensive and self-contained way he more resembles Tatum. He was another virtuoso, "prone to romance, complete and self-centered in his musical concept" (Horricks, 84). From Tatum he incorporated a skill at making radical harmonic and rhythmic changes, especially in his playing of ballads, and an ambition to succeed as a solo pianist. From the be-boppers with whom he was surrounded from the early 1940s on, he took in the longer melodic line, and in his improvising he was "normally . . . concerned with line rather than mass, with geometry, not colour" (Harrison, *Modern Jazz*, 20). In language quite reminiscent of earlier commentary on Tatum, Max Harris said in a review of his recordings, "These are taken at the sort of headlong tempos in which only great executants are at ease, and, while the dazzling flow of ideas Powell throws off in these circumstances has often received comment, one cannot help wondering if non-pianists realize how demanding such improvising is in terms of physical energy and mental concentration, quite apart from the exorbitant rate at which musical ideas must be produced" (p. 21).

Powell never had the kind of cub-pack relationship with Art that so many others did (Wiggins, Rowles, and Taylor, for example). Tatum, it seems, kept his distance from the be-boppers. It's impossible to say whether this had more to do with their music or their life styles—drugs other than alcohol seemed to figure much more prominently in their lives than it had in his generation (both Parker and

Powell had severe addiction problems), and often they approached jazz more with anger than joy, and more with introspection than outgoing exuberance. They aimed more to "be creative" and different than to "swing." In any case there are a few anecdotes that illuminate a Bud Powell in his twenties, trying to engage the older man in the tried and true way, by "cutting him up." Billy Taylor has described how, sometime around 1950, he was the house pianist at Birdland in New York, playing with a trio, while on the same bill were Bud Powell with his own trio and, finally, Art Tatum as the star of the show:

> Bud was drinking a lot. It was one of those periods where he was into the bottle. He loved Art. He had great respect for him. He and I used to argue about Art because it was frustrating to him—he loved Art, but he loved Charlie Parker more. He wanted to make the piano sound more like Charlie Parker than he wanted to sound like Tatum, and he succeeded in that.
>
> Here we are, all on the same bill—two young guys who'd been arguing about the merits of this older player. And Bud's whiskey told him to challenge Art. Art had just played a brilliant set. And Bud said, "Man, I'm going to really show you about tempo and about playing fast. Anytime you're ready." Art laughed, and he said, "Look, you come in here tomorrow, and anything you do with your right hand I'll do with my left."   ["Tribute," 9,11]

Taylor says that Bud never took up the challenge, although Doerschuk reports that "The next day, Powell actually did spend hours limbering up in preparation for the encounter . . ." ("Art Tatum Biography," 26).

Horricks has described another encounter between the two, at about the same time (1950) and maybe during the same double-billing at Birdland. He claims that earlier Tatum had said, directly to Powell's face, that he was "just a right-handed piano player." Most of the pre-bop pianists were scornful of the minimal role given to the left hand by bop-style players—and not just piano players; Louis

Armstrong once complained about younger players who brought the bop influence into his group: "Sometimes I feel like paying them half a salary!" (Hilbert, "Memories . . . ," 6). Powell had been hurt by that insult from a man he admired so much, and he was determined to prove him wrong during this engagement, where Tatum was a captive audience. "For the first number he played "Sometimes I'm Happy"—improvising at a lightning tempo entirely with his left hand. Tatum didn't know which way to turn. After the set he whispered to a friend, 'Don't tell the kid I said it, but . . . I was wrong. He's got one helluva left hand.' The friend did tell Bud, though. And in this instance the pianist knew his own ability." It may have been another part of his answer to Tatum's challenge that in 1950 Powell recorded what was considered a brilliant version of a tune that had virtually been Tatum's own since the 1930s, the venerable "Tea for Two."

While the be-boppers were moving jazz along a different track from the one Tatum had been on for many years, he remained a force and many retained their respect for him. And in spite of what was happening in Harlem and on 52nd Street, life went on in a familiar way for Tatum in the latter half of the 1940s. Musicians of the pre-bop generation, most of whom had been drafted into the military and were now being released, still venerated him. The tenor player Bud Freeman recalled stopping over in Chicago to see Tatum on his way home from his military discharge. He arrived at the Three Deuces just as Art was coming off from a set, and he stopped him, told him who he was, and asked if he would play just one tune for him before going off. Art went back to the piano and played a full 40-minute set, which so astounded the manager he came over to find out who Bud was, saying "I can never get him to do that!"

If Art (and many others of his generation) was being neglected in some quarters, there is no sign now that it depressed him. In both 1945 and '47 he was the second-ranked pianist in the *Esquire* poll of jazz experts. He was frequently on the radio, appearing on the Oxydol Show and repeatedly on Piano Playhouse, a Saturday morning showcase for pianists run by Cy Walter and Stan Freeman. In 1947 he was given a few more seconds of film visibility in a 16-minute movie "short," a quasi-documentary called "The Fabulous Dorseys" in which he is shown playing in a night club with the piano surrounded by the Dorsey brothers and other well-known musicians, who finally join him in an ensemble blues. And he still had more energy for life than almost anyone around. Bobby Tucker, Billie Holiday's accompanist in those years, remembers Art in Los Angeles in the later 1940s:

> He loved pianists, I don't care how bad they played. And he was interested in us as kids, you know. He came by one night at Billy Berg's and he said, "Look, I'm gonna be over at Stuff Crouch's," which was a spot over on the east side, an afterhours joint. So when he says I'm gonna be someplace, that's an automatic, you must appear. So, he's just gonna go over there and hang out. So we got through, [Jimmy] Rowles and I went over. He's up at the bar drinking boilermakers, and we say, "Come on, Art, play," you know. And he says, "No, Rowles, you go play 'Miss Jones.'" So I thought, "Well, he ain't gonna play for a while, so Jimmy went up to the piano and after he got through we said, "Come on, Art," and he says, "No, Bobby, you play 'Some Other Spring.'" So we would play until the customers would say, "We want Art," and we would say, "So do we!" I played "Some Other Spring" with Billie Holiday. And "Miss Jones" was one that Rowles had played. In other words, he's just letting you know that he had heard you play something. I mean, he'd even go to the extent of stealing something that you played, you know, it's like to compliment you in a manner. He wouldn't "steal" it, he'd thought of it before we even walked down the street, but, something he heard us play he would identify it with us—as a way of saying, "Look, kid, I know you're around."
>
> So then this night—we would go right from work, and he wouldn't start playing until about 4 o'clock, but then he wouldn't stop. And as long as he was playing you couldn't leave. So, I think we must have gotten out of there about 8 or 10 o'clock in the morning. And Rowles went home, and

he came to work that night—I was all right because I wasn't at home, I was away from home and nobody knew where I was. I mean as far as hanging out all night I didn't have nobody to report to. So the next night, we were talking about what a wonderful thing it was, and this night he comes around with a chauffeur, just as we're getting through, and he says, "Come on, let's go back over to — ——" and Rowles says, "Oh my God, Dorothy [his wife] is going to kill me." So, we go over, and it's even later this night. And Jimmy says to me, "Look, you're going to have to go home with me." He's living in Burbank, and we're coming down the street, and his wife is out, and he's explaining half-way down the block, he says, "Bobby'll tell you!"—and she says, "Both of you guys get the hell out of here!"

Along with the energy, amazingly, went the drinking. Johnny Smith, the guitarist, remembers seeing Art on 52nd Street in this postwar period:

When I got out of the service after WWII I went into New York as a staff guitarist with NBC. And at that time 52nd St. was in full bloom. Every doorway would be a jazz place and you'd go from door to door, and that's where I first met Art personally. And I, of course, hero worship, I got up close to the piano, and I got to know Art, met him, and he took me in back between sets and we talked. And one of my most vivid memories was the fact that people, you know, would send drinks up to Art. He drank straight Scotch with a beer chaser. The place where he was playing had this upright piano, it wasn't a grand or anything like that, it was an upright. And people would send up drinks and the whole top of this upright piano would be covered with shots of Scotch and bottles of beer. And Art would be playing some incredible piece, and he'd go on with his right hand and with his left hand he'd reach up on top of the piano and get a shot of Scotch and a swallow of beer, and put it back and never stop playing. It was just something that you couldn't believe.

Mel Clement, a Washington-based pianist who knew Art well, has guessed that in these years it was routine for Art to drink two quarts of whiskey and a case of beer in any 24-hour period. The pianist/ writer Don Asher remembers seeing him in Boston about this time: "The bartender was pouring bottles of Pabst Blue Ribbon beer into a glass pitcher. When it was nearly brimful he handed it to Mr. Tatum. The pianist raised the pitcher to his mouth; he tilted his head, opened his gullet. Down the hatch in three or four stupendous swallows. Some of us were just starting to drink—glasses of beer and ale, swigs of Four Roses in back of the garage. But this was man's work."

"Man's work"—these are the kind of respectful terms in which most people referred to Art's alcohol consumption, and they tend to camouflage an almost inescapable conclusion. The bass player Pops Foster in his later years said it straight out: ". . . he was a liquor-head. Even that didn't stop Tatum. He was so good he could walk out of a place or get fired and walk right into another place and the people would be glad to have him, juice-head and all." Even in the late 1940s Tatum was making no concessions to his diabetes, nor even to the general idea of taking care of himself. The amazing thing is that it was not until 1953 that a doctor finally presented him with a life-or-death choice. Until then nothing seemed to slow him down.

In 1947, Marnette Jackson (the mother of Art's then fourteen-year-old son Orlando) popped into his life again, briefly. On June 26, 1947, a Toledo paper ran the headline, "Swing Pianist Sued for Nonsupport of Son." Once again we run into Art's automobile; the *Toledo Times* noted, "The suit was filed hurriedly in an effort to tie up Mr. Tatum's auto during his visit to the home of his parents. . . ." It seems that Art had agreed in May 1933 to pay $5 a week for child maintenance—but in the fourteen intervening years had paid only $14. While this makes it sound as though Art had no interest in Orlando, we shouldn't forget Arline's insistence that Art visited him and gave him "everything he wanted." Since Orlando was being raised by someone other than Marnette, I can't help suspecting that Marnette was trying to increase her own income, rather than looking after Orlando's support. In any case, some arrangement was apparently worked out in 1947, and the suit was dropped. (There is another parallel with Fats Waller here, since back in 1928 Fats had been sentenced to a brief jail term for a similar disservice to a former mate.)

Art and Orlando figure in a story that Page Cavanaugh, the pianist, relayed to me. If it were even partly true it would be deeply poignant, because it suggests that Orlando might have had a power no one else had, the power to make Art Tatum question himself. I have found no support (or contradiction) for this story, but will quote it for the record because at least one person thought he had heard it from Art himself:

> It came about in New York, I guess it was in a conversation with Art. Yeah, I'm pretty sure about this. I don't think I'm wrong on this. This was when the bebop thing happened, you know, late '40s, early '50s—the kid [Orlando] had told his dad that the guys at school were saying, "Yeah, your dad's a good player but he's pretty old-time, you know, like, bebop's the thing." And this had upset Art a great deal. And the story goes—as I recall, now I'm trying to dig way back into this one—as the story goes, Art called his own record date, just for his own benefit, I think up at the Nola Studios. And he hired the bebop players, they'd come up and just sit and play, for I don't know, a regular session, a 3-hour session I guess. He called 'em and just let 'em record. I don't think it was for commercial purposes at all, I think it was just for Art's edification. He was telling me afterwards—that's what it was, 'cause the story was, he said, they think you can't hear—you know, you're not sighted, so they forget that you can hear everything. He said, "I was hearing things like, 'Yeah, well, what are we here for?' Well, Art called us, you know and he's wonderful, and the whole thing, and he's the old man, you know"—it's almost a case of everyone saying, you know, like, "humor him." And apparently they sat down, and at the end of three hours he had apparently wasted the entire collection of them. Wiped them out. Even things they had no comprehension of. Did the entire instructional three

hours, and said Thank you, fellas, and they were paid and that was that!

The idea that Art might have actually acted on his impulse to corral his challengers and whip them all at once (although not in Madison Square Garden) is provocative and sounds like him, but the call to a session at the recording studio is probably too much to swallow. Surely if there had been a recording made it would have surfaced by now—more obscure items have been found. And even if some kind of session took place, without recording, the story would have circulated and turned up in some jazz interview. I can't explain Cavanaugh's memory, but I'm left wondering if Orlando's adolescence could have touched Art Tatum in this particular way.

There were those who thought that in his late thirties Art was becoming more magisterial, more Olympian in his personal style. Joe Howard, who much later would write the first doctoral dissertation about Tatum, told me about approaching him for an autograph:

> I was in the army, stationed in Brooklyn, Fort Hamilton, this was '46, '47, and that's when 52nd St. was in its heyday. We spent all our time down there, we'd buy a beer and nurse it for 4 hours. I remember going down there to hear Tatum many times, and one night I said to my buddy, "I'm gonna go get his autograph." So when he finished his set I walked up to him and introduced myself and said, "Mr. Tatum, may I have your autograph?" I think I was a 19-year-old GI, I had my uniform on, and he said, "Sure, baby," and out of his left pocket he pulled a stamp pad and out of his right he pulled a stamp, and he stamped his name, Art Tatum. He had a stamp! I never forgot that.

I was ready to read a kind of condescension or aloofness in this—until I came across a copy of Art's 1938 application for a passport and found that he had signed it with an X, as he also had signed his contract with William Stewart in 1932.

There's another story perhaps more suggestive of an Olympian attitude. Bill Randle, who at the time was an influential disc-jockey and impresario in Cleveland, remembers going to a club in Washington, D.C., possibly the Bengazi, with Art and Willis Conover, America's international disc-jockey (via the Voice of America). Ben Webster was appearing with a trio. Webster was more than just a fan of Tatum's, he idolized him—years after Tatum's death Webster was still carrying Tatum tapes around the world with him. And it went deeper than merely admiring his playing; Whitney Balliett has told of visiting Webster once when he found him shaving: "Some Art Tatum records were on and he kept running out of the bathroom and mimicking fantastic Tatum figures. Then he started telling me what Tatum was like . . . and the next thing I knew he was crying." On this night in Washington, Webster wanted Tatum to sit in, but Tatum (according to Randle) didn't like to play for nothing, at least not in a commercial club (Harlem after hours might be another matter). Webster finally prevailed, by giving Art a hundred-dollar bill (Tatum checked to make sure it wasn't a ten). Tatum then climbed onto the stand but immediately set an impossible tempo for Webster to play with, so fast that Webster had to drop out after a chorus and a half. It was another of Art's non-verbal, musical commentaries on the proceedings around him, and hardly a warm response to Webster's admiration. And it was Art's never-yielding stance of independence, which Randle learned something about in his two years of dealing with him: "He wanted to do everything in his own time. You almost had to learn how to lead him, in his own way, and even then you couldn't predict what he would do. You might think you were manipulating him, and he'd just be manipulating you up the wall. He was blind, and he developed all kinds of very sensitive apparatuses for insulating himself from hassles and a lot of things."

IN 1942 FATS Waller had appeared in a solo piano concert in Carnegie Hall, before solo jazz piano concerts had become one of the conventional ways in which jazz might be presented. In this he was a little ahead, once again, of his good friend Art Tatum (although the Waller concert was not very favorably reviewed). But in 1945 Tatum made his own first appearance in a jazz concert format, and from then on he was on the concert circuit regularly. For most of these concerts Tatum was but one star in a whole constellation, but in 1946 and '47 he did a series of solo concerts organized by Bill Randle, who was then an important disc jockey in Cleveland (who has since had several other careers and recently been awarded an honorary Doctor of Humanities degree by Bowling Green State University).

> As a solo artist, and as a true artist, they were the only concerts he ever did. The rest of them were jazz concerts, where he'd play with guys and stuff. These were just solo piano. He was a piano [pause] player, a concert artist, just like Horowitz and Rubinstein. I was the only person who ever put him on in that format. For the rest of them he had a trio or he'd play and then they'd have a jazz group. They were jazz oriented, put on by jazz promoters and that sort of thing. He didn't like to play as a concert artist. That was a lot of work. He had to be fairly disciplined, you know, he had to be on time, and he had to play an hour and then have an intermission, or 40 minutes and intermission, and then play again. You know, sometimes in a club setting he'd play four hours in a row, and sometimes he'd play five minutes. He was a very loose cat.

Even if there was something in Art that liked the concert format there was something else that wanted more spontaneity, and probably wanted a more social atmosphere. There was also something that wanted its usual ration of beer, and Randle did what he could: "I used to have literally a galvanized washtub full of beer, Pabst Blue Ribbon, backstage." Still these concerts were enormously profitable for Art. At a time when the Art Tatum Trio was getting $2000 a week, to split three ways and for playing five or six sets a night, Randle managed to pay Art alone $2500 for the same number of nights—more than three times his usual income and for many fewer hours of work.

As he lost his hold on 52nd Street he was compensated to some degree by a move into university and community concert halls all across the country—not only in such cities as Boston (at the renowned Symphony Hall), Philadelphia, Chicago, and Pittsburgh, but also in less obvious places like Altoona, Dayton, Gary, and Milwaukee. Norman Granz, a onetime film editor (he had a hand in the making of an early and now-classic jazz film *Jamming the Blues*) had begun promoting jazz through his Jazz at the Philharmonic (JATP) concert series. Granz was an aggressive promoter and he hit upon a format which turned out to be hugely successful—and which in effect rescued a lot of great musicians whose careers were in free-fall, as a result of either the be-bop phenomenon or the demise of the big band era.

> I'm sure Norman paid him a lot of money. Norman paid musicians very high. JATP took over people like Tatum and Lester Young and Coleman Hawkins and Howard McGhee and Roy Eldridge, Flip Phillips, the guys from those big bands that were kind of breaking up at the time. JATP was touring all the time. I mean all the time, so they were playing 80–90 concerts in a six-month period. That was full-time work when you consider the kind of money they were getting. Tatum worked for Granz a lot. He did a lot of JATP, 'cause I remember that.

One might not agree with the Granz aesthetic (one acquaintance quoted him as saying, "I'm not selling music, I'm selling excitement"), and one might suspect that the gruelling schedule and the nightly requirement of whipping audiences into a frenzy had something to do with pushing musicians toward burnout. Nevertheless most musicians who worked for Granz would probably agree that he couldn't have come along at a better time. (One wonders, however, what Art did after those concerts, at least in such places as Gary or Salt Lake City or Seattle.)

None of these concerts was recorded, and nothing Tatum did on the JATP circuit was ever released (if any recordings were even made of Art's performances). There are recordings made at a jazz concert in April of 1949 at the Shrine Auditorium in Los Angeles, organized by West Coast disc-jockey and promoter, Gene Norman. Tatum never adapted his repertoire to the changing and now bop-oriented tastes of the public, and for this concert (which was presumably typical for him) he chose such well-worn articles from his closet as "Humoresque," "Someone to Watch Over Me," "Yesterdays," "Willow Weep for Me," a Gershwin medley, and "The Kerry Dance." Never mind—the audience for Tatum standards was still out there and he was in superb form; the concert was a success and the recording was bought and issued by Columbia Records. Whitney Balliett praised these live performances to the sky:

> . . . Tatum is a perfect whole in the 1949 Los Angeles concert. Almost every number has passages to ponder and weep over—the runs being poured back and forth between the two hands in "Someone to Watch Over Me"; a "Yesterdays" that is a complete rebuilding of the tune, from the first note to the last; a tidal-wave, up-tempo "I Know That You Know"; a delicate and (so rare for Tatum) fond version of "Willow Weep for Me"; an incredible light and deft takeoff to boogie-woogie in "Tatum-Pole Boogie"; and a "Man I Love" with an arpeggio, lasting some eight bars, that no other pianist would dare because it is impossible. [*Ecstasy*, 114]

In 1949 Tatum signed a contract with the newly formed Capitol Records and recorded twenty-six, mostly familiar, titles for them. Gunther Schuller, echoing Balliett on the concert, has referred to these first three sessions for Capitol as an announcement of Tatum's maturity, and they clearly included several masterpieces: "Willow Weep for Me" (a studio version this time) and "Aunt Hagar's Blues," performances that Schuller thinks may be Art Tatum's "crowning achievements." He devotes several pages to a close analysis of them. What he likes about them is clear:

> . . . "Willow" is Tatum at his most eloquent and concise. Here everything is of a piece. Whereas often in earlier performances, despite whatever brilliant playing, one can get nervous with the constant intrusions and deviations of decorative runs and harmonic detours, in "Willow" every musical gesture evolves organically out of its predecessor.
>
> . . .

> Another new element in Tatum's playing at this time . . . was a more mature, more clearly delineated use of the chorus structure. From this period on Tatum seemed to have understood the need to give each chorus its special character, even mood perhaps, rather than his more helter-skelter earlier approach of allowing any and all ideas to be crowded into a single chorus at will. In this more discriminating approach . . . Tatum gains a firmer grasp on the "compositional" lucidity of his improvisations.
>
> [*Swing Era*, 492–93]

There is more than a little irony in the fact that Art's trajectory of musical growth reached a high point while his public acclaim was on the decline. It is also ironic that while Tatum received relatively little exposure through solo concerts, his arrangements are now (1991) starting to show up in serious concerts played by young, highly versatile pianists (for example, Steven Mayer and Jon Kimura Parker) who include Tatum classics such as "Runnin' Wild," "Hallelujah," or "Gang of Nothin" along with such standard classical fare as Liszt, Beethoven, Schubert, and Max Reger.

TATUM WAS NOW, in 1949, forty years old. This was the year that Miles Davis recorded his landmark album, *The Birth of the Cool,* and Tatum may have been considered a throwback in time by the younger bop generation. There is no doubt that he was in the middle of some lean years, with regard to club dates and recordings, but in terms of his own musical development and in the judgment of critics with a larger perspective he seems to have been in his prime and still going strong.

Tatum's "Other" Children

"Say, you look like me! Who's your momma?"

FATS WALLER

AT LEAST THREE people, including Orlando, have been characterized as children of Art Tatum. Any children of Art's deserve mention, and might even throw some light on his life, so it was necessary to follow these leads. And indeed the stories turned out to be interesting.

Most people I talked to believed Art had no children at all. The first inkling I had of Tatum offspring was when several people mentioned meeting "Tatum's son" in Germany, in military uniform . . . At first I wondered whether someone was trading on the Tatum name to sell mutual funds to musicians, or some such scam. Eventually, however, Rudolph Perry, Russell McGown, and Art's brother and sister all vouched for Orlando's existence and his career in the military, and there was no doubting his authenticity.

However, knowing about Orlando did not clear up my confusion when others reported meeting "Art Tatum, Jr." here in the States, always in civilian clothes and usually around Baltimore. I began to believe there might be two sons. But the few people who were able to report with authority about his marriages insisted that neither of his two wives, Ruby and Geraldine, had had any children. Pursuing a few slender leads led indeed to Baltimore and to an interesting person, but not necessarily to a clear conclusion.

In 1983, *Cadence* published a fascinating interview with "Art Tatum, Jr." (Whitehead). The careful reader will note that this should have been an interview with Art himself, since he was born Arthur, Jr. But it was an interview with a man who claimed Art Tatum as his father. I asked the interviewer how he came across him:

> I went to see him—he was playing around town quite a bit, and I had seen him—he was playing at a free afternoon concert at an old folks' home, and I went to see him. He was like a really good cocktail piano player. He wasn't gonna make you forget Art Tatum, Sr., but—I talked to him a little bit and he seemed like a very interesting guy, and so I just decided what the hell, do an interview, so we set it up. . . .

In the published interview "Art Tatum, Jr." sounded intelligent, articulate, and intense. He also sounded like a man who had been through extremely severe psychological trials, which he attributed not only to his having Art Tatum for a father but to having a highly religious mother who was determined "Art, Jr." should not follow in his footsteps. This conflict, he said, had dominated his life, and at his father's death there was a crisis. He gave up the piano for twelve years and worked and traveled abroad, especially in Africa, where he "lived as a primitive for about three years," ate poorly and drank contaminated water, and also taught English and music and wrote stories and plays. But, he said, "I was able to get a lot out of it, I was able to come into my own as an individual. I was able to search my soul, and have my soul search for the reality that was lacking, and by the time I got back to the States (April 1981) I was together, whereas before I went I wasn't really together." Somewhere "Art, Jr." received a degree in literature, and also a Ph.D. in etymology (or else they were the same degree, it was hard to tell). "I did this because I had to build a personality apart from the legendary heir of a genius."

He also claimed to have a degree in theology, and while in Egypt he registered at the University of Cairo for a year, "because I wanted to find out about the God thing." (Had he been listening to George Bush speeches?)

There is more. He made an heroic decision to put God to the test, "to prove or disprove his concern about me as an individual . . . either he was gonna relate to me personally, like he did to Moses, or I'm gonna' tell the world it's phony, that it's a whole lie . . . I mean after all, he allowed my old man to die, a true inspiring genius to die, a true inspiring genius to die prematurely; there must be some breakdown in communication, and I'm gonna find out what it is."

And he got his hero's reward:

> The seventh day of my fast, I did have an encounter with a power that is inexplainable. I was taken totally out of my physical mind, without losing perspective of the material world. But I was set in that kind of realm where beings made themselves known to me. I had heard about angels but I never really believed they would make themselves known in this day and age. I thought it was totally of a different dispensation, of a different dimension in time. But I experienced what few men can truly witness. I was given a perfectly new body. My system inside was totally renovated. I was cured of the ulcer . . . and when the X-rays were taken again of my quote unquote malignant system, there was no sign of the slightest infection. And from the seventh to the tenth day I thought that I was being transformed from a human into a spirit, and I did not expect to live beyond that time . . . It took me 60 days after that to come back down to earth, mentally, and relate as a normal human being."

This person gets your attention. He said he was born July 7, 1935, in New York City (which would have been two years after Orlando's birth and one month before Art married Ruby), but that Art and his mother separated very early. "Art, Jr."'s mother was "an early convert to Christianity" and she "was prone to be dedicated as missionary in the Protestant faith, and didn't want me into the nightclub circuit . . ." Mother kept father and son apart, and it was only in his 'teens that he was able to sneak into New York to hear him and to get acquainted with him, secretly.

There was a second interview in 1986, where he is described as a man who "has earned a bedrock peace that is earned only through excruciating self-examination, through questioning everything around him" (Warren). Here we learn that Art, Jr.'s mother was named Lillian, and a marriage is claimed:

> When Lillian Tatum left New York for Sumpter County, S.C. in 1935, she was not accompanied by her husband, although she was carrying his child. They had separated, their son says today, because Lillian had tired of Art's way of life. Deeply religious—she later became a missionary—Lillian no longer could abide being the wife of a jazz man and all that it implied . . . She and the baby stayed in South Carolina until he was 3, when they moved back to New York.

There are several inconsistencies, within the interviews and between them, and the question of where Art, Jr. was born, New York or South Carolina, is just one of them. (The Eubie Blake Center established that there is no birth record for "Art Tatum, Jr." in Sumter County.) We learn that he attended Hunter College (but Hunter College says they have no record of the attendance of an Art Tatum, Jr. Of course he may have used a different name, as he told Whitehead he had done at one time. For that matter, whatever name he may have used at Hunter may have been his real name.) He said that he now prefers teaching to playing in public, although "it's made me not as secure financially as I have been. I can get up to $10,000 a week when I'm playing." (Where, and how, a lot of musicians would like to know!) In this interview, surprisingly, there is no mention of the odyssey into Africa, but he does refer to a revelation about twelve years after his father died: ". . . in 1968, he dreamed three straight nights that his father talked to him and encouraged him to make his own career." In both interviews Art, Jr. claims an association with the famous blind vocalist, Al Hibbler, who indeed was a friend of Art Tatum's. (Unfortunately, Hibbler in a personal interview disclaimed any knowledge of this alleged son of Art's and denies that "Art, Jr." was ever his accompanist, as he claimed to have been.)

This second interview was part of an announcement that Art Tatum, Jr., was to play a concert at the Eubie Blake Cultural Center in Baltimore. Within days the paper received four calls questioning his claim to be Art Tatum's son, and both the paper and the Cultural Center made efforts to resolve the issue. Karl and Arline both denied any knowledge of Lillian or her son. "Mr. Tatum, Jr.," the paper said, "acknowledged earlier this week that he does not have a birth certificate, although he does have a Maryland driver's license in the name of Art Tatum, Jr. 'I am who I say I am,' he said. 'They [doubters] don't know who my father is. I know who my father is.'"

Who *is* his father? I've been unable to locate "Art Tatum, Jr." to discuss this with him. One of the people who called the *Sun* to protest this person's appropriation of the name Tatum claimed that he or she had known him under the name Cato. The Director of the Eubie Blake Center remembered that a pianist named Cato was working around Baltimore in the early 1980s, but could not remember whether this was the same person who later approached him as "Art Tatum, Jr." Whoever he is, he sounds complex and interesting and severely troubled. He knows a lot about Art Tatum and, what is even more persuasive, he sounds as though he truly believes what he says. But one can't help noticing a number of contradictions and essential ambiguities in his story, and the absence of even one other human being who can confirm his parentage seems damning.

But no final word is really possible. Might Art, especially flushed with his successes in the years 1933 to 1935, have had an affair with a woman who turned out to have serious guilt about it, who even turned to religion to manage the guilt? And passed the guilt and conflict on to her son? To tell the truth, nobody ever knew where Art was when he wasn't at the piano. As Leroy "Snake" White said to me, explaining why he didn't know anything about Art's private life: "Well, see, I was married. After 8 or 9 in the morning, I'd go on home. See, I don't know where he would go." Maybe he did have a liaison with a Lillian, and maybe he did spend some time with "Art, Jr." when he was adolescent. I doubt it, but I'd like to know more. We may have heard the last of him, however. He has disappeared from the Baltimore area. It's rumored that he headed out to San Francisco, but it's doubtful he would use the Tatum name in California, since somewhere along the way Art's widow and/or some close friends threatened "Art, Jr." with a lawsuit.

SEVERAL PEOPLE TOLD me about hearing Tatum's "daughter," Mai Tatum, play and sing, usually in St. Louis. She impressed them, and they liked her. I eventually made contact with a man who had spent a lot of time with her, in the 1980s, and was utterly convinced that she was a real Tatum. She certainly did not fit into the picture of Art's life as I understood it, but it was another lead that had to be followed.

In several of the annual issues of *The Music Index*, a guide to musical subjects in periodicals, I had noted but only out of the corner of my mind that Art's entry was followed by one for "Mai Tatum." When I first saw these I ignored them because I had no reason to think that Tatum had fathered a child. But after talking to several people who were reasonably convinced that Mai was indeed related to Art, I dug up the references noted in those entries.

In 1960, *Variety* ran the following item under the heading "New acts":

> We went to see Frank Driggs at Columbia and were directed to the recording studio on the seventh floor, where he was auditioning a lady who sang and played piano. The piano solos between vocals, though not performed with comparable facility, contained runs and ideas reminiscent of Art Tatum's. There was good reason for this. The pianist was Tatum's daughter. Mae Tatum was singing "I Waited Too Long," and song and voice were familiar to us. We have a 78 single on the Trumpet label . . . and it couples "I Don't Care" and "I Waited Too Long" by the Beverly White Trio. The latter composition, a ballad with good,

lovelorn lyrics, is by Beverly White, Mae's professional pseudonym. The other side, "I Don't Care," is a swinger and it gave us a better clue to where we had heard her before. Remember the 1937 records by Claude Hopkins of "Sunday," "Swingin' Down the Lane," "Honey," "June Night," and "My Kinda' Love"? The singer was Baby White, the same girl. Though never awarded critical favor, these vocals had an infectious and individual quality. Some she sang with restraint and a kind of transparent sophistication, but there were lines of climax and rhythmic emphasis that were punching home with a vigorous and earthy conviction. Everybody's ears then were full of Ella Fitzgerald, Billie Holiday, and Mildred Bailey, of course.

It turns out that Mai (or Mae) Tatum, alias Beverly or Baby White, had also done some professional appearances on the same stage with Pearl Bailey, and I was able to ask Pearl's husband, the drummer Louie Bellson, about it.

Yes, Beverly was on the road with us—she played the Apollo with us, the Howard Theater here in Washington, also the Royal Theater in Baltimore, and she did quite a lot of travelling with us. Pearl always thought—and me too—that she just had a marvellous voice. I don't think she played the piano with us . . . Maybe one tune or so—mostly singing right up front, at the microphone. . . . We're talking about, oh, the '50s, this was after I left Duke's band, so it had to be around '55, '56, '57. She told Pearl and I then that she was Art Tatum's daughter. She took a lot of pride in it, and her great association with him. . . . She was a very dear person, very talented person, surprised us, we didn't know that Tatum had a daughter, you know. . . . She was marvellous to work with, and she broke it up on the solos—she had great audience reactions. Well, you know, Pearl was a perfectionist when it came to talent. She wouldn't allow another, especially another lady to sing on the show with her if she wasn't talented, you know. She sang things like "Pretend," all the standard tunes, you know, the old goodies. Beverly went on the front part of the show, and then Pearl closed the show. I would say that Beverly was around, maybe, 40, something like that. I'm just guessing.

The dates Bellson mentions signal a problem. To have been 40 in 1956 is to have been born in 1916, only seven years after her alleged father. Of course Louis was only guessing at her age.

In 1972 the *St. Louis Post-Dispatch* published an interview with Mai, identifying her unquestioningly as Art Tatum's daughter. In the article she claims a master's degree from the Juilliard School of Music (Juilliard searched its records for me and found no registered student with the names of either Mai Tatum or Beverly White) and mentions that she is writing an autobiography. The writer of the article (Richmond) reported that she had worked for ten years, 1950–60, at the Victorian Club, "one of the most exclusive spots in St. Louis," and she was now re-opening in St. Louis, presumably after an indeterminate absence, at Benedetti's Tumble-In, a piano bar that was not quite so exclusive. (The era 1950–60 includes the period when she was working in theaters with Pearl Bailey and Louis Bellson, but nothing was said about that in the article.) In the interview she emphasized her singing:

> I didn't make a name for myself with my piano playing. I started as a singer and even changed my name to Beverly White. I didn't want to trade on my Daddy's fame. As a matter of fact, early in my career my piano playing got me fired from the Duke Ellington band. I was Ellington's vocalist, and we were playing at the Zanzibar Club in New York. I heard this blind singer from Little Rock named Al Hibbler and arranged an audition with Ellington for him. Al came to the club and waited around, but Ellington was in no hurry. He spotted Betty Grable and Harry James at one of the tables and went over and chatted with them. I felt sorry for Al just waiting like that and when one of the band members suggested that I play piano for Al to give him his chance, I did. Al brought down the house and was

hired, but Ellington wasn't happy with me. He let me know that he was the only piano player in the band. One of the other members of the band spoke up and told Duke he was mad because I played better than he did. A little while later I got a note saying I was fired. But I stayed on. The club owner hired me and I still sang with the band. It didn't seem to bother Ellington. . . . But after that I gave the piano a wide berth.

After that she sang, she said, with a number of big bands and was in the original cast of *Cabin in the Sky*. She took up the piano again, and acknowledged the family name of Tatum, only at the urging of Nat King Cole and Macdonald Carey.

When I talked with Al Hibbler about "Art, Jr." I also asked him about Mai. Al remembered her as Baby White, said she was indeed singing with Duke at that point and he used to love her voice, and even confirmed that she left Duke about the same time that he joined him. But he denied she had anything to do with his New York audition:

Betty [Roche] and Ray [Nance] and Ben [Webster] told me one night, said "Man, come on down and listen to the band." So I went down there, and I went back, I said, "Duke, can I have an audition with your band?" [He said] "I'm busy, I ain't got no time, and the show's about to go on. I'll tell you what you do, you go on out in the audience, and order what you want"—and that's it. So I went on out there and I sat down. And Duke was back in the dressing room, before the show went on, you know how you piddle around, gettin' himself together for the show. So Ben Webster go get on the piano, start playing "Summertime." And he say, "Root," he call Ray Nance Root, "go get Hibbler and bring him over here. Put him on the bandstand, hear him sing 'Summertime.'" The band's playing, you know. And I start to sing, and the house broke up. Duke hear all this racket, you know, they applaudin' and hollerin' and carryin' on. Duke ran out on the bandstand, said, "What you doin' on my bandstand? Do you know

'Solitude?'" I said, "Yeah." So he played "Solitude," and I sang that. He played "Mood Indigo" and I sang that. Then he say, "You go on back there in the dressing room and cool it." Later on he came back there, say, "You really know how to turn it on, don't you?" I said, "Well, I try, you know." "Come on back down tomorrow night." So I went down the next night, and he come up with this, "Ladies and gentlemen, we got a singer up here who thinks he can sing, and we're gonna bring him out and see what you-all think about him." "Sunny Side of the Street," playing different songs, I was singin' em all. So anyway— do you know I was in the band two weeks before I knew it?

Officials at the Musicians' Union in St. Louis were skeptical of Mai's claim about her relationship to Tatum and confirmed that her real name was Beverly White, but were understandably reluctant to accuse her of any blatant deception. She had failed to give them a birth date when she joined and the last year she paid any dues was 1978. They claimed that "In 1971 we knew she was over 40"; if that's true she could not have been born any later than 1931 (when Art was twenty-two, and before Marnette and Orlando). It might of course have been earlier.

I talked with Charlie Fox, a St. Louis piano player born in 1920 and still active (he often tours with Clark Terry, another St. Louisan), and he was adamant: "She couldn't be Art Tatum's daughter, she's as old as he is!" He remembered that Beverly was working at the Plantation Club in St. Louis when he (Fox) was only about ten, and thought she must have been eighteen or twenty then (i.e., 1930). According to Charlie, the name she was born with was not Beverly but Magnolia. And I talked to an authentic old-timer, Gus Perryman, born in 1901, who lived across the street from Magnolia in the mid-1920s and he remembers her as "a few years younger" than he was.

The evidence seems to put Magnolia White's birth in the general vicinity of 1910, which clearly rules out Art Tatum as a parent. The state of Missouri has no birth recorded under that name, so her real origin remains unknown. Al Hibbler thinks she came from Peoria, Illinois.

Mai's voice on those early Claude Hopkins recordings sounds adorable, and in privately taped interviews done around 1980 she still sounds charming as she talks about her "Daddy." Her life-story is poignant, even if there was a bit of the "con-woman" about her. (She once sold a piano to a well-known St. Louis pianist and band leader, Russ David, on the strength of its having belonged to her "father," Art Tatum. David paid dearly for it, but now believes he was "conned.") She seems to have been a talented lady, capable of achievements on her own without any need to invoke the reputation of a more famous "relative." Her career seemed once to have had some substance to it, based on her very real musical talent, but it crumbled and the name Tatum did her little or no good in the long run. She died around 1988 or 1989, after some years of illness, in complete poverty and obscurity.

1950–1956

"Won't you tell her please to put on some speed,
follow my lead, oh how I need,
someone to watch over me."

"Goin' home, goin' home . . ."

SOMETIME IN THE early 1950s Art and Ruby's marriage collapsed in a nasty heap. They had set up house in Los Angeles in the late 1930s and had been married for more than fifteen years, but almost no one knows anything about Art's life at home. Whatever his domestic arrangements were, Art was absent from them for much if not most of those fifteen years. Karl, Art's younger brother who traveled with him between 1939 and 1942, has said that Art generally got back to Los Angeles at least twice a year, for anything from two to five weeks at a time. Ruby almost never traveled with him, according to all reports, and even when she was with him he hardly seemed to include her in his life, as Red Norvo told me: "I probably saw her on the streets a dozen or more times, and never associated her or didn't know [she was his wife]. But—

you know, Art's not the kind of guy that would introduce his wife to you. The average guy would say, 'Here's my wife.' She might be standing right there and he'd talk to you and never say a word about her." There were many people who knew Art professionally but who didn't know for sure whether he was married or not.

One of the few people I've talked to who knew Ruby at all, Bernice Lawson, has said that she was outgoing and likeable, but that she hardly ever left the house. She had no children, and Bernice never mentioned any interest of Ruby's that might have given her life some meaning or content during her many months—years when you add them up—apart from Art. Ruby's mother lived with them in the beginning, and that might have postponed the growth of loneliness and resentment on Ruby's part, but we don't know how long she was there. Ruby took as good care of Art as she could when he was around, and tried to give him the foods recommended in light of his diabetes (although in view of his life style away from her that would be like pushing back the tide with a broom). The point is that those who knew her say she cared for him, and he apparently cared for her, in his way. Ernie Lewis says that although she had no musical training Art taught her piano—"He had her playing some nice changes. Yeah, he told me about it, he used to talk about her all the time." But one wonders: did Ruby want to learn the piano, or did Art Tatum require the piano as a bridge to the people in his life?

There is no point in lingering over Art and Ruby's relationship. There is simply too little to go on. All we know for sure is that in the later years Ruby began to drink more and more, to the degree that the few people who knew her considered her an alcoholic. Art's sister Arline talked about Ruby's problem drinking and some of its consequences:

> No, she wasn't too bad. But when she'd start, I mean, she'd just keep goin', but otherwise she was a good girl, very well talented, you know, and very well educated, and—she just liked to drink. I guess she be by herself so much, I guess that was maybe the reason why, it accumulated, because she was by herself. They didn't have any kids. I don't think Art's a kid fella. He only had that one. Eventually they got

a divorce 'cause Art—there was lots of things that Ruby would do—see, Art was like Poppa, he believe in takin' care of home. And Ruby did so many things, he was afraid to leave the money with her, afraid she wouldn't pay the bills right—that's why he sent for me—afraid maybe somebody would come in, rob her or something. And then when he would go away, then she started—when she got out there in California there was some guy, I met the guy, he didn't tell me his name, there was some guy, the guy didn't know I was there. And this guy came by the house, and then someone told me about the guy. He just had Ruby, you know—every time that he'd want something done he'd come to Ruby and git it done. So finally I found out what was going on, you know, different things, he would go this place and that place and git things on Ruby, you know what I mean, clothes, at the stores where they traded. I found out she was givin' 'em to him, so I, I didn't fault him as much as I did Ruby. But then she told me the truth. She thought the world of me, anyway, and I thought the world of her. She told me—I said, "Ruby, why you do things like that?"—you know, we sit and talk—I said, "You're satisfied—" She says, "You know I love Art, you know. I don't know why I do it." She says, "I never do it when I'm sober." She says, "I only do these things when I'm drinkin'." And she did. She only did these things when she be drinkin'. And that's the reason why I think this guy would see that she had drinks in her before, you know, before he approached her to do, you know. But she, she'd tell me anything. So then Art started fooling around with Geraldine . . .

Bernice believes it might not have happened if Art had devoted more time to her (just as she believes Art might still be alive if somebody had taken better care of him), but we can't know that. The situation that swamped Art and Ruby was nothing unique—perhaps most jazz musicians were gone from their wives for long stretches. Lots of marriages survived this, and lots did not. Many musicians either opted for studio work, which kept them in one city, or got out of the business altogether in order to have a conventional family life; Tatum did not have these options. Things turned completely sour and bitter between the Tatums, and Ruby sued for divorce. Her complaint was "That on or about the 25th day of February, 1951, and continuing for more than one year preceding the commencement of this action, the said defendant disregarding the solemnity of his marriage vows, wilfully and without cause deserted and abandoned the plaintiff, and ever since has and still continues to do wilfully and without cause desert and abandon said plaintiff, and to live separate and apart from her, without any sufficient cause, and/or reason and against her will, and without her consent."

The interlocutory decree was awarded in January of 1954 and the final decree on February 2nd, 1955. The property settlement they agreed upon apparently awarded everything to Ruby including the house and even (although this is hard to fathom) Art's piano, which he used to brag was the best piano on the West Coast. Art was deeply angry with her (according to Ernie Lewis) and it sounds like it was mutual. From then on Ruby drank even more—Bernice Lawson said she saw her on the street several years after the divorce and could hardly recognize her, she looked so bad. She died within a few years of the divorce.

Art was married for a second time, to Geraldine Williamson, in November of 1955. He had apparently been living with her for some time before that, so Geraldine could not have been surprised by his ways, which had not changed. Jay McShann, the pianist, remembers driving Art's car for him, touring the Los Angeles after-hours spots with him in this period: "It'd be getting around six a.m. I'd keep telling him we'd better be getting on home. His old lady would be good and mad. But Art would say to me, "Oh, don't you worry none about my old lady. I'll think of something to tell her." Mrs. Tatum [the year of McShann's story is not clear]—she was a very nice lady. And because of our late hours and her staying up until we got in, she had already confronted me earlier. She'd said to me, "Mr. McShann, I don't know about you—why are you keeping my husband out so late, every night?" (Is this what Art thought up to tell her?) On this particular night McShann finally got Tatum home. "Mrs. Tatum met us at the door and she had blood in her eye. She looked at me, as I handed her the keys to the car, and she said, 'Mr. McShann, I always thought you were a nice man. But from the way you've been keeping Art out I just don't know what kind of man you are!' So I told her as I was backing out the door, 'Don't worry. Everything's all right,' and I took off. . . . The truth is, I couldn't do much about the situation" (Spellman, p. 23).

Ernie Lewis says that Geraldine had worked as a telephone operator, was tall and good-looking, and that Art was "crazy about her." In fact the only time Ernie ever saw Art down in the dumps was once when he was having some kind of trouble with Geraldine, before they were married. She was a close friend of two of Art's closest friends, Lois and Rozelle Gayle, and she may have been paired with another of Art's intimate friends, Eddie Beal, before taking up with Art. She was a very different person from Ruby, much more quiet and socially distant. She was retiring with everyone, but people have implied to me that she had little or no use for most of Art's musician friends, who were too rough for her taste, and almost none of the ones I talked to knew anything about her. She apparently had no particular interest in music or in the fact that Art was a musician, and Ernie Lewis remembered an incident that surprised him: "I remember a time he brought her to San Franciso. Both of them were staying at the St. Francis Hotel, he was playing in the neighborhood, down the street there. She wasn't concerned about him playing, she never would go, she stayed up in her room. I'll never forget that." Art and Geraldine were married for only a year and ten days before she was widowed.

ART STAYED BUSY with club dates in the early 1950s, but from the session for Capitol in late 1949 until December of 1953 he made not a single solo studio recording. There was never a very strong demand for his recordings, but it seems terribly unfortunate that just when his conception of jazz piano had reached the zenith of "maturity" and "lucidity" the interest in recording him should reach a nadir. There was one studio effort in 1952 with a trio (including Slam Stewart and Everett Barksdale), but the only other recordings from these years were all done live, especially at Cafe Society and at the Embers, and released long after his death.

Art was still listening to every piano player around, and even a few words of encouragement (he seldom gave more) still carried enormous weight. Tommy Flanagan said that Tatum's description of his playing as "very nice" was one of the greatest compliments he ever received (Ullman, *Jazz Lives*). Don Asher, Hampton Hawes's biographer, has passed on Hawes's account of his encounter with him in 1956, when he was twenty-seven:

> I was working with Stan Getz at the Tiffany Club in L. A. when Art Tatum showed up at the bar. Didn't even know he was in the club till he came lumbering out of the shadows, head turned to the side and up—like Bela Lugosi coming at you, scare you if you didn't know who it was. Moved right up to me and said, "Son, you hot. I came down to hear you." Well, I knew I was playing good, getting there, but in the overall rundown of players I considered myself comparatively lukewarm at the time. And here's Art Tatum looking weird at me out of the corner of one eye, saying, "Son, you hot." I said, "I'm glad you came and I wish you'd show me some of that stuff you do with your left hand." He said, "I will if you'll show me some of your right-hand stuff. Why don't you come by my house?" Gave me the address and we shook hands on it. I kept thinking, "Son, you hot." From Tatum—that's like the king telling you you're one of the most loyal and courageous subjects of the land. Man came down to hear me play, shook my hand, said I was hot. It messed up my mind . . .

Somewhere in the early 1950s Norman Granz came into play, in a big way. Granz, the founder and producer of the fabulously successful (in commercial terms) "Jazz at the Philharmonic" series of concerts, and owner of his own record label (Clef), decided that Tatum had not been adequately presented on records. This seems to have been a very personal, subjective decision; Granz simply wanted to make a monument to what he saw as Tatum's genius. His plan for Tatum was unprecedented in the recording industry: invite him into the studio, start the tape, and let him play whatever he felt like playing. In two days in December 1953 Tatum recorded 70 solos, and in two more sessions he completed a total of 124 solos, 121 of which were issued on fourteen 12-inch LP records (they have recently been re-released on compact discs). At the time this was an astonishing enterprise, the most extensive recording that had been done of any jazz figure. The tunes were largely standards from Tatum's repertoire, a potpourri of some of the best of American popular songs, most of which he had recorded before. Granz set no time limits, and many of Tatum's performances in this setting run to five and even six minutes. All the same it's surprising how often in this completely free situation he voluntarily limited himself to a three- to four-minute treatment, the kind he had learned to provide under the constraints of the old 78-rpm recordings.

Granz also had the idea of combining Tatum with various groups of all-stars of Granz's own choosing, such as Lionel Hampton, Buddy Rich, Benny Carter, Louie Bellson, Roy Eldridge, Harry (Sweets) Edison, Buddy DeFranco, and Ben Webster, and this led to a further seven recording sessions and a release of some fifty-nine cuts.

To be given such an opportunity—to immortalize oneself in whatever way one chooses—might this not make a performer at least self-conscious, if not nervously paralyzed? Even such established artists as Stan Kenton and Nat Cole had severe anxiety about making even one solo album. What was Art Tatum's attitude to the proceedings? Barry McRea has given us the best picture we have (a better picture might come from Norman Granz himself, who is still alive, but I've been unable to penetrate his outer defenses, a pleasant lady known to me only as Mary Ann):

> Granz was . . . a little unsure of the great pianist and the first session was approached with some trepidation. He laid on a good supply of beer and did everything possible to foster a good atmosphere. Such preparations were unnecessary and the outcome was very different from that which

Granz expected. Tatum, an inveterate basketball fan brought with him a portable radio and between each number he left the piano stool and tuned into a game in which he was particularly interested. The beer flowed steadily and a feeling of genuine cordiality was maintained throughout. At one stage, Granz realized to his horror that he would run out of tape in mid-chorus. At first he conjured with the idea of scrapping this number without telling Tatum but finally elected to admit his oversight. Tatum was highly amused and, after establishing exactly where the break had occurred, started a new tape at that exact spot without even the minutest change of tempo. In recounting this story, Granz failed to nominate the title but added that such was the pianist's complete mastery that the tape join did not arrest the swing of the solo concerned. It was also perhaps typical that such a perfectionist should decline to hear playbacks. He explained that this was because he was always aware when an error had occurred.

Not only aware, one should add, but probably able to make it sound like no error at all.

Tatum's approach to this remarkable situation was simply to do what he did every other day and night of his life, exercise his talent at the keyboard, in as natural and unself-conscious a way as breathing in and out. He did it in the same spirit that he might have done it at Harold Brown's house, or Bernice Lawson's. I have no sense that this was an occasion that Tatum felt stimulated to live up to, or that he brought any particular ambition to these sessions at all. And maybe that's easy to understand; after all, he himself had been the occasion up to which others had to live for many years now. Tatum knew what Tatum was supposed to sound like, and he knew he could do it. In fact, in Bill Randle's opinion, "He knew he was a great player, in fact he thought he was the greatest player of all." But at the same time he was completely unself-conscious about it; it was a fact of nature, just a given in the universe. As Eric Larrabee wrote, Tatum was "generous of himself with a prodigality that seems almost naive and childlike, as though he couldn't imagine being otherwise. . . . He took himself as he was; if there was any divine discontent stirring in Art Tatum, it escaped the attention of those who knew him." I'm reminded of the remark that France's General Charles DeGaulle made in his autobiography: "Whenever I'm uncertain what to do I simply ask myself, 'What would General DeGaulle do?' "

This whole unusual recording project received a lot of critical attention. The solo recordings in particular provoked a minor storm of controversy. Granz called the series, "The Genius of Art Tatum," and immediately upon their issue he was chastised, by the French critic André Hodeir, for abusing the term "genius." That started it. Billy Taylor then rushed in to defend Tatum, and Martin Williams argued that "Hardly anyone attempted to deal with M. Hodeir's real point," which was that the world could have expected more from Art Tatum (*Art,* 173). Years later Gunther Schuller called Hodeir's remarks "petulant, cavilling, unreasonable, and often incoherent." Schuller expressed his own opinion of Tatum's "heroic effort": "Even the least of these belong to Tatum's mature work, and the best of them may be numbered amongst his very finest life-long achievements." Hodeir, on the other hand, while praising much in Tatum, had given as his summary opinion of the Granz project: "Equipped with greater technical means and a better imagination than one finds in any other pianist, he has an easy time doing superbly what I would have preferred not to have seen him bother with at all" (quoted in Williams, *Art,* 176). It's clear that not only jazz harmony, but also jazz criticism, involves some dangerous waters that make navigation difficult.

On the whole the critical reaction to this panorama of the Tatum style was mixed; listeners found it hard to feel wholeheartedly one way or the other. The effort to evaluate the massive output brought out the conflicting themes that had characterized assessments of Tatum over two decades, and made some of them much clearer. I think they are worth sampling here.

Whitney Balliett, reviewing the first four LPs, said,

It takes about six hours to hear the albums through, and the cumulative effect, at one sitting, is unnerving. For here . . . is a new kind of Tatum, a Tatum unfettered by rhythm accompaniment, a kind of whooping, damn-the-torpedoes Tatum who was allowed to do just what he pleased, and did. It is also a Tatum who, a little overripe on the bough, exhibits, within the confines of his materials, an extraordinary set of pianistic exercises that are, simply, demonstrations of how to play the piano perfectly.

["Art, and Tatum"]

The same review, however, went on to assert: "Unfortunately, little of the astonishing crystal palace of sound that Tatum has created here is jazz. It is, in fact, difficult to find a single complete chorus of jazz improvisation in the whole series. One hears, rather, a weird cross between a jazz-oriented pianist and one who is, at various times, decked out in Chopin, Debussy, cocktail filagrees, and Frankie Froeba."

John S. Wilson, an esteemed jazz critic for the *New York Times,* said in his review of the first five albums:

Listening to Tatum must be undertaken as an active role, not a passive one, otherwise the man is not really being heard. It is the passive listener, the listener who doesn't hear beyond the surface, who is apt to become annoyed with Tatum's repetitious use of runs. Given the time, as he is in this series of disks, Tatum can woo a willing listener step by step from surface sounds down into the heart of his kaleidoscopic imagination and hold him there enthralled.

Michael Gibson, writing in *Down Beat,* was not wooed. He was moved, perhaps, but not in the way Wilson had in mind. After charging that "Tatum was content to serve up florid, virtuoso performances that deserve to be anathemised if only for their effect upon his admirers, Oscar Peterson in particular," and offering the Granz solo recordings as evidence, he went on to make a poignant point:

The real pity of the Tatum story, however, is that by the time he found someone who was prepared to record him in a variety of moods and surroundings, the vital flame which had sparked his earlier greatness was already waning. Art's last recordings sound very old and very tired, with an air of almost decadent wistfulness about them: when you've done everything possible on a jazz piano in 1940, then doing it again in 1954 can't give much satisfaction. . . . Art Tatum deserves the title of immortal genius, both for performance and for influence, but one feels that it is by his earlier recordings that he would like to be remembered most.

Mait Edey, reflecting on Tatum's last years, wrote: "Norman Granz deserves a lot of our gratitude for recording him so prolifically during this period. Indeed, it was wise to record Tatum in quantity if you wanted much music of quality, because of all the very great jazz players Tatum had the most frequent and horrible lapses of taste . . . and these lapses make almost half the material on the 'Genius' series . . . hardly worth hearing." "Few musical experiences," he said, echoing Hodeir, "are as discouraging as hearing Tatum wasting his time on inappropriate material, as he did too much of the time."

The various group sessions evoked similar commentary: playing with Tatum brought out the best in some of them (especially Jo Jones, Lionel Hampton, and Ben Webster) but seduced others into trying to match Tatum's virtuosity rather than playing in their own most comfortable style (Buddy DeFranco, Sweets Edison, perhaps even Benny Carter, who one might have assumed had enough experience to avoid the challenge of a cutting contest). Tatum, for his own part, did not seem to adapt in any particular way to the various people Granz brought in; his approach to the sessions, in Edey's view, was "undeviating" (Tatum being simply a fact of nature). The key to whether the collaboration worked or not seemed to be in the attitude of the other players. To a man other players never blamed Tatum for any difficulty they had in playing with him; if there was any problem it lay in their own inadequacy. He was above reproach.

The first group session involved Benny Carter (saxophone) and Louie Bellson (drums). Louis told me a little about that afternoon:

> We got there early so we could visit. He seemed to me to be the kind of man that when you meet him, you felt like you knew him before. And he was a very kind man, who expressed beautiful thoughts—and confirmed my conviction about anybody who's that great, always had to be beautiful personalities—very caring people, who, you can talk to them, they take time, this kind of thing. Of course, Tatum could see a little bit, you know. And Benny Carter and I happened to drive in together that day and we came in the studio together. When we walked into the studio and opened the door, there was Tatum sitting at the piano, he turned around and saw Benny Carter and I, and his comment was, "Oh, oh, I hope you guys don't play nothing fast." Benny and I looked at one another—he hopes we don't play anything fast! But that shows you how humble he was. But on that record date, where we spent three hours together, Benny Carter, Tatum, and I, I was just in awe. I think we could have done it in less, but we just took our time. But something happened on that record date, Benny Carter asked Tatum if he knew this one particular song, and Tatum said, "Well, Benny, you stumped me that time"—because he had the reputation of being able to tell you every verse in every song, he just had it in his head. But this is one that kind of slipped by him. He told Benny just to play the melody on the saxophone, which Benny did, you know, no chords or anything. And Tatum says, "OK, Norman, let's put one on." And when he played it, Benny Carter looked over at me and he said, "Do you realize this man didn't know the chords and he played all the right chords and went way beyond that!" It just shows you the magnitude of an Art Tatum. What a joy it was to work with that man—he mesmerized you—'cause he played so well, he almost made the good players during that time sound mediocre.

"Magnitude" *and* humility would be an attractive combination; I hope the gods will forgive me for seeing something other than humility here. It strikes me as the De Gaulle syndrome popping up again. Tatum simply had a vision, a totally compelling image of how a Tatum ought to sound, and he was incapable of *not* following that vision. Tatum played the way a Tatum should play, and adapting to other players was not a high priority. For example, Benny Carter was a senior figure (even in the '50s) and because of his musical knowledge and experience other musicians usually looked up to him and deferred to his wishes. On this Granz session, Carter wanted to do some second takes; he felt he had either made mistakes or could do better than he had done on certain numbers. But Bill Douglass, who was there, says Tatum would not defer. He didn't like to do second takes, he almost never did them, he didn't want to do it for Benny Carter, and there were no second takes. Douglass thinks Art may have said something to Benny about "getting his act together."

Art had to know that others often found his way too fast for them, and in Bellson's story of the recording session Art makes a joke about it. Perhaps after all there is a little humility in that; maybe it was all he could do. He apparently couldn't, or wouldn't, change it. And other players didn't expect him to change it—his vision was as compelling to others as it was to him. Sweets Edison was part of one of the Granz group sessions in 1955 and his account of the experience is typical:

> He was just the world's greatest jazz piano player, the world's greatest piano player, you know, he could play anything. Of course I worked with him on a couple of albums. And naturally everybody was so excited working with him, because after he got through playing there wasn't anything anybody else could play. He just played so much, and you listened so intently, when he finished you had lost your trend of thought. He was such a magnificent piano player, gee whiz, words can't express his genius on the piano.

Slam Stewart had more experience trying to collaborate with Tatum than any other musician, and he once said, "At times when I was taking a solo he would more or less sound like he was taking a solo himself. But it didn't bother me hardly at all. I kept my ears open and my mind closed to the fact that he was also soloing at times too" (Spellman, 22). Most people who played with Tatum weren't with him long enough to get so good at coping.

One of the very few players I talked to who ever challenged Art on his approach to collaboration was the irrepressible Les Paul, an ardent admirer of Tatum all his life: ". . . I remember vividly the day we made an album with Art, and Art played the first run, and he says, 'Whatta you wanna do?' And I said, 'I don't care.' He says, '"Lady Be Good".' I says, 'OK.' He started out on piano and he played the run, and I says, 'Hold it!' I says, 'Hey, Art, if you're gonna play like that there's no reason for me even to be around!'"

Jo Jones had the technical facility on drums to be completely comfortable with Art's level of playing. In fact, in Balliett's view, "if Tatum had played with more musicians of Jones's strength and inventiveness, he might in time have pocketed some of his insuperable fireworks and got down to business." Hampton, too, was at home with speed and fireworks and the sessions with him and Buddy Rich must be jazz at some kind of summit. But many think the day on which Ben Webster joined Tatum, Red Callendar on bass, and Bill Douglass on drums, provided the most precious moments of the whole Granz marathon. Benny Green thought that this recording session was "probably the most successful attempt of all time" in which another soloist matched his personality against Tatum's. The key to Ben's success, Green asserted, was that Webster had mellowed as a soloist to such a point that "he could create authentic jazz just by playing the tune, for his tone was so redolent of the jazz spirit, and his sense of time and rhythm and harmony so profound, that he could take a ballad . . . and merely by rocking it gently in the arms of his style, squeeze more jazz out of it than a great many young men" who bury it under substitute chords and technical bravura. Ben apparently felt that his rendition of "Night and Day" with Tatum was one of the best recordings he had ever made. Ben loved

Art's playing; he played some piano himself and had never given up his interest in it. He had often jammed with Art in the past, and he too, like Les Paul, was not afraid to challenge Art's tendency to swamp soloists. According to guitarist John Collins, Ben and Art had in the past had "mock" disputes about it: " 'Goddamn it, Art, back off. You're playing more than me.' To which Art, continuing to shower down a profusion of notes, would reply, 'Oh, man, go ahead and play your horn and quit worrying about me' " (Spellman, 47). And that is apparently exactly what Webster did on the Granz session in 1956, a session of which Webster was hugely proud, and the last studio session of Tatum's life. Granz has claimed that another session was planned, and even scheduled, pairing Tatum and Charlie Parker. What an education in improvising that might have been— but it never happened.

This outpouring of recordings put a spotlight on Tatum for a new generation, and reminded an older generation of his stature. The effect showed in the polls: For three straight years (1954, '55, '56) he was voted the top jazz pianist by the *Down Beat* critics, over Teddy Wilson, Erroll Garner, Nat Cole, Oscar Peterson, and all the be-bop pianists. The eclipse of the late 1940s had passed and he was again in the limelight. In 1954 or '55 he and his trio (with Stewart and Barksdale) traveled for some six weeks giving jazz concerts together with the Shorty Rogers and Stan Kenton bands. Bob Fitzpatrick was playing trombone with Kenton on that tour and was able to reminisce about Tatum:

> He'd sit on the bus and sing [advertising] jingles, from the radio. He knew coins by feel. I don't think he ever had pennies with him because he'd use phone booths, he had nickels, dimes, and quarters. He'd always wear a suit with a vest. And then Art's valet would put the money in his pockets for him, he'd have ones, fives, tens, twenties, each in different pockets. . . . He didn't fly, he would not fly. The tour started in San Francisco, and when the concert finished that night he got on a train to go to Salt Lake City, and we stayed over, got on the plane the next morning, went to Salt Lake City, and he got in just before the

concert that night. He'd been on the train all that time. But he always made it. He had a problem with Slam. Slam was really—well, Slam called it "ignorant oil." Whenever Slam would show up at the concert hall juiced, Art would take every tempo twice as fast. And Everett [Barksdale] would sit there in the middle, you know, he didn't know what the hell to do. And then Art [who had himself given up alcohol at this point] would growl at Slam, "You son of a bitch, why do you do this to me?" Unbeknownst to the audience, pretty much. But finally he'd get the tempos on certain things up so fast that Slam would have to play in half-time, he really couldn't handle it. He probably couldn't even have handled it sober. Just ridiculous tempos.

Johnny Smith was another artist featured on the Kenton-Rogers-Tatum tour, and he remembers a different aspect of it:

We did 70 one-nighters in a row. . . . At that time Art had serious health problems, and I sat right across from him on the bus, and he never complained one minute on any of the legs of the tour that we did. But I could see that the poor guy's ankles were swollen up something terrible and he must have been in terrible pain, but he never complained. He used to be after me, he said, "Teach me to play the guitar," and I said, "No, I certainly won't," I said, "I won't do that, I got enough problems without Art Tatum playing the guitar." And finally I leveled with him, I told him, "Art, there's no way that you can play the guitar." And he says, "Why not?" I says, "Because your fingernails are too long." His nails were very long, and as a matter of fact they had a lot of trouble recording him because his nails would click on the keys. But he wouldn't cut his nails, because he says, "The strength of my fingers is in the nails." And when I told him that he'd have to cut off his nails, well, that kind of ended that project that he had in mind.

He continued to work on the night-club circuit, but he remarked to a friend that he was getting too old to play in bars (Spellman, 24).

He was only in his mid-forties, but the night-club circuit meant train trips around the country, hotel rooms, and more than a few uncongenial surroundings, and the fact is that he was not well—*really* not well. His weight had dropped from his normal 230 to around 180. In 1953 a doctor friend of his in Washington, D.C., diagnosed Tatum as not only ill but fatally ill. That news may not have been communicated to Art, but Everett Barksdale, who was with him at the doctor's office, was told (and, for some odd reason, sworn to secrecy; it must have been a heavy burden for him to carry around). Even if the words "fatally ill" were not used certainly Art was led to understand that something serious was happening. Still, he did not give up alcohol immediately. It was only the following year, after a joint three-day binge in New York with Barksdale, that he quit and started drinking orange juice instead, and began making a serious effort to control his weight. (I can't help wondering whether the death of Charlie Parker in 1955, "fat and drunk and doped up all the time" as Miles Davis described him, might have strengthened his resolve).

He presented no solo concerts between 1952 and 1955, and then appeared in one at Brandeis University in late 1955 (near the time of his marriage to Geraldine), which went very well in spite of his condition (medical, not marital). *Down Beat* reported that "He was surrounded at the end by students who pressed close to thank him for appearing, and perhaps touch him" (Cerulli, "Giants of Jazz"). Earlier this same year Art had been privately recorded playing at the Hollywood home of Ray Heindorf, at a party celebrating the completion of a movie Heindorf had been working on. These recordings were not released until years after Tatum's death, but they show him in surprisingly good spirits and wonderful form. "Every cut," Michael Ullman wrote, "contains passages no other pianist would have thought of and few could imitate." Martin Williams, too, addressed some of the Heindorf moments in rare superlatives. A jazz critic who did not give praise either lightly or superficially, and who complained early in the review that "Tatum's melodic taste is so banal" and that there is "structure-less haphazardry" in some of his playing, wrote about one of the performances from this session: "'Too Marvelous for Words' may convince you that Tatum knew everything there is to know or could be discovered in jazz about the European harmonic system . . . It is very likely that 'Too Marvelous' is the greatest single Tatum performance we are fortunate to have" (*Jazz Masters*, 38).

In September of 1955 he recorded for Granz in Los Angeles. In November he was in New York playing with the Trio at Basin Street. In January of 1956 he was back in Los Angeles to record with Red Callender and Jo Jones, and in February with Red, Bill Douglass, and Buddy DeFranco. DeFranco himself was almost too ill to make this session, but he refused to be left out (somewhere in the session he forgot to come in after one of Tatum's solos, illustrating Edison's remark that "when he finished you had lost your trend of thought"). In March he played the London House in Chicago, again with the Trio.

In August 1956, Art played before a far larger audience than he ever had before, some 19,000 jazz fans who filled the Hollywood Bowl for a major concert. This was another Norman Granz extravaganza, and it featured many of the same artists who had made up the 1944 Esquire All-Stars concert, for example, Louis Armstrong, Sweets Edison, Roy Eldridge, but also Ella Fitzgerald, Buddy Rich on drums, and Oscar Peterson and his trio (Ray Brown and Herb Ellis). Art was on his own home territory but it must have been a major effort for him, because by now he had an advanced case of uremia, a toxic blood condition resulting from severe kidney disease.

Granz had further plans for promoting Art's career and was putting together a prestigious solo concert tour for the fall, on which Art was to be billed simply as "Tatum." Art had even bought the white tie and tails for it, and Spellman says such a tour "had long been his dream." If, in fact, Tatum's playing had always been at least in part designed for serious listening, then this tour would have been a culmination of a kind. (Pearl Bailey once said, "Tatum should have been dressed in tails and heard by everyone in the world.") But he didn't live long enough to enjoy it.

In September he recorded with Webster, Callender, and Douglass, and in October he had at least two more engagements with the trio, one at Olivia's El Patio Lounge in Washington, D.C. and one at the Red Hill Inn in Pennsauken, New Jersey. On one of the nights in New Jersey he told Barksdale he wasn't sure he was strong enough to go on for the second set (but he did). Mel Clement spent a night with him during the Washington gig:

> I was with him 10 days before he died, until way into the morning. I played a job someplace, and he was playing at Olivia Davis's El Patio, on 13th St., that's where the Chinese restaurant is now, above G St. on 13th. He was waiting for me, it was, like, after 2 in the morning when I got there. He and I were the only people there. The guy was running the vacuum cleaner, we got him to shut it off, and we sat there and talked, 'til about 6 in the morning, and played back and forth a little bit. We didn't do a lot of playing at all, just sat and talked, reminisced a little bit—one of the best conversations we ever had. I remember the last tune he ever played for me. It was one I learned from him, and I've never seen any music to, and I don't believe that anybody else in town would know it, never heard anybody else play it, tune that goes back to about 1923, called "Just Like a Butterfly Caught in the Rain." He recorded it several times. Beautiful tune. Then, I took him back to his hotel . . .

Tatum had to break off his tour with the Trio to return home to Los Angeles for "a rest." Interestingly, one report (Balliett, *Musicians*) says that in early November he was getting ready to travel to his sister's home in Milwaukee, and it sounds like he was ready for truly "going home." But there wasn't time for travel. On November 4th or 5th Geraldine began calling his friends, asking them to come over if they could. There was hardly time for any except those who were already in Los Angeles to respond. Rozelle Gayle, who had named Art the godfather of his son, and Eddie Beal were there, of course, and Sweets Edison, Benny Carter, Bill Douglass, and lots of fellow pianists. Art sat on the edge of his bed and they talked, and the pianists all played for Art, on his new Steinway-B grand piano. For the first time in his life, Art did not play. Gerald Wiggins was there:

I was talking to his wife, Gerry, the day before he died, we were all up at the house, and I said, "Can't something be done about it?," and she said, "No," and I said, "Something's got to be," 'cause he looked all right. He's there sitting on the side of the bed, all the piano players in town are there playing for him. She knew he was dying. Sure, he knew, too. He was lucid—he looked great sitting there on the side of the bed. He didn't look sick. He didn't look that thin to me. Everybody played—he always encouraged the guys, you know. And the next day he was gone.

There is no indication that Art tried to reach Orlando, his son. He did however request someone to reach Oscar Peterson and ask him to come down from San Francisco, but Oscar was unable to make it to Los Angeles before Art died.

ART'S SISTER ARLINE has given this account of the night of Art's death:

My husband and I were living in Milwaukee then, and the phone rang and it was my mother, calling from Toledo. She said, "You're going to have to go to Los Angeles on the airplane. Art's sick and he wants you." I called Art on the telephone [apparently Geraldine had not called Arline], and he said, "Can you come out?" I told him I'd take the first plane from Chicago in the morning, and Art said, "I'll be looking for you," and he began to cry. I told him not to cry—that I'd be there—and hung up. While I was doing my little packing, I heard the screen door open and shut, and I asked my husband did he hear that? He said yes and went to the door, which was latched, as always. I finished packing, and the phone rang and it was my mother, and she was crying. She told me there was no need for me to go, that Art had passed. My husband and I looked at each other and said it must have been just when that screen door opened and closed.

[Balliett, *Musicians*, 208–9]

Art's mother wanted to bring him home to Toledo for burial, but Geraldine wanted him buried in Los Angeles. Geraldine won. The funeral was held on November 10th at the North Neighborhood Community Church, with some 300 people attending. (The audience at Fats Waller's funeral had numbered at least 4200.) Al Hibbler was invited to sing but was unable to get out of a contract to do a television show. Ella Fitzgerald sang "God Will Take Care of You" (finally, someone!), and Sarah Vaughan sang "The Lord's Prayer." Stuff Smith (violin) and Jimmy Lyons (piano) played "Sweet Lorraine," among all Art's recordings the tune issued more often than any other (24 times), and "Without a Song," and Art's good friend Buddy Cole played a number of songs on the organ. After the funeral, Ben Webster and several others stayed on at the church and without any audience "played a little thing of their own, for Tatum."

He was buried at Rosedale Cemetery in Los Angeles. Art's pallbearers were Eddie Beal, Benny Carter, Bill Douglass, Ed Brown, Ralph Roberts, and Edgar Hayes. Honorary pallbearers and guests included Oscar Peterson, Erroll Garner, Billy Taylor, Dizzy Gillespie, and Cozy Cole.

Art's gravestone is inscribed simply, and cryptically, "Someone to Watch Over Me."

The English pianist Alan Clare was once intrigued with a workman who was carrying out some remodeling inside his house. Clare was playing some recordings, and he began to notice that the workman was whistling along with whatever music he put on—Beethoven, Rachmaninoff, it didn't seem to matter. Even if he hadn't heard it before he had the natural musical ability to follow a melody closely and almost automatically. Clare decided to give him a real test and dug up his recording of Art Tatum doing "Tea for Two," with the ground-breaking chord changes Tatum introduced into the tune. The workman never lost a beat nor did he lay out for a bar or two to figure out what was going on. He tracked Tatum flawlessly through all his changes, and when the record ended, he spoke for the first time. He glanced at Clare and with classic English understatement said, "Tricky fucker, ain't he?"

References

Asher, Don. "Keys of the Kingdom." *Jazzletter,* March 1990 (1–5).

Balliett, Whitney. "Art Tatum." *American Musicians: Fifty-six Portraits in Jazz.* New York: Oxford University Press, 1989.

Balliett, Whitney. "Art, and Tatum." *Saturday Review,* 29 Oct. 1955.

Balliett, Whitney. "One Man Band." In *Ecstasy at the Onion.* New York: Oxford University Press, 1971.

Bechet, Sidney. *Treat It Gentle: An Autobiography.* New York: Da Capo, 1975 (originally published: London: Cassell, 1960).

Blesh, Rudi, and Harriet Janis. *They All Played Ragtime,* Rev. Ed. New York: Oak Publications, 1971.

Bookspan, Martin, and Ross Yockey. *André Previn: A Biography.* Garden City, N.Y.: Doubleday, 1981.

Bower, Helen. "Toledo Is Still Home to Pianist Art Tatum." Unidentified newspaper, 22 Dec. 1949.

Cerulli, Dom. "Giants of Jazz." *FM Program Guide,* May 1967.

Chilton, John. *Who's Who in Jazz: Storyville to Swing Street.* Time-Life Records Special Edition, 1978 (first published: Philadelphia: Chilton Books, 1972).

Collier, James L. *The Reception of Jazz in America.* Brooklyn, N.Y.: Institute for Studies in American Music (Brooklyn College).

Conover, Willis. "An Art Tatum Interview." *Keyboard,* Oct. 1981 (28–31).

Crow, Bill. *Jazz Anecdotes.* New York: Oxford University Press, 1990.

Dance, Stanley. "Tiny Grimes." In Dance, *The World of Swing*.

Dance, Stanley. *The World of Swing*. New York: Scribners, 1974.

Davis, Miles (with Quincy Troupe). *Miles: The Autobiography*. New York: Simon & Schuster, 1989.

Doerschuk, Robert "An Art Tatum Biography." *Keyboard*, Oct. 1981 (20–27).

Edey, Mait. "Tatum: The Last Years." *Jazz Review*, Aug. 1960 (4–5).

Ellington, Duke. *Music Is My Mistress*. Garden City: Doubleday, 1973.

Feather, Leonard. *Inside Bebop*. New York: J. J. Robbins, 1949.

Finklestein, Sidney. *Jazz: A People's Music*. New York: Citadel Press, 1948.

Fisher, Renée. *Musical Prodigies*. New York: Association Press, 1973.

Foster, Pops (and Tom Stoddard). *The Autobiography of Pops Foster, New Orleans Jazzman*. Berkeley: University of California Press, 1971.

Gibson, Michael. "The Paradox of Art Tatum." *Jazz Journal*, Oct. 1960 (3–4).

Giddins, Gary. *Riding on a Blue Note: Jazz and American Pop*. New York: Oxford University Press, 1981.

Giddins, Gary. Liner notes for Verve CD 827–901–2 or LP VE 2–2506 ("The Genius of Bud Powell").

Gitler, Ira. *Jazz Masters of the '40s*. New York: Collier, 1966.

Gitler, Ira. *Swing to Bop: An Oral History of the Transition in Jazz in the 1940s*. New York: Oxford University Press, 1985.

Green, Benny. *The Reluctant Art: The Growth of Jazz*. New York: Horizon Press, 1963.

Harris, Rex. *The Story of Jazz*. New York: Grosset & Dunlap, 1955.

Harrison, Max. *Modern Jazz: The Essential Records 1945–70*. London: Aquarius Books, 1975.

Hilbert, Bob. "Memories of Phil Napoleon," *Journal of the International Association of Jazz Record Collectors*, Winter 1992.

Hildesheimer, Wolfgang. *Mozart*. New York: Vintage Books, 1982.

Hodeir, André. "The Genius of Art Tatum." In Martin Williams, *The Art of Jazz* (173–80)

Hoefer, George. "The Hot Box: Tatum." *Down Beat*, Oct. 24, 1963 (24 +).

Hoefer, George. "The Hot Box." *Down Beat*, Jan. 9, 1957.

Horricks, Raymond. *These Jazzmen of Our Time*. London: V. Gollancz, 1959.

Howard, Joseph. "The Improvisational Techniques of Art Tatum." Ph.D. dissertation (Musicology), Case Western Reserve University, 1978.

Howlett, Felicity. "An Introduction to Art Tatum's Performance Ap-

proaches: Composition, Improvisation, and Melodic Variation."
Ph.D. dissertation, Cornell University, 1983.

James, Burnett. *Essays on Jazz*. London: Sidgwick and Jackson, 1961.

Jasen, David A., and Trebor Jay Tichenor. *Rags and Ragtime: A Musical History*. New York: Dover, 1989 (original publication, New York: Seabury, 1978).

Jones, Hank. Interview by Doug Long, *Cadence*, July 1983.

Keepnews, Orrin. "Art Tatum." In Shapiro and Hentoff, *The Jazz Makers*.

Korall, Burt. "Tatum . . . Like the Wind." *Saturday Review*, Oct. 12, 1968 (67).

Larrabee, Eric. "The Tatum Magic." *Saturday Review*, Nov. 1, 1975 (44–45).

Laubich, Arnold, and Ray Spencer. *Art Tatum: A Guide to His Recorded Music*. Metuchen, N.J.: Scarecrow Press, 1982.

Lees, Gene. *The Will to Swing*. Toronto: Lester and Orphon Dennip, 1988.

Levant, Oscar. *A Smattering of Ignorance*. Garden City: Doubleday, 1942.

Loesser, Arthur. *Men, Women and Pianos*. New York: Simon & Schuster, 1954.

McPartland, Marian. Liner notes for Verve MGV83601.

McRea, Barry. "Tatum: The Clef Recordings." *Jazz Journal*, Oct. 19, 1966 (11–12).

Miller, Paul Edward (ed.). *Miller's Yearbook of Popular Music*. Chicago: PEM Publications, 1943.

Nanry, Charles, and Ed Berger. *The Jazz Text*. New York: Van Nostrand, 1979.

Ramsey, Frederic, and Charles Edward Smith (eds.). *Jazzmen*. New York: Harcourt, Brace, 1939.

Reisner, Robert G. *The Jazz Titans*. Garden City, N.Y.: Doubleday, 1960.

Richmond, Dick. "Mai Tatum Plays Big Piano." *St. Louis Post-Dispatch*, March 16, 1972.

Roberts, Betty. Quoted in the *Toledo Blade*, Jan. 21, 1992.

Rosenkrantz, Timme. "Reflections on Art." *Down Beat*, July 5, 1962 (15).

Rothman, Seymour. "The Art of Tatum." *Toledo Blade Sunday Magazine*, June 14, 1970.

Rothman, Seymour. "Art Tatum's Toledo Years." *Toledo Blade*, June 30, 1985.

Sargeant, Winthrop. *Jazz: Hot and Hybrid*. New York: Da Capo, 1975 (originally published 1946).

Scheer, Julian. "Charlotte Close-up," *Charlotte* (N.C.) *News*, March 27, 1956.

Schuller, Gunther. *The Swing Era: The Development of Jazz, 1930–1945*. New York: Oxford University Press, 1989.

Shapiro, Nat, and Nat Hentoff (eds.). *Hear Me Talkin' to Ya*. New York: Dover, 1966 (originally published 1955).

Shapiro, Nat, and Nat Hentoff. *The Jazz Makers*. Westport, Conn.: Greenwood, 1975 (originally published by Rinehart, New York: Rinehart, 1957).

Short, Bobby. *Black and White Baby*. New York: Dodd, Mead, 1971.

Southern, Eileen (ed.). *Biographical Dictionary of Afro-American and African Musicians*. Westport, Conn.: Greenwood Press, 1982.

Spellman, A. B. "Art Tatum." Notes on the recorded music included in the Art Tatum boxed set issued by Time-Life Records, one in the Giants of Jazz series.

Spencer, Ray. "Art Tatum: An Appreciation (Chapter One, The Tatum Story; Chapter Two, The Tatum Style)." *Jazz Journal*, Aug. 1966 (6–16).

Spencer, Ray. "Art Tatum Recordings." *International Association of Jazz Record Collectors Newsletter*, April 1988 (31–34).

Stearns, Marshall. *The Story of Jazz*. New York: Oxford University Press, 1970. Originally published 1955.

Stewart, Rex William. "Genius in Retrospect," in Stewart, *Jazz Masters of the 'Thirties* (181–91).

Stewart, Rex William. *Jazz Masters of the 'Thirties*. New York: Macmillan, 1972.

Stewart, Slam. Jazz Oral History Project, funded by National Endowment for the Arts, Interview by Stanley Crouch, on file at the Institute for Jazz Studies, Rutgers University, Newark, N.J.

Stokes, W. Royal. *The Jazz Scene*. New York: Oxford University Press, 1991.

Taylor, Billy. *Jazz Piano: A Jazz History*. Dubuque: Wm. C. Brown, 1983.

Taylor, Billy. "An Art Tatum Recollection and Analysis." *Keyboard*, Oct. 1981 (36–40).

Taylor, Billy. "A Tribute to Art Tatum." *Toledo Blade Sunday Magazine*, June 30, 1985.

Trotter, James M. *Music and Some Highly Musical People*. Chicago: Afro-American Press, 1969.

Ulanov, Barry. *A History of Jazz in America*. New York: Viking Press, 1952.

Ullman, Michael. *Jazz Lives.* Washington, D.C.: New Republic, 1980.

Ullman, Michael. "Art Tatum: 20th Century Genius" (record review). *High Fidelity,* Sept. 1986 (84).

Vance, Joel. *Fats Waller, His Life and Times.* Chicago: Contemporary Books, 1977.

Waller, Maurice. *Fats Waller.* New York: Schirmer, 1977.

Warren, Tim. "Art Tatum, Jr.: Peace at Last." *Baltimore Sun,* Sept. 21, 1986.

Warren, Tim. "City Demands Proof that Musician is Art Tatum's Son." *Baltimore Sun,* Sept. 27, 1986.

Whitehead, Kevin. "Art Tatum, Jr.: Interview." *Cadence,* May 1983 (15–22).

Wilder, Alec, with James Maher. *American Popular Song: The Great Innovators, 1900–1950.* New York: Oxford University Press, 1972.

Williams, Martin. *The Art of Jazz.* New York: Oxford University Press, 1959.

Williams, Martin. "The Real Art Tatum." In Williams, *Jazz Masters in Transition* (originally published in *The Jazz Review,* July 1960).

Williams, Martin. *Jazz Masters in Transition: 1959–1969.* New York: Macmillan, 1970.

Wilson, John S. "The 'Autobiography' of Art Tatum: Chapters 1–15" (record review). *High Fidelity,* Aug. 1954.

Wilson, Russ. "Art Tatum Gone But Music Lingers." *Oakland* (Calif.) *Tribune,* Nov. 11, 1956.

Wilson, Teddy. "Still More of the Greatest Piano of Them All" (liner notes). Los Angeles: Verve MGV8360.

Wilson, Teddy. Jazz Oral History Project, funded by National Endowment for the Arts, interview by Milt Hinton, on file at the Institute for Jazz Studies, Rutgers University, Newark, N.J.

Young, Gavin. "Three Pianists Discuss Art Tatum (and Other Matters)." *Jazz Journal,* Nov. 1963 (22–24).

Notes

Chapter 2

1. This information comes from Mr. Tatum's obituary and from statements made by Art's brother Karl, who appeared on a BBC television documentary about Art and also is quoted in Whitney Balliett, "Art Tatum," in *American Musicians*. Tatum's birth certificate gives his father's age as twenty-eight, but a little arithmetic applied to data in the obituary argues that Art's father was twenty-four at his birth.

2. This address is from the birth certificate, and Arline recently gave me this address as well. However, one of Seymour Rothman's feature articles for the *Toledo Blade* gives the address as 218 Mitchell Street. I believe the Tatums owned both houses but lived on Mill Street.

3. A pianist who eventually became an assistant to James Petrillo, then head of the Musicians' Union, and was responsible for integrating the separate black and white local union chapters.

4. One of Art's childhood acquaintances, Steve Taylor, stoutly maintains that the incident involved a fight in a pool hall and not a mugging, but he didn't personally witness the pool hall incident and it may be no more than the final result of a cumulation of those distortions that come with repeated re-telling of a narrative.

5. Rothman (1970). There are so few stories of Tatum's childhood that I felt obliged to include this one, but it has the ring of invention. Consider the similarity to Graham Greene's lines about a fictional child destined for

sainthood: "We must not think that young Juan did not laugh and play like other children, though there were times when he would creep away with a holy-picture book to his father's cow-house from the circle of his merry playmates" (*The Power and the Glory*, New York: Bantam Books, 1940/1954, p. 21).

6. Rothman in 1970 wrote that Karl later played basketball with the Harlem Globetrotters, but he was mixing him up with "Goose" Tatum, who is no relation. Karl did, however, win a basketball scholarship to Benedict College, Columbia, S.C., and has been active in athletics for most of his life.

7. On Oct. 13, 1990, the *Toledo Blade* carried a short article remembering his birthday, but claimed that "it is just 91 years ago today that he was born . . ." This roused his 7th and 8th grade teacher, Mrs. Henry Morrison, to write in to say that this had to be wrong, as she herself was only ninety-four. The *Blade* put me in touch with Mrs. Morrison, just months before she died.

Chapter 3

1. In 1970 Rothman wrote, "Art was not yet six years old when he discovered the piano." In 1985 his account said, "Until 1969, the piano on which Art started playing at age 3 and showed his real genius by 6 was still in the living room."

2. The statement is also found in Reisner, *The Jazz Titans,* and in Chilton's *Who's Who in Jazz.* No source is given in any of these books. Chilton states that he also studied guitar in Columbus.

3. Of course the story has been repeated in other publications, but the fact is we don't know where it originated.

4. Queries to *Time-Life* about the files on which Spellman's piece was based finally elicited the intelligence that the organization had no idea how to find them.

5. I say "may" because I have not personally authenticated the documentation on Blind Tom that is the basis for the description here: Trotter, *Music and Some Highly Musical People,* and Fisher, *Musical Prodigies.* Milt Hinton first called my attention to Blind Tom.

Chapter 4

1. Spencer says that Lester Smith played with Speed Webb's band in 1925, but since I don't know whether that was before or after Art's Toledo

group it doesn't help to date this six-piece band. In 1925 Art was fourteen.

2. Most of my information about this early relationship comes from the Teddy Wilson interview, Jazz Oral History Project, funded by the National Endowment for the Arts and housed at the Institute for Jazz Studies, Rutgers University, Newark, N.J.

3. Neil Leonard's book, *Jazz and the White American,* is full of interesting information about the resistance to jazz. For the other side of the coin, James L. Collier's *The Reception of Jazz in America* is a useful book.

Chapter 5

1. As already noted, Spencer believed Tatum first went to New York in 1930.

2. A copy of the contract is on file in the Toledo Public Library.

3. All datings of Tatum recordings are taken from the excellent discography by Laubich and Spencer.

4. In a Freudian slip that made me chuckle, when copying out this passage I wrote "polar beers."

5. Throughout this interview Arline spoke as if she believed Orlando was still alive. Karl has stated (1991) that Orlando died "about a year or so ago."

6. John Chilton, in *Who's Who of Jazz,* says it was Zutty Singleton, and when I talked to Collins he first thought it was Singleton, but later felt sure it was Winston. Winston now lives in Hawaii, but I haven't verified this with him.

7. Collins went on to a remarkable and mostly unsung career, working with the trios of Slam Stewart, Nat Cole, and Billy Taylor, as well as in the larger groups of Lester Young, Fletcher Henderson, Benny Carter, Coleman Hawkins, Artie Shaw, and Bobby Troup.

8. A number of fellow musicians have told me he was and have given me specific instances in which Tatum took a train while the rest of the show he was in flew. Unfortunately for me, Arline claims that Art had no fear of flying, but says that both she and Karl do.

Chapter 6

1. Marshall tells this fascinating story in considerably more detail in a book of his own, which is forthcoming.

Chapter 7

1. An excellent place to start in getting acquainted with these fascinating characters is Rudy Blesh's *They All Played Ragtime,* and another useful book is Jasen and Tichenor's *Rags and Ragtime.*

Chapter 8

1. All the information in this paragraph appeared in *Jazz Information,* vol. 1, 1939–40, issues for Sept. 19 and 26, Oct. 31, Dec. 8 and 29.

2. Stepin Fetchit, whose real name was Lincoln Perry, was a performer who made a career in films out of acting the comedy role of a ludicrously lazy and slow-moving black fellow. Anyone born before 1935 is likely to remember him.

3. Seymour Rothman, "The Art of Tatum." Rothman got this figure from the owners of the Latin Club, where Tatum was playing, but it seems improbably high.

4. Jazz Oral History Project interview, Institute of Jazz Studies, Rutgers University, Newark, N.J.

5. Results were probably obtained in 1943 but when announced they were called the 1944 *Esquire* poll.

6. Laubich and Spencer in their discography list twenty solo sides which may have been recorded in 1944, but the documentation is inconclusive and they choose to place them in 1945.

7. Jazz Oral History Project interview, Institute of Jazz Studies, Rutgers University, Newark, N.J.

Chapter 9

1. This is Gitler's account. But Stearns says that Bird went to Eldon, Mo., in the Ozarks, where he "practiced alone from 1932 to '33 between odd jobs running errands" (p. 161). Parker would have been thirteen in 1933.

2. Interview, Jan. 15, 1963, done while Bud was in a hospital in France being treated for tuberculosis. Quoted in liner notes for Elektra Musician recording E1–60030 (Jazz Masters Edition); the interviewer is not identified.

Index

Printed in the United States
101098LV00002B/54/A